PRAISE FOR *SOLILOQUIES ON FUTURE POLICING*

Astonishing revelations which should whet every reader's appetite.

—M. K. Narayanan, Former National Security Advisor and Former Governor of Bengal

A fascinating peep into the fantasy world of digital technology;

A timely though stark alert of ever-emerging challenges which confront the police in combating cybercrime;

A roadmap for police and governments on how and what to equip the police with to handle such crime;

A primer and guide for compulsory reading by policemen and teaching in police training institutions; and

An incredible and loving bequest to police and policymakers by a police officer with no formal learning in the science of 'bits and bytes'.

—P. S. Ramamohan Rao, Ex-Governor of Tamil Nadu

Valuable addition to the knowledge that every policeman requires.

—Dr R. K. Raghavan, Former Director, CBI, and Former Indian High Commissioner to Cyprus

Soliloquies on Future Policing is a gripping read. The author is so upto date that he has visualised and chipped in a chapter on policing in Metaverse.

—Walter Isaac Davaram, IPS, Former Director General of Police, Tamil Nadu

Soliloquies on Future Policing is a compendium on the emerging technologies in the world in general and their applicability in the police force, particularly in its various functions pertaining to Crimes, Law and Order and Security. While graphic on the various technologies, the author has not failed to project the flip side. The wide reading of literature, and extensive acquaintance with cinemas on the looming technologies by the author, as quoted in each chapter, is evident and impressive. The illustrations of employment of a few of these technologies in various countries and a few states in India in police and other organisations in the anthology will compel many to follow suit. Chapters on cybercrimes throw lucid light on daily happenings in this field worldwide. As Roger Bacon would say, all the chapters in part three of the anthology 'Law Enforcement' deserve to be 'read, chewed and digested' by police officers.

—A. X. Alexander, Former Director General of Police, Tamil Nadu

For the Indian Police, these are exciting times in the throes of a digital transformation. Visionary police officers like Jayanth Murali, who are spearheading that transformation, bring hope and clarity even as there is increasing realisation that the police cannot remain impervious to today's mind-boggling technological disruptions. Jayanth Murali's new book *Soliloquies on Future Policing* is a veritable feast of ideas and a huge inspiration. A lucidly written treatise and a must-read to understand the minefields and opportunities that lie in the path ahead, especially the promises of unprecedented efficiencies in police service delivery, investigation, prosecution, crime prevention, security management, intelligence gathering and its analysis, with speed, accuracy and transparency.

—N. Ramachandran, Former Director General of Police, Assam and Meghalaya, and President, Indian Police Foundation

As an academic who wears the uniform of a top cop, Dr K. Jayanth Murali brings a rich and vivid imagination to non-fiction. The scenarios he builds of the future of policing with cyborgs and robots are not beyond the realm of the possible; they are very believable and must show the way to planners of a society free of major crimes.

—R. Mohan, Resident Editor, *Deccan Chronicle*, Chennai

Through his articles, many of which were carried in the column he wrote for *DT Next*, Dr Jayanth Murali has used his decades of experience as a police officer to elevate technology from the world of gadgetry and geeks and married it with the concept of the future of policing. These essays reveal not just Dr Murali's expertise as a senior police officer and keen personal interest in advancements in technology but also the possibilities that would be explored in the near future.

—Gopu Mohan, Editor, *DT Next*

The prescription of the erudite Justice V. R. Krishna Iyer that the police should use their 'wits and not fists' races to one's mind whenever Dr Jayanth Murali churns out his masterpieces on the prevention and detection of crime. In a cynical world where the police are often unfairly portrayed as the last to arrive at the crime scene, this top cop's encyclopedic knowledge and prolific enunciation of the latest investigative techniques infuse hope for a safer tomorrow. A salute for a work that would make Scotland Yard sit up and notice.

—Sanjay Pinto, Advocate, Columnist and Author,
and Former Resident Editor, NDTV 24X7

The author's accessible and engaging writing style and stories from the field make this book an essential and compelling read.

—S. R. Jangid, Former Director General of Police, Tamil Nadu

Soliloquies on Future Policing is a comprehensive and delightful compendium of exponential technologies and miscellaneous policing issues.

—J. K. Tripathy, Former Director General of Police, Tamil Nadu

Soliloquies on Future Policing is a delightfully written page-turner. Like a sci-fi thriller, it takes the reader on an exciting journey through a smorgasbord of new technologies.

—Jaffar Sait, Former Director General of Police, Tamil Nadu

The current era of technological disruptions, the rise of artificial intelligence, blockchain revolutions, and the growing cybersecurity threat pose severe challenges to the Indian state and the police. Our success in dealing with these will depend on how equipped we are to counter these emerging threats. The author, a seasoned police officer with rich field experience, has a futuristic toolkit to help build professional capabilities and state capacity in a follow-up to his earlier work. This book aims at ensuring that policing in India, be it at the field level or on the technology front, is alive to the needs of a modern state and economy.

—Ashish Bhengra, Former Director General of Police, Tamil Nadu

Soliloquies on Future Policing results from fruitful mulling by Dr K. Jayanth Murali over the inseparable issue of Urban Policing and interwoven aspects of challenges thrown by ever-evolving cyberspace.

He has churned through various vulnerabilities and the reality of security breaches to present a doable response solution by proactive and reactive policing.

Dr Murali has already elucidated new patterns of technological facets in his *42 Mondays*, and his current book assumes yet another pedestal, a notch up, forcing us to rethink and align our tactics and strategies.

The pre-requisites of policing aim are to sense this system holistically, to stay ahead of cybercriminals and to have a disaster recovery plan to mitigate the damage. Police should leverage a collaborative platform in this fight against cybercrimes. I wish Dr Murali, IPS, a great success in his literary journey

—Shankar Jiwal, Director General of Police, Tamil Nadu

Soliloquies on Future Policing is a riveting page-turner that gives the reader a deep sense of the policing that will unfold in the future. It offers a glimpse into a cornucopia of emerging technologies having incredible and mind-blowing applications, besides providing a peek into burgeoning and emerging trends of cybercrimes and fascinating aspects of law enforcement. The author's engaging writing style with stories from the field makes this book an essential and compelling must-read for police officers and lawmakers and is highly futuristic. My advice to all police officers, especially, is to read and keep a copy of this for ready reference as this will be the future of law enforcement.

—C. V. Anand, IPS, Commissioner of Police, Hyderabad

SOLILOQUIES ON FUTURE POLICING

AN ANTHOLOGY ON EMERGING TECHNOLOGIES, CYBERSECURITY AND LAW ENFORCEMENT

DR. K. JAYANTH MURALI

Director General of Police (Retd.)
Bestselling Author, Marathoner, and
Peak Performance Coach

Forewords by

M. K. NARAYANAN

Former Governor of West Bengal and Former National Security Advisor

DR R. K. RAGHAVAN

Former Director, CBI, and Former Indian High Commissioner to Cyprus

and

S. R. JANGID

Director General of Police (Retired)

INDIA • SINGAPORE • MALAYSIA

ISBN
Hardcase 979-8-89233-574-4
Paperback 979-8-89233-572-0

In loving memory of my batchmate SHRI DEBASHISH PANIGRAHI, *who crossed over to the celestial world after valiantly battling covid.*

CONTENTS

Part 2
Cybersecurity

Part 3
Law Enforcement

M.K.Narayanan
Former Governor of West Bengal
Former National Security Advisor

FOREWORD

I am delighted to write the Foreword for this book, as the Author is not only one of the most perspicacious thinkers among Police Officers of his generation, but has written a book that is highly relevant for our times. Apart from an in-depth analysis of new emerging technologies, the Author has laid bare not only the perils that confront law enforcement agencies, but also the technological challenges they are likely to confront in the future.

Technological advances have contributed immensely to the betterment of the world we live in. There is, however, a dark side to this progress, which criminals and others tend to exploit. Cyber space today is teeming with cyber-voyeurs, cyber-stalkers, cyber-extortionists, etc. This situation is only likely to worsen, given the current pace of technological progress and the unprecedented proliferation of surveillance techniques. In short, every new technological innovation expands the scope for cyber penetration and attack.

The book is not a piece of science fiction. Given his long career in Law Enforcement, the Author has attempted to convey to his readers how criminals can exploit the world of exponential technologies. The book demonstrates how cyber criminals already have the ability to hijack new technologies, including robotics, synthetic biology, virtual reality, and artificial intelligence. In short, the book succinctly conveys that the future contains many threats that we are presently unaware of, but it does also offer a way forward on how to counter them.

There are certain astonishing revelations which should whet every reader's appetite viz how using the latest technologies a criminal could download a blue print of the Glock pistol and 3D print it in the comfort of his home. Also, how it is possible for a terrorist to download the genetic sequence of a virus (the Ebola virus for instance) and use the tools of synthetic biology to unleash a bio-terror attack etc. The Author also enunciates his own version of Moore's Law, and states that the speed at which criminals adopt new technologies today exceeds the rate at which Law enforcement can adapt. Furthermore, that in the last 30 years the explosion of new technologies has far outpaced those that took place in the previous 1000 years.

The book is a valuable edition to the many tomes already available to technology and cyber security professionals. It has also tried explain what motivates cyber criminals and how they carry out their criminal activities. This book should encourage CEOs and Corporate Boards to recognize how critical it is in today's world to erect defenses against cyber security threats and vulnerabilities if they wish to protect their Company's assets. The more data that is generated the bigger is the threat potential, and the book highlights what needs protection and how best it can be achieved.

Finally, the Author makes a fervent plea that Humanity should take back control over our gadgets, and channelize technology's tremendous power for the betterment of human kind.

FOREWORD

The first decade of the 21st century has thrown up far too many complicated challenges to field policing. Each day brings new surprises and problems. The chaotic political scene in many countries and the growing tendency to disobey well established and constitutionally endorsed laws are too much for the police to cope with. This is why we are witnesses to the police fumbling with dynamic situations that permit no latitude. The recent incident in which our Prime Minister was held up en route to a public meeting in Punjab is a supreme illustration of how policing fails on crucial occasions. The political heavyweights can legitimately raise the question why the Punjab State Police proved wanting despite all technological tools available to them. The one lesson drawn from this single happening is that technology cannot handle all police problems, and that the human element will still be critical to making the police to act fast and act intelligently.

The book by Jayant Murali, a senior IPS officer from Tamil Nadu, examines all aspects of the police use of technology in present times. Technology is not a panacea to all ills in policing. Nevertheless, it can help the police to remain on rails.

The author discusses cybercrime and Artificial Intelligence in some detail. The phenomenon of an exponential growth in technology that is useful to policing is also mentioned. This is as it should be at a time when misuse of the Internet has become outrageously frequent.

Gratifying to many of us who retired from the Police several years ago is the passion, among some who joined the force much after we had hung up our boots, for reforms and innovation. The author is one of them. His writing reveals his zeal to take advantage of recent technology not only as an academic exercise but to educate all rungs of the police on how they can adapt themselves to fresh challenges by using technology. The author has not stopped being curious and innovative. He remains planted on earth so that he is not too dreamy or impractical. He is clear that technology in police can go only some distance and not all the distance. Commendable is his practical approach to policing issues.

What is distinctive about policing in modern times is that new forms of crime have not totally replaced conventional crime. This is why a policeman of the present times cannot transform himself totally. He should be adept at everything that the community expects in terms of crime detection. This is one theme that is not overlooked by the author who writes lucid prose. His book is a valuable addition to knowledge that is required by every policeman to make his presence felt.

Dr R. K. Raghavan

Former Director, CBI
Former Indian High Commissioner to Cyprus
13th January 2022 at Chennai

S R Jangid IPS, Director General of Police (Retired)

FOREWORD

I am glad to write this foreword because Mr. K.Jayanth Murali is an officer of Tamilnadu Police, an organisation I belonged to and proudly served till my retirement. And also because I had the opportunity to observe him from close quarters, from his very first posting till my retirement in 2019.

Just because the author was my junior officer, I don't want this foreword to end up looking like a performance appraisal. But, a prelude racks up enormous legitimacy and authenticity when someone who writes it knows the author as intimately as any teacher would know his student. When a teacher comes to know that his pupil has offered his gift to the world in the form of a book, it's but automatic for his heart to swell with pride. As I write this foreword, I feel the same emotions that a teacher would feel over the accomplishment of his student.

As a former police officer, I have recently noticed a transition in the character of the crimes. Traditional crimes such as burglary, theft, and robbery are dropping drastically, but technology-enabled crimes such as fraud and cyber-crime are increasing exponentially. Making the threat hard to deal with since transgressors of these new types of crime can launch disproportionate attacks from all over the world, presenting a unique challenge to police agencies worldwide. Thereby emphasising the importance of equipping police forces with new technologies to tackle them. Only by harnessing the latest technologies the government and police would be able to combat this evolving new threat more effectively.

Jayanth Murali, in the present book, has dealt exhaustively with a cornucopia of emerging technologies whose applications are incredible and mind-blowing. As I read on, I found the book inundating me with game-changing technological advancements which are transforming and redefining policing today, such as Artificial Intelligence, Virtual Reality, Nanotechnology, Predictive Policing, 3D Printing Technology, Microbial Signatures or Human Microbiome, Synthetic Biology, CRISPR Technology or Gene Editing, DNA Fingerprinting, Police Robots to name a few. I am sure the reader will find this book not only one-of-its-kind but comprehensive for having covered more than a dozen emerging technologies, including technologies such as CRISPR, Microbial Signatures or Human Microbiome, which are awaiting their turn to bob up on the radar of emerging technologies vis-à-vis law enforcement. Most of the emerging technologies described in the book have unlimited potential for police applications and can unleash tremendous impact.

For instance, Virtual Reality (VR) we are witnessing today is better than anything we've seen in days gone by, and the promise of what VR could become in a few years is compelling. VR is becoming as disruptive as the Internet has been, especially with the ongoing leap from Web 2.0 to Web 3.0. . A Metaverse is getting built in the VR space, which has forced Mark Zuckerberg to change the name of Facebook to Meta. We live in a magic time when technologies are no longer a limiting factor in solving the significant policing challenges we face. The book is so up to date that I find the author has surprisingly chipped in here with his views on policing the Metaverse. The incredible ways by which various technologies are helping police solve crime is unceasingly fascinating to me.

Jayanth Murali, with his explosive insights based on a long career in law enforcement, makes an excellent attempt to take his readers on an exciting journey through the world of exponential technologies, pointing out its upsides as well as its pitfalls. The book reads like science fiction while firmly leaning on scientific facts. But technology is not solely beneficial; It is a double-edged sword. The author recognises the harm and destruction the misapplication of technology can bring about. He brilliantly reveals the downsides of technology by uncovering - How organised criminals, hackers, substate actors and terrorists are accessing the latest technologies for their benefit and how criminals have progressed well beyond cybercrime into new and emerging fields of technology such as artificial intelligence, 3D Printing, Virtual Reality, Synthetic biology, Drones etc. At the same time, several law enforcement agencies worldwide are unaware of these looming technological developments, let alone their exploitation by both organised crime and terrorists. He thereby makes a strong case for the police organisations to stay abreast by leveraging technology.

This book would be valuable for law enforcement professionals, cybersecurity professionals, and technology students aspiring or seeking to understand what motivates the cyber-culprits to perpetrate crimes and how they do it. This book will also encourage CEOs and corporate boards to realise that it is crucial to consider cybersecurity vulnerabilities and threats related to their organisation's IT assets, employees, products, and the cyber supply chain. The author accomplishes all this in a captivating style in each chapter by introducing the technology in question, then describing its potential benefits and highlighting how the new technologies are being exploited or will enable the criminals to capitalise on it nefariously in future.

The technologies in the conglomerate give a deep sense of the kind of things that will unfold in policing in the future. The authors' accessible and engaging writing style, combined with stories from the field, make this book an essential and compelling read for law enforcers, corporations and the community alike. The author's startling overview of the applications of emerging technologies, their likely impact on policing, and how the criminals could exploit the technologies make "Soliloquies on Future Policing" a must-have for police institutions. The book is cutting edge in its content. This masterful page-

turner, much like a sci-fi film, gives the readers a glimpse into policing systems we are building with our technological tools and the possibility of criminals using the same implements against us.

Best Wishes.

(S R Jangid)

Chennai
07.02.2022

ACKNOWLEDGEMENTS

Publishing a book is a laborious and gruelling job. It cannot be accomplished singly by a person. For me, it took several months of nudging, prodding and shoving from my family, friends and well- wishers to thrust this book into this world.

To start with, first, none of this could have happened without my greatest ally, my wife, Jayanthi. For her immense patience, unsolicited assistance and unwavering support despite her arduous dual commitment of simultaneously being a homemaker and a bureaucrat, I owe her a ton of gratitude.

To my Dad and Mom, who laid a stable foundation for me and taught me the invaluable life lessons of integrity, hard work and grit. Words aren't enough to adequately express my gratitude to both of you. This book would not have been possible without your blessings, guidance and con¬tinual benevolent presence at home.

To my daughters, Tanya and Sonya, who mean the world to me and whose love and support have made every day of mine more beautiful than the previous day. I am super grateful to both of you for making my life meaningful and purposeful.

To my siblings, Ashok and Priya. I feel blessed to be on this incredible voyage with both of you. You guys, in your ways, helped me shape this book, mostly because I wouldn't be me without you. Thank you very much for the same.

To my dear Rafiq Bhaiya for being my true Bhaiya in need and for standing by me through thick and thin, and for keeping the ship sailing while this book took shape. To Bhaskar for constantly inspiring and moti¬vating me to deliver my best even when my world appeared upside down. My heart overflows with gratitude for both of you.

To Ms Vidhya, a Corporate Strategist par excellence for Invent SoftLabs, Legal Magic and several other companies, for making this book a reality by voluntarily pivoting herself into a bridge between the publishers and me. Please accept my sincere thanks.

With reverential awe, I bestow my sincere gratitude upon the entire constellation of souls at Notion Press, most importantly luminaries like Ms. Surekha Thamannan who painstakingly worked on my manuscript under the visionary leadership of Mr. Naveen. Their orchestration of efficiency, commitment to excellence and dedication have propelled this project to soaring heights, where dreams manifest into tangible reality. I am forever indebted to their stellar contributions.

To my team, Murali, Madhan, Partiban, Govindan and Suresh, who were invaluable in helping me manage the hundreds of moving parts needed to create this book. My heartfelt thanks to all of you.

Last but not least, many have contributed and helped me in this book in ways they don't even realise. Their names could not be mentioned here due to space constraints. To them, I owe a deep sense of gratitude and appreciation.

INTRODUCTION

My entry into the world of law enforcement began innocuously in 1991 when I joined the Indian Police Service as an Assistant Superintendent of Police. Since then, I have been an enthusiastic observer and student of the transformative power of technology despite having no technology or engineering background whatsoever, as I had opted for the biological sciences stream during my college. Even after finishing my undergrad studies in Agricultural Sciences, I decided to pursue my postgraduate studies in Microbiology. I completed my PhD in Microbiology just before stepping into the Lal Bahadur Shastri Academy of Administration, Mussoorie, in September 1991 to enrol myself in the foundation course, which is mandatory for all civil servants. It was here that I had my first exposure to a computer, but when I joined my first posting, none of the police stations in my jurisdiction had any computers, not even my office. Mobile phones were also non-existent then.

Today, technology has become ubiquitous. Policing worldwide, including India, has undergone a fundamental transformation in the years by the many new types of technologies that are helping police to work more efficiently. Such rapid development of modern technologies is having profound implications on modern-day policing. Computers have become vital for police work in the 21st century as it affords the police the capability of searching extensive, international criminal information databases. Today's police officers can pull up information about suspects on computers. They can analyse data about crime and offenders, even predict the likelihood of a commission of crimes. Many of these technologies are relatively young, and some in many countries like India are still waiting for adoption. Besides allowing the police to plot crime incidents and patterns to anticipate and prevent recurrences, technology is also rendering help in interrogating criminal suspects, persons of interest and identifying suspects using such innovations as biometrics. New technology has equipped police to perform more effective audio and visual surveillance and expeditiously analyse forensic samples such as blood, DNA and toxins. Technology also has advanced police mobility, communications and weaponry.

Technology, like in the rest of the world, can play a significant part in India. It can act as a force multiplier, as the police to population ratio in India is less than 150 per 100,000, compared to the United Nations recommendation of 222 per 100,000. By adopting technology, we might bridge this wide gap in India. Besides, in India, there is a stigma attached to stepping into a police station; most citizens dread going to a police station. By providing digital access to the citizens, it will be possible to access services from the comfort of their homes. Most States are already providing such online services to the citizens. In addition, police can use social media to reach out to citizens to educate and inform them on traffic diversions, caution them about new types of crimes perpetrated in cyberspace or dispel rumours. The police can also use technology to detect crimes and nab criminals. Call detail records (CDR), mobile tower location, emails, SMS and web browsing history are providing valuable clues and helping police detect cases expeditiously. Apart from the existing technologies, there are several new emerging technologies like Artificial Intelligence (AI), Nanotechnology, 3D Printing, to name a few, the full potential of which are yet to be exploited by police organisations. AI in India is used in facial recognition technology in CCTVs to analyse footage and match fingerprints. AI is also being used to detect false vehicle number plates and recognise the car's make and model. But, the use of AI for predictive policing, which several Western nations are employing, is yet to come about in a big way in India. Big data could be helpful to integrate data from various sources such as location data, travel data, bank and credit card data, to help draw connections between crime and the criminal and create a 360-degree view of the criminal. Although this is happening now, productivity and functioning of the police organisations can be enhanced immensely in India if more technology is inducted in day-to-day police work to enhance the public–police interface by deploying emerging exponential technologies, by improving the internal operational efficiency of the organisations through better HR management and by integrating the five pillars of the criminal justice system namely the police, judiciary, prosecution, prison and forensics. Such real-time integration between information technology systems of the five pillars can significantly increase efficiency and drastically reduce the time taken to deliver justice.

But, still, not everything is hunky-dory with technology. On the one hand, technological advances benefit our world in myriad ways, but there is a sinister flip side, as criminals spin the same technologies against us. New technologies help generate illicit employment for millions of hackers, spammers and scammers who steal our personal information, bank account information and social media accounts. Further, hackers are accessing classified government information, breaching banks' firewalls and siphoning off millions of dollars. They are hacking into home CCTV monitors to spy on families, wiping out servers, scrutinising Facebook posts to conspire home invasions and using the GPS on mobile phones to tail their victims' every move. Man is yet to create a not-hackable computer, which is a worrying fact considering our dependence on computers for everything from financial services to air traffic control to the water/electricity grid for our essential services.

In my long law enforcement career spanning three decades, I have seen criminals establish themselves as early adopters of technology. Cybercriminals sought the online world long before the police could consider it. Cyberspace today is teeming with cyber-voyeurs, cyber-stalkers, cyber-tyrants, scam artists, cyber-extortionists, bullies and so on. As days go by, the cyber situation is likely to worsen at the current rate of advancement of technology coupled with the unprecedented proliferation of surveillance cameras, geo-location services, RFID tags and wireless networking technology. Every new technological innovation benefits cybercriminals by expanding the surface area available for penetration and attack, delighting and pleasing the cyber-offenders who are only too happy to exploit the unique vulnerabilities of the new technology. Cybercriminals continue to maintain the lead in cyberspace worldwide and remain ahead of the police.

Cybercriminals over the years have not paused but have kept pace and continued to evolve with the advancement of technology. Today, cybercriminals have also started to foray into emerging technologies such as robotics, virtual reality, AI, 3D printing and synthetic biology. Such ominous trends that are now becoming conspicuous all around is disturbing, because our world today is run mainly and maintained by technology. Today, the Internet could be as minuscule as a grain of sand, but tomorrow's Internet could be the size of the towering Himalayas.

Although the Internet has helped us improve our infrastructure, it has put us at tremendous risk. Our air traffic controls, railways, stock markets, electrical grid, sanitation systems, drinking water grid and so on, are all dependent on the Internet to function correctly. Just imagine the consequences of hacking any of the critical infrastructure systems. If a city's electrical grid gets hacked, the city would be thrown into total mayhem as it would get blacked out without lights, elevators will become non-functional, there would be no Internet, no cell phones, and air traffic control wouldn't be able to establish contact with the aeroplanes in the sky. Such an incident did take place in South Houston, USA, where a hacker hacked into the Water and Sewer department grid. Luckily, the hacker didn't do too much; he only caused the water pumps to fail. If the hacker whose IP address got traced to Russia had decided to poison the water supply system or mixed the wrong proportions of chemicals to treat the water, thousands of people would have easily gotten killed. Connecting our infrastructure to the Internet is beset with risks. The time has come to ponder if it is worth the serious risks.

The world is yet to realise that more extensive connections bring more significant risks as they allow hackers to play in a more widespread playground. The Internet of Things (IoT) is proliferating unimaginably and getting every physical object online. The trend has been to connect our devices randomly without any thought to make our lives easier. There are currently more devices connected to the Internet than people in the world. The Internet connects a staggering 10 billion devices today. The IoT devices connected worldwide will likely be 30.9 billion units by 2025. Homes or residences, on average, have ten connected devices, which the analysts' project will rise to 50 by the end of 2021. Devices such as smartphones, speakers and 5G will significantly affect our management and interaction in our homes and professions.

And, when it comes to technology in policing, technology imperceptibly expands police authority which the community and the courts most often fail to note. Technology also exacerbates the very problem the police recruit them to solve. The law enforcement system the world over is in a crisis. Police brutalities, discrimination and custodial deaths happen with the regularity of the days turning to nights and vice versa. The answer to the vexing question of reforming the police and curbing misconduct is sometimes innovative technologies. Body cams, hot spot policing and Tasers have been the answer in the past. An antidote to police murders seemed to be the Taser that could incapacitate a suspect without firing a bullet. Almost all 18,000 police units in the US issue their officers Tasers, or stun guns, as a non-lethal alternative to restraining or subduing people who appear to be threats. But, Reuters has documented more than 1,000 incidents since 2000 in which Tasers have killed people. In 2018 alone, 49 people were killed by Taser in the US. Technological devices may make policing more convenient, but they do not necessarily steer to better outcomes. Technology can never substitute for compassionate policing based on trust between cops and the citizens.

Further, in law enforcement, big data, on the one hand, has the inherent ability to reduce bias and inequality, while on the other, it has the potential to deepen inequality, threaten privacy and challenge civil liberties. Many in the world fear that data-heavy law enforcement supervision may impose a hefty price on the citizens in the name of objectivity, efficiency and public order. Predictive policing, which several Western nations have adopted, devours humongous quantities of ancient data or historical data. Based on such data, the tendency to conclude that the predicted hot spots are at risk for high crimes may be absurd because old data is not an accurate record of all crimes committed in a particular area; it is just the data that has come to the notice of the police. The problem of relying on such data is bias permeation given the historical patterns of police in India to over-police the poor and the minorities. In Western countries, the tendency of the police might be to over-police on racial considerations. Hence, such technologies are risky because they concretise the past biases into current and future prejudices.

Although police are adopting new technologies to combat crime in sophisticated and detailed ways, surprisingly, there has been a little perceptible transformation in police tactics and strategies at some places. Few police organisations appear to be acquiring new technologies not to affect more efficient crime control or organisational change but to simulate and propagate established police practices. Many such as Matt Shroud, the author of *Thin Blue Lie*, have been busy pointing out that tools of some new technologies may be overhyped and, in many cases, ineffective. The general lament that the police leaders, instead of grappling with fundamental questions about police work, have been looking to technology as a silver bullet has been growing louder with the simultaneous belief that salesmanship and spin of corporate interests have seduced the police leaders to think that technology will solve society's deeply entrenched biases and injustices.

I have been vociferous in simultaneously vilifying and hailing technology with the same zeal because everything, including technology, has two sides. It is better to look at both before we commit to either. For instance, computers and phones have been transformative tools. Still, on the flip side, they have rendered us susceptible to cyber-attacks, despite which we continue to contemplate having thousands of hackable devices on top of them. Some of us are just becoming aware that our phones, laptops and security systems could stream live data to someone thousands of miles away without our knowledge. Newly emerging technologies such as robotics, AI, genetics, synthetic biology, nanotechnology and 3D printers will likely have an incredible impact on our lives. Whether these technologies affect society positively or negatively depends on who controls them. Our techno-driven world is highly vulnerable and can be brought to a grinding halt by bad actors who know how to leverage the same technologies and turn them against us to our detriment.

The more we connect ourselves to the global information grid through smartphones, autonomous cars, social media networks, IoT and so on, the more susceptible we become to the machinations of the bad actors or terrorists. I am not striving to be a pessimist here, and I am not implying that cybercriminals thrive because of technology. Technology is essential for humanity to develop, progress and transform itself. But what I am trying to infer is that technology is a double-edged sword. If we don't guard ourselves and our technologies, catastrophe could be inevitable. Hence, this book intends to point out the positives and pitfalls of the technology. So the present book is about the new emerging technologies like AI that can transform law enforcement, their present and possible future applications, and their benefits and drawbacks. Besides, it also briefly dwells on how cybercriminals exploit cyberspace and the safeguards we can contemplate to prevent their misuse.

I have titled the present book 'Soliloquies on Future Policing: An Anthology on Emerging Technologies, Cybersecurity and Law Enforcement' as it is a series of weekend rooftop soliloquies I had choosing, researching, pondering before finally getting the draft out on paper for submission to the newspaper for publication. Some of them are possibly endorphin-tinged as those chapters took shape and form due to oxygen-infused high octane soliloquies during my weekly long runs. So, the book you are holding in your hands is a compilation of articles that I published in the *Deccan Chronicle* and *DTNext* (English dailies) in the last two years following my maiden book, *42 Mondays*. Therefore, *Soliloquies on Future Policing* becomes a sequel to *42 Mondays*. The first volume, *42 Mondays*, dwelt on game-changing technologies such as AI, Augmented Reality, Virtual and Mixed Reality, Nanotechnology, Autonomous Technology, Predictive Policing, 3D Printing Technology, Microbial Signatures or Human Microbiome, Synthetic Biology, CRISPR Technology or Gene Editing, Brain Fingerprinting, GPS, DNA Testing, Police Robots and Police Drones which are transforming policing. Therefore, *Soliloquies on Future Policing*, besides including new versions of a few of the technologies presented in *42 Mondays* such as CRISPR Gene Editing Technology, AI, Microbial signatures, Virtual Reality and 3D Printing, also has several other emerging technologies, for instance, Blockchain Technology, Behaviometrics, DNA fingerprinting technology, GIS, Infra-red Technology, Robot dogs, Cognitive Computing and 3D Imaging to name a few.

The chapters in the present volume have been compiled based on relevance and not chronologically according to the publication dates. I have divided the book into three parts. The first part deals with the emerging technologies and their application in policing, the second part deals with cybersecurity and cybercrimes, and the third part deals with different aspects of law enforcement. In the first part of the book, among the various emerging technologies, I have devoted a chapter on the emerging technology of 3D printing that will impact policing big time in the future. On the positive side, I have illustrated how 3D printing is being used by police forces to simulate detailed models of crime scenes, car crashes, footprints and fingerprints and to make architectural models for planning raids and courtroom use. On the flip side, I have highlighted how 3D printing can be the devil's playground. Guns have already been 3D printed, and I have highlighted how criminals use 3D printers to unleash unusual modus operandi of deceitful schemes.

Metaverse is a virtual world where people socialise, work and play through their avatars. Metaverse is projected to grow into a 10 trillion to 30 trillion dollar industry. Any ecosystem will become a breeding ground for criminals when so much is at stake. Hal Lonas, CTO of Trulioo, believes that to counter the potential threats of the metaverse, we will need a virtual version of Interpol to police it for fraud and financial crimes. Or we may have to bring the metaverses under the purview of the real world's national or international legal systems. Given the potential for cross-border payments of various sizes through the metaverse, we may need international agreements on what can go on and what cannot. Metaverse would require policing because human behaviour in the virtual world will reflect human behaviour in the real world. I have therefore included a chapter titled 'Who Will Police the Metaverse' in the book.

Elon Musk has claimed that humans are already cyborgs because of our integration with phones and computers. I reveal how humans turn into cyborgs and the implications in the chapter titled 'Are We All Cyborgs Already'? In the chapter 'Does Cloud Computing Have a Silver Lining', I have recounted how cloud computing is attracting cybercriminals and the vulnerabilities of the Cloud to hackers because of a high volume of data flow between organisations and cloud service providers. Virtual reality belonged to the realm of fantasy a few years ago. In the chapter on this subject, I have discussed how online interactions lead to real-world crimes. I have also divulged how terrorists use virtual spaces to radicalise, train and recruit followers.

Recently a powerful unique technology has emerged called CRISPR. CRISPR is a term employed in microbiology that stands for Clustered Regularly Interspaced Short Palindromic Repeats. These are segments of DNA with bizarre sequences found in microorganisms to serve an adaptive immune function. In 2016 US director of national intelligence James Clapper placed 'genome editing' among six top perils listed in the section on weapons of mass destruction as terrorists could use the technology to develop a virus that shears out segments of DNA in the human genome or create bio-weapons. Another fear police officers harbour is that criminals could use this technology to evade DNA tests. In the chapter on newly emerging CRISPR technology, I have delved into all the above.

Today, in the 21st century, nanotechnology is skyrocketing us into a new era of technological power, one that extends enormous promise for the future and colossal dangers – a chapter on Nanotechnology details how the new technology transforms forensics and police investigation. Nanotechnology is helping police differentiate forged products from originals. The use of nanofibers and nanodots is helping police prevent and detect counterfeiting crimes. Bio-Nanosensors are also finding applications for the detection of bioterror agents, drugs, explosives and identification of toxins.

Blockchain technology is emerging as a valuable technology to investigate illegal activity. In the chapter on Blockchain, I have shown how it is turning out to be a useful investigative tool and how the public nature of the Blockchain would allow the police to access criminals misusing technologies, mobiles, the Internet and so on. In the chapter 'Can Advanced Exoskeletons Turn Police into Robocops?', I have delved into how exosuits for cops can enable different enhancements, ranging from resistance to various forms of assault to superior combat capacity and faster movement.

The 3D Imaging technology, which has been around for decades, finds a place in the book as it is today proving helpful to law enforcement agencies because of its capability to identify and detect weapons among milling crowds. Similarly, in the chapter on infrared technology, I discuss how infrared cameras are helping police officers and security professionals to track, locate and capture criminals more efficiently in adverse weather, under dense foliage and in woodlands. Also, it can record, even in complete darkness, for surveillance. In the chapter on Geographic information system (GIS), I have brought out how GIS maps are helping police analyse crime patterns, manage special operations and assist law enforcement agencies in keeping their communities safe.

Police departments have been using robots to perform tasks they consider hazardous to humans, such as detonating bombs or gathering intelligence in hostage, robbery or active shooting situations. In the chapter devoted to robots, I have divulged how police use robots in law enforcement. Besides, I have raised issues on future legal implications of autonomous robots in law enforcement. In the chapter on Voice biometrics, I have discussed its emergence as an Audio Forensic tool to analyse and identify voice and its use for crime prevention and detection – and how the new technology shapes law enforcement.

Dataveillance is gaining prominence, so I have included a chapter on it in which I have explained how police are using Dataveillance to predict potential terrorist threats. As Dataveillance aggregates data, the enormous amount of amassed data proves beneficial for predictive policing. In the chapter on Astroturfing, I have revealed how it has become a manipulation tool for political and commercial ends. Several countries are now resorting to Astroturfing as a weapon to counter propaganda or stifle dissent. Cognitive computing is the development of a computer that can think and reason like humans. I have highlighted how researchers simulate thought processes in a computerised model and its future application in a chapter on the subject.

The microbial signature, which is the unique impression of bacteria and other microorganisms that criminals leave at the scene of the crime, is evolving as a new tool in the arsenal of law enforcement. Because the variety of species and strains in a person's microbiome is unique, we can use such molecular signatures to locate someone at a crime scene. I have therefore devoted an entire chapter to it to reveal its potential as the DNA sequencing technology, which facilitates investigators to analyse crime scene microbes, is becoming increasingly cheaper. The chapter on AI underlines how AI, facial recognition systems and so on are now being used by police forces worldwide and how they are revolutionising the war against crime. I have also highlighted the future likelihood of use of AI by criminals and the consequences.

The second part has a collection of articles on cybercrime and its impact, besides a few chapters on the dark web and its criminal misuse by criminals. The emergence of the dark web has brought a lot of crime to the global online community. Law enforcement agencies worldwide should police the dark web in their fight against crime, illegal weapons, illegal explosives, child pornography, illegal human trafficking and so on, through ingenious and effective ways. In chapters titled 'Darknet Weapons Market' and 'Human Trafficking on the Dark Web', I have highlighted that the dark web is getting exploited for human trafficking and the sale of firearms and explosives.

And in a separate chapter 'Are Biometrics Safer Than Passwords?', I have discussed the pros and cons of biometrics vis-à-vis passwords. Passwords have their advantages though biometrics like fingerprints, face and iris, is a lot more challenging to crack than passwords. The reader can uncover the newly emerging field of Behaviometrics that can identify a person uniquely based on a person's behaviour rather than physical characteristics in a separate chapter on Behaviometrics.

In the book's third part, the reader will find a few chapters on terrorism, such as bioterrorism, agroterrorism, cyberterrorism, and a couple of chapters on policing strategies. During the onset and the course of the pandemic, I published a few articles about policing during the pandemic, which the reader can access in Part 3 of the book. The reader will also find a few chapters of general nature which may not have a significant connection to technology, such as the chapter on the problem of police suicides in India and chapters on safeguarding data, and on the Police Commemoration Day, which police in India observe on October 21 every year. A chapter on crowdsourcing reveals how police forces worldwide embrace it to aid their criminal investigation.

Emotional Intelligence (EI) is a significant factor in day-to-day police work because a policeman's job involves dealing with hostile and aggressive criminal elements while maintaining good rapport and relationships with law-abiding citizens. A policeman's job also entails examining witnesses and comforting the victims. All of which requires good interpersonal skills, a high latitude of empathy and excellent communication skills. Hence, I have included a chapter on EI as it is important for a police officer to regulate his emotions and also comprehend the emotions of others, because an officer with high levels of EI would be able to remain calm, collected and relaxed even in the face of the gravest provocation.

Last but not least, I have deliberately included a chapter on the importance of spirituality for police officers in the final part, as police officers work in a realm where there is an endless struggle between good and evil. More than any other profession, those in the field of law enforcement are in an unusual position to make a spiritual difference in the lives of both colleagues and citizens with whom they interact. However, without a solid spiritual foundation, the stress involved in a law enforcement career can pull the officer down emotionally, thus leading to issues in the family, divorce, addiction, and in extreme cases, even suicide.

The present compilation is highly relevant today for both laymen and professionals. It offers a peek into various emerging technologies bursting forth on the policing scene while also highlighting the pitfalls and positives equally engrossingly. Police organisations around the world are embracing new technologies at a fast pace. Drones, facial recognition systems, robots and automatic number plate readers have become standard policing tools the world over. New technologies have discernibly transformed police work.

Law enforcement agencies can now uncover, accumulate, generate and share troves of data and integrate it across organisations and devices. In the coming years, the world will further witness the invention of many new technologies with applications in policing. The challenges of the coming decade in law enforcement will include identifying technologies that are most effective in reducing crime and using those technologies properly.

Furthermore, humans and law enforcement authorities will have to decide the quantum of technologies they would optimally need. If they fail to ask this question and go about blindly acquiring technologies, either because they fancy them or because some corporate is willing to offer it free, it will only lead them to disastrous consequences because the speed at which exponential technologies are evolving may modify the path of humankind forever. For instance, a person dreaming of owning an autonomous self-driving car should assess before buying one whether or not he would be willing to entrust his and the lives of his family members to a car that someone in another part of the world can hack to carjack or murder remotely. Similarly, if technology like autonomous robots or CRISPR is let loose without proper safeguards and regulations, nothing but catastrophe awaits humankind.

Finally, there are many technologies available today. Some are expensive, while some are complicated. Hence, police departments will have to make correct and good choices to invest the limited resources available. Further, the speed at which criminals are taking to new technologies today exceeds the rate at which law enforcement can adapt. Therefore, the book makes a case for law enforcement to guard, embrace and leverage new technologies faster than the velocity at which criminals are progressing with adequate caution and safeguards to stay miles ahead of the criminals in the race.

PART 1

TECHNOLOGY

Chapter 1
A REALITY CHECK ON CRIMINALITY IN VIRTUAL REALITY

Way back in the 1970s, my cousin heaved me into a video arcade, exposing me to the virtual world for the first time. Once inside, I was blown away by the surreal ecosystem of flashing lights, eerie phantasmagorical sounds flaring off weirdly flickering lights and glinting game cabinets with shimmering screens beckoning me to have a go. At 50 paise a game, I grabbed the joystick, wrenched it in delight while simultaneously tugging the buttons. In the process, I discovered myself transforming and becoming things I always dreamed about – a Tarzan who knocks the living daylights out of the jungle's marauders, a saviour slaughtering the demons with machine guns. I also found myself turning into a dragon slayer butchering the evil dragons. My time at the arcade was sheer bliss, a kind of rapture. Video games transported me into a bizarre world where I could be someone I craved and dreamed of while remaining who I was. It was a world where men could become women, women men, adults could become children, and human beings could transform themselves into animals, superheroes or monsters. A world where I could kill and go unpunished. A world where I could die but still be alive.

So, when boredom overtook me during the recent lockdown, I decided to check out *Virtuosity*, one of Denzel Washington's less well-known films that was pending on my bucket list. In the sci-fi flick, Washington plays Parker Barnes, an imprisoned police officer employed to hunt down a Virtual Reality (VR) killer played by Russell Crowe who gets out into the real world. The villain in *Virtuosity* is not a human being but a computer program named Sid 6.7, who turns a criminal in the VR simulations. In 1995, when *Virtuosity* got released in theatres crimes happening in the virtual world seemed far out and unreal.

Today, what got portrayed as sci-fi has turned into reality as criminals have joined these virtual worlds, and a full range of criminal activities are now present in the virtual space. Traditional 'real world' crimes happen every day in virtual worlds, including money laundering, stealing intellectual property, traffic of child abuse pictures and even suspected terrorist activities. Yet the concept of 'virtual reality' is new to law enforcement agencies around the world. Therefore, the new virtual worlds and societies extend a quirky set of challenges for the criminal justice system. Besides, the near-total absence of essential jurisprudence means that outlaws are always free to act with impunity.

Virtual worlds often encompass components popular to other online activities, such as MMORPGs (Massive Multiplayer Online Role-Playing Games). MMORPGs are video games that enable thousands of players to enter a virtual world and interact concurrently. Participants can operate their own 'cities and countries', set up armies to win wars and go on a diversity of 'quests' with their avatars. There are several virtual worlds and MMORPGs in existence today, with new ones appearing increasingly often. One of the most prominent virtual worlds is Second Life (SL), created by Linden Labs in 2003. Among MMORPGs, the World of Warcraft (WoW) is probably the most popular in the world. Tens of millions of people explore these spaces every month. Blizzard Entertainment's WoW independently has over 11 million active subscribers.

Surprisingly, to many players, the virtual world is central, and the real world is lesser. Many have come to comprehend that their virtual world is the natural world and vice versa. For a few, their avatars are so realistic that anything that happens to their avatar in the virtual universe makes a deep imprint on their actual persona. As a result, the virtual universe witnesses all types of crimes reported in the physical world. Gamers could suffer from cyberbullying to identity theft. In Japan, the police apprehended a man for virtually perpetrating mugging sprees with software 'bots' in the online game Lineage II.

The world's first virtual rape was reported in a world called LambdaMOO, in which a character named Mr Bungle using a 'voodoo doll' took control of the two avatars and then forced them to engage in sexual acts. In October 2016, a journalist by name Ms Belamire reported that she suffered sexual assault while playing the VR game QuiVR, using the HTC Vive. During the game, a gamer with the onscreen name of 'BigBro442' first started to rub her breasts and later followed it up by rubbing her virtual crotch. Several other users of VR have reported similar experiences.

In the game 'The Sims Online' a 17-year-old boy, going by the in-game name 'Evangeline', was discovered to have built a cyber-brothel, where customers would pay sim-money for minutes of cybersex. In Japan, a 43-year-old woman grew so enraged after her online husband 'divorced' her in the interactive 'Maple Story' game that she committed a virtual murder by eliminating him. The woman, Mayumi Tomari, was later arrested by the Japanese police.

Then, there was the killing in Russia of a 33-year-old member of the Platinum clan of an MMORPG guild by a 22-year-old member of the rivalrous Coo-clocks clan. When the two virtual gang members confronted each other in the physical city of Ufa, Russia, the 33-year-old got severely beaten to death. In South Korea, a 22-year-old student named Choi and an accomplice manipulated a virtual world server and made approximately US$1.2million. There have also been other instances where online game interactions have sparked real-world crimes. For example, Kimberly Jernigan of North Carolina, USA, was arrested for trying to kidnap a boyfriend she'd met on SL.

In future, VR may be increasingly used not only by criminals but by terrorists and antisocials as well. Hezbollah has developed its own shooter computer game named 'Special Force 2', which acts as a radicalisation medium for young jihadis. In the game, players earn points by launching Katyusha rockets at Israeli towns and becoming 'suicide martyrs'. A document leaked by Edward Snowden revealed that both the USA and UK were spying on gamers by creating undercover avatars to snoop, recruit informers and perform mass interception between players in various games.

Most police officers in the world may not have investigated any case involving a virtual world or MMORPG. Though it may be tempting to ignore MMORPG crimes considering them virtual, therefore not 'real', police must remember that virtual crimes have real-world victims. The psychological and economic impact of virtual crimes on their victims is every bit real to their inhabitants, as is the physical world to most investigators.

Finally, VR could be akin to spiritual reality. When we die in a video game, it's not game over; we can start a new game and play and die in as many games as we want, just like spiritual rebirths. But if you die in physical reality, you're dead. Besides, VR, like spirituality, helps us have adventures in consciousness and explore our psyches through the mind-altering, dream-changing, ego-breaking VR technology.

Chapter 2
THE EMERGING FACE OF FACIAL RECOGNITION TECHNOLOGY

Face recognition technology (FRT) has long been employed in science fiction films to depict a futuristic world of advanced technology. In the 1960s, *Star Trek* dazzled audiences demonstrating retina scans and facial recognition scans as a part of their digital security system. *RoboCop*, a 1987 Hollywood movie, unveiled futuristic police checking digital facial recognition instead of a driver's licence. Steven Spielberg's *Minority Report*, made in 2002, showed Tom Cruise, who is on the run, walk into a retail store. The retailer has technology that recognises each arriving shopper and instantly displays the images of clothing by the taste and preferences of the customer.

FRT is a relatively new technology that law enforcement agencies worldwide have started adopting to identify persons of interest. Face recognition identifies or verifies an individual by comparing and analysing patterns, shapes and proportions of their facial characteristics and contours. Police organisations are regularly utilising facial recognition to uncover probable crime suspects and witnesses by skimming through millions of photos. Authorities are also exploiting this technology for surveillance at public venues like concerts and stadiums and to gain entry into specific properties. Most police departments are today considering face recognition to be an indispensable tool to solve the most heinous crimes like terrorist attacks and violent assaults.

For instance, in New York City in 2019, a man followed a young woman home from work. He attempted to kidnap and rape her at knife-point, after hauling her into a grassy area before ultimately letting her go. Investigators employed FRT to compare pictures from surveillance video at a food shop close by with a mugshot database. A little more investigative work enabled the police to identify a suspect and arrest him within 24

Andrey_Popov/Shutterstock.com

hours. The 27-year-old suspect arrested previously for raping a 73-year-old lady was on bail when the offence was committed. In February 2021, the Delhi Police used FRT to identify more than 1,500 rioters who had created communal unrest in the north-east region of Delhi.

Further, the use of FRT in India helped the Delhi Police find 3,000 missing children in only four days. Scanning 45,000 children in New Delhi would be an almost ridiculous chore using conventional methods. But FRT could sift through the data in a matter of hours, enabling thousands of children to be identified, matched to missing person complaints and reunited with their families.

The Interpol Face Recognition System (IFRS) contains facial images from more than 179 countries, making it a distinctive transnational criminal database. Since 2016, more than 1,000 criminals, fugitives, persons of interest or missing persons have been identified using IFRS.

Back in India, there have been several FRT endeavours. The Telangana State Police have created a facial recognition system that enables them identify offenders by comparing the suspects' faces with digital photographs in a central database called Crime and Criminal Tracking Networks and Systems (CCTNS). Chennai city police used a face recognition software called FaceTagr developed by a Chennai-based company to monitor the Diwali shopping crowds. Similarly, Amritsar police uses an FRT developed by a Gurugram AI company Staqu Technologies called Punjab Artificial Intelligence System (PAIS) that could detect a murder case within 24 hours. The Staqu-developed PAIS claims that it can match images with a precision of 98 per cent if the database has five photos of the person. Elsewhere, the Surat police is using the state-of-the-art NeoFace technology of the NEC Corporation for solving crimes. In July 2018, Andhra Pradesh launched e-Pragati, a searchable database of millions of people containing e-KYC Aadhaar numbers. Uttar Pradesh police in December 2018 attempted 'Trinetra', an AI-based application with face recognition capabilities and a database containing details of 5 lakh criminals.

Unlike DNA technology, facial recognition is not expensive and time-consuming and, once installed, the facial system needs little overheads or expenses. The relative ease of the process makes it easy to incorporate it as a part of daily work. Much of the fear about FRT is because the public knows little about how police are using the technology and whether it has effectively lessened crime. The police departments that use facial recognition have not been forthright about how they use the technology. As long as police departments continue to use face recognition under this information void, the retaliation against the technology will likely grow more robust, no matter the potential upsides. Unfortunately, most of the time, the police have been found using the technology to solve routine crimes and identify people they see as suspicious quickly.

The technology can add value if used properly. At present, people do not have a good understanding of technology; hence a little education could help in gaining acceptance. Civil liberties groups have been crying themselves hoarse that facial recognition contributes to privacy erosion, bolsters bias against minorities and is susceptible to misuse. San Francisco, Boston and a prominent police body camera manufacturer have banned

FRT by law enforcement. IBM too has backed away from its work in this area. The biggest fear is that the government might misuse the technology for surveillance. Hence some more US states are contemplating a ban on technology in certain areas.

The Boston Marathon bombings brought out the limitations of FRT. This technology is less accurate on people of colour. Further, the error rate of FRT is higher for men than women. CyberExtruder, a reputable company supplying facial recognition software to some law enforcement agencies, has accepted that some skin colours give high error rates. Some facial recognition systems available today have an accuracy rate of 99.31 per cent on the still frontal face. Modifications in lighting, face positioning, facial expressions, profile pictures, makeup, hairstyle, facial hair, glasses and other accessories diminish the precision rate. A big smile can render the system less effective.

Facial recognition being a powerful technology, the State should consider its use only for law enforcement and national security, that too, with adequate safeguards. Aadhaar has iris and biometric information; there appears to be a move to strengthen it with facial recognition. Once that is done, Aadhaar will have total surveillance infrastructure. Usage of FRT in the absence of any data protection or data privacy law could result in misuse of the technology. There is no legal provision to stop the misuse of FRT in India. The Information Technology Act, 2000 does not have provisions to deal with the abuse of technology. Cybercriminals appear to be taking advantage of this situation by making such data available on the darknet.

Finally, recognising our spiritual nature or spiritual recognition technology could go a long way in overcoming FRT concerns. If we treat faces as just another unit of data that is to be harvested by the global surveillance machine, something sacred and spiritually deep within us gets transgressed. Counteracting the consequent dystopia recognising our spiritual nature and connecting to the divine blueprint of the soul could help us experience utopia even in a dystopian world.

Chapter 3
ROBOTICS IN LAW ENFORCEMENT

RoboCop, released in 1987, tells the story of a Detroit police officer Alex Murphy killed in action and resurrected as a cyborg super-cop with a built-in program to restore law and order. Today science fiction has become a reality. Police in different parts of the world is using robots for law enforcement. The world's first operational 'Robocop' officially joined the Dubai police force in May 2017. Since then, robots have been deployed for policing in different parts of the world, including China and USA, and in some states of India.

We initially exploited robots for meeting industrial needs. We deployed them for improving the efficiency and quality of production in industries. We have eventually used them to meet military and law enforcement needs. Policing today is being touched by technology like every other field of human endeavour. Unlike factory bots sliding onto a production line, robocops today are strolling our neighbourhoods and wielding weapons.

Looking back, Israel first used unmanned aerial vehicles (UAVs) successfully in their conflict with Syria in the early 1980s. It was not until the late 1990s that the US military fully endorsed the use of UAVs for surveillance and conducting airstrikes from a distance. The application of this technology got widely witnessed during the Gulf war conflict in their fight against Al Qaeda and ISIS because of the intention of the USA to curtail troop casualties during surveillance and intelligence gathering missions.

The USA is now using this technology to fight their enemies efficiently and effectively with minimum collateral damage, using a few trained men from remote locations. The Americans and several other countries have now come to accept robotics as a tool for policing, like the way it was adopted in the US military. Although some are cautioning the potential dangers of using robots for policing, eventually, robots

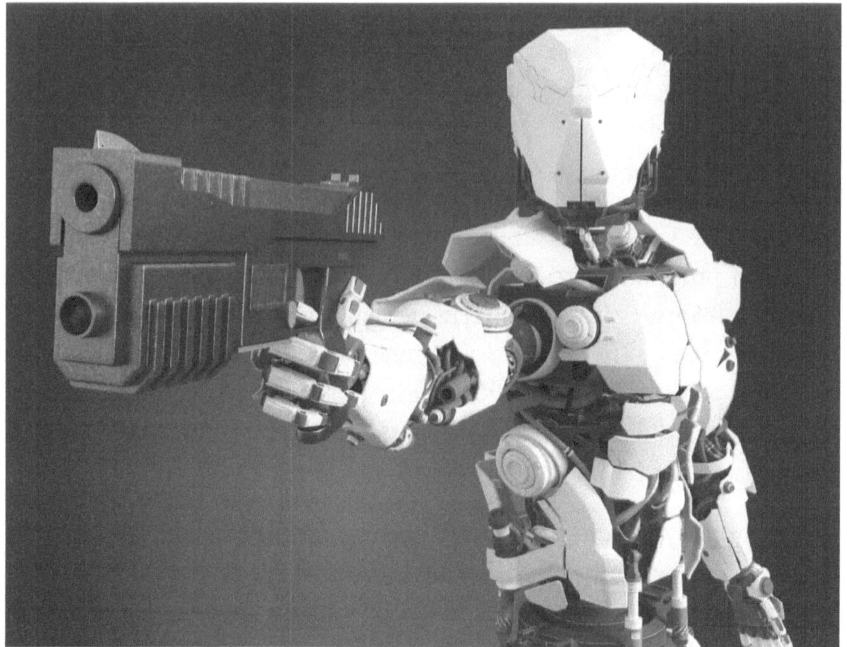

Sarah Holmlund/Shutterstock.com

are gradually and steadily becoming part and parcel of the police-toolkit. Over thirty years ago, the science fiction film *Robocop* featured a memorable scene in which a giant mega-corporation unravels a law-enforcement droid called ED-209. Launched as 'the future of law enforcement', the new robot's debut during a demo gets met with an unmitigated disaster when the robot cannot recognise when its identified threat has dropped his gun, resulting in the disastrous obliteration of its target, proving a point that putting one's trust in autonomous armed police robots could prove catastrophic.

However, there are several areas of policing where robots are being used, such as patrolling, surveillance, anti-terrorist operations and intelligence collection. Patrol robots could monitor the roads/streets for reporting and detecting crimes to human officers. The robots also accurately record the happenings witnessed during the patrol for immediate and future review. The Chinese robot, called AnBot, which they have rolled out into airports and train stations, has facial recognition technology that can track potential criminals and forward information to a central command manned by human operators. Dubai police introduced its first robot police officer in May 2017. Wearing a police cap and moving on wheels, the robot features a computer touch-screen on its chest that can report a crime or inquire about speeding tickets. Police robots are also making stops, arrests and other serious situations less dangerous. They are also clearing debris from accident scenes.

Robots are also being used in law and order and violent situations to control and safely assess conditions remotely from a safe distance to enable the human officers to develop reliable tactical plans for execution. Atlas robot recently unveiled by Boston Dynamics can move like humans with self-sustaining energy and is controllable remotely. We could use such robots for patrolling in hostile situations. Police in Uttar Pradesh has acquired a set of Skunk drones built to spray crowds with pepper spray and paintball. The drone, manufactured by South African firm Desert Wolf, hovers mid-air over a protest and fires up to 20 paintball (or other 'non-lethal' ammunition) per second while simultaneously dispersing tear gas pellets onto people. It's also fitted with onboard speakers to let police communicate with crowds, and has bright strobe lights and 'eye-safe' lasers to disorient and disperse a gathering.

Robots can also restrict and restrain armed suspects who are likely to hurt humans by opening fire or by using any other weapon or weapons. A robotic firm in Israel has built a Roomba-like gun-toting robot with a built-in 9 mm Glock pistol called 'Dogo'. This small land rover can enter a house quietly, climb stairs, and even manoeuvre over obstacles. Ready with eight cameras and two-way audio, the Dogo allows police to communicate with and fire upon suspects without risking their lives. Robots could also access inaccessible crime scenes and generate crime scene reports, mahazars, and collect evidence from the scene of crime (SOC). Robots also seem to have a better ability of electronically recording victim, witness and accused statements without misinterpretation or human bias.

Without putting humans at risk, it would be possible to defuse and dispose of bombs using bomb disposal robots remotely. Brazilian police, to inspect suspicious packages during the Olympics held in their country, acquired 510 PackBots, that are military-grade bomb detection and reconnaissance robots. PackBots have capabilities of bomb detection and disposal. The PackBot climbs stairs, manoeuvres in water, and can crawl around at about 6 miles per hour, faster than most adults jog. Similarly, Cleveland police have recently inducted a new robot named Griffin, created by students from a local college, which stands 12 inches tall; the six-wheeled rover reaches places that police can't, such as under a car or behind dumpsters, to look for explosives. Griffin has been fitted with a camera and light, which allows police to monitor and act on a situation remotely from a safe distance. Unlike the military-grade robot, which the police deployed in Dallas, Griffin is light enough to get around quickly and easily.

The Los Angeles Police Department (LAPD) has inducted a Bat Cat which is short for Bomb Assault Tactical Control Assessment Tool. Bat Cat is a radio-controlled monster that has been designed to pick up a car bomb with its massive, 50-foot telescoping arm. The Bat Cat also can tear through a house in minutes. In 2011, LAPD used it to obliterate the walls of a home during a standoff.

In July 2016, police in Dallas modified a non-lethal bomb disposal robot to deliver explosives to kill a gunman. They clamped a bomb to an explosive-detonation robot and boom: a non-lethal robot became an assassin. Police Chief David Brown allowed his SWAT commanders to plan an ingenious strategy to neutralise a deadly suspect. In response, the Dallas Bomb Squad devised a plan which envisaged innovative use of delivering explosives through a robot to neutralise the deadly sniper Micah Xavier Johnson, a 25-year-old military veteran from Mesquite, Texas, who had unleashed sniping attacks one after another which killed five Dallas police officers. After a 45-minute shoot-out and a failed two-hour negotiation, the Dallas SWAT team decided to put a stop to the man who swore to slay even more officers. The team put to use a bomb squad robot and halted the siege with no more police officer casualties. This ploy, however, earned attention as the anti-militarisation groups came out and vocalised their displeasure.

Human rights activists worry that these robots lack social awareness critical to the decision-making process. For instance, during mass uprisings in Egypt in January 2011, the military declined to shoot and kill the protesters, an action that needed inherent human compassion and regard for the rule of law. Several anti-robotics activists, including Elon Musk and Stephen Hawking, were signatories to a letter that threatened the use of gadgets that can choose targets without human management. Using explosives is bringing up new concerns over the reasonableness to launch a robot to eliminate dangerous suspects instead of continuing to mediate their surrender. Such deadly use of explosives may get the approval of the court, for using it under the conditions of confronting a significant threat. But police organisations must give serious thought before executing such a choice. Most tactical commanders would have green-lighted the alternative of using a police counter-sniper if there had been a window in that cabin in Dallas. In which case, it would have been a successful risk elimination by a police sharpshooter. In the days to come, robotic weaponry is likely to get used more often; therefore, we may need more officer training and rules of engagement – along with constant legal analysis. Many continue to condemn the use of bomb robots, solely because they perceive it as too hostile.

Robots are of different types. Humanoid robots may seem scary, but they have been with us since 2000. Robots may be autonomous or semi-autonomous and range from humanoids such as Honda's Advanced Step in Innovative Mobility (ASIMO) and TOSY's TOSY Ping Pong Playing Robot (TOPIO) to industrial robots, medical operating robots, collectively programmed swarm robots, UAV drones such as General Atomics MQ-1 Predator, and even microscopic nanobots. By masquerading as a lifelike edifice or automating motions, a robot may show the existence of intelligence or thought of its own. Autonomous robots are likely to increase in the days to come.

Telerobots are appliances remotely operated from a distance by a human operator. They get used when a human cannot be present on-site to execute a task because it is hazardous, remote or inapproachable. The robot may be in another country, or maybe in a different locality. For disabling a bomb, the operator may send a small bomb disposal robot to cripple it. Teleoperated robot aircraft, like the Predator Unmanned Aerial Vehicle, are increasingly being employed by the army. These pilotless drones can scan terrain and fire on targets. Several robots such as iRobots PackBot and the Foster-Miller TALON are being used in Iraq and Afghanistan by the US Army to defuse roadside bombs or improvised explosive devices (IEDs) in action known as explosive Ordnance disposal.

Sustaining a growing police force requires huge expenditures which several countries cannot afford; so, robotics could become a viable alternative to augment an expensive human police force. Today the governments spend crores of rupees of taxpayer's money towards recruitment, training and salaries for police personnel. Besides, the police personnel incur crores of recurring expenditures in terms of travel bills, medical bills and other benefits. None of these expenses will accrue if we deploy robots. The United Arab Emirates has big plans for the future. By 2030 it wants robots to make up 25 per cent of its police force,

Eventually, robotic technology will become cheaper and more energy-efficient. A robot called EATR has generated public concerns as it does not need an energy source, as it continually refuels itself using organic materials. Researchers have devised an engine for the EATR capable of fuelling itself on biomass and vegetation available on battlegrounds or other local environments.

Can robots evolve and become spiritual like humans? As human consciousness is nonphysical, it may not be possible for humans to create consciousness in machines. Raymond Kurzweil, an American inventor, futurist and the author of the book *The Age of Spiritual Machines* believes that the future machines will 'proclaim to be conscious, and thus to be spiritual'. He further concludes that 'twenty-first-century machines' might go to church, meditate, pray and be able to connect with their inherent spirituality.

CHAPTER 4
UNCHAINING BLOCKCHAIN FOR POLICING

The US government was the first to use blockchain technology to investigate and bring down a dark-web marketplace called the Silk Road, which sold drugs, weapons, and everything illicit on this planet. The blockchain also helped nail two corrupt investigators investigating the black-market site. Authorities often criticise bitcoins and cryptocurrencies as enablers of crime as they give criminals anonymity and a way to bypass highly regulated financial channels. But the blockchains that power the cryptocurrencies are now being mined by criminal detectives. The most famous case detected by using blockchain technology reads like an Agatha Christie thriller.

Silk Road was a mysterious marketplace. Nobody knew who was behind it. All that the investigators knew was that he went by the username: DPR or Dread Pirate Roberts. Sometime soon, however, an undercover agent could become friends with DPR and the two began messaging almost daily. The undercover user name was NOB. In 2015, two Silk Road users namely Death from Above and French Maid began handing out threats to DPR informing him of exposing his identity if he did not cough up 'hundreds of thousands of dollars, in bitcoins'. At the same time, French Maid was selling information on the federal investigation of Silk Road back to DPR. Around the same time, 21,000 bitcoins vanished from Silk Road accounts and DPR through his own investigation figured out that credentials of a Silk Road administrator named Curtis Green had been used to steal the money. After the discovery, DPR approached NOB to kill Green. But Green by then had turned approver for the federal authorities, and in their protective custody had handed over his computer information, including his Silk Road credentials. Federal investigators still did not know who 'Death from

Zapp2Photo/Shutterstock.com

Above' or 'French Maid' was and had no clue what had happened to the 21,000 bitcoins. A God-sent tip from one member of the cryptocurrency community occasioned the top Federal authorities to investigate their own agents investigating the case discreetly. When they looked into NOB's accounts, they found he was moving humongous amounts of bitcoins to his personal accounts. Blockchain makes the bitcoin possible. Blockchain tracks every bitcoin transaction. Blockchain's audit trail with federal subpoena power revealed that the bitcoin payments from NOB's accounts were coming from the Silk Road. NOB was the owner of both 'French Maid' and 'Death from Above'. He was playing both sides all the time. Upon further investigation, the agents found that the 21,000 bitcoins had gone to the account of a secret agent on the task force investigating Silk Road. The agent had been in the room when Curtis was handing over his password. Both NOB and the secret agent had done a great job of concealing their criminality. Today, both are cooling their heels in the prison. Without blockchain, they would still be undercover agents.

Similarly, blockchain technology is today helping detection of crimes in new ways without face-to-face interactions. In a blockchain, we store data in blocks, linking each block in a chronological order in a line with a hash that forms a unique identifier linking the blocks together. We cannot alter data in a blockchain, we can only add it on to the chain with timestamps and no single stakeholder can control it as they distribute it over a large network of computers. This is basically an e-ledger. By using technology, it is now possible to keep tabs on and analyse transactions that we can connect to crimes and criminals. With blockchain technology we can make crime reports on a distributed ledger, through which we can automatically update the victim or the complainant every time there is a development in the case. This could even apply to cases under trial, where we can intimate warrants and summons to registered users in real time. Exchange or sharing of data between different law enforcement agencies or with different components of criminal justice system becomes simple helping multiple users to access the data with varying levels of permission.

Blockchain provides an unalterable chronological clandestine storage of records and documents by which police can analyse criminal activity. Further, the public nature of blockchain falls outside of potential third party doctrine issues. Blockchain therefore would not raise third party doctrine issues which revolves over anticipation of privacy over information one shares with the third party such as a bank or ISP. Hence, mobile records, Internet history, transactions and so on would become admissible as evidence in an investigation as the public nature of the blockchain would allow the police to access criminals using such technologies to commit crimes. Further, law enforcement and Internet providers who have problems with keeping customer and transaction data could keep any quantum of data without needing to erase it.

Blockchain can also play several book-keeping roles like securing a chain of custody to inter-organisational data sharing and more by which it can free up enormous funds for more important aspects of police work. Samples of evidence collected during an investigation sometimes go missing or get disintegrated or get stolen or mishandled or get thrown away. The chemical examiners' report in the sensational Sister Abhaya case was found fudged. This brought to light the scowling verity of manipulation even in high-profile cases.

Though we may not physically store a blood-stained knife on the blockchain, it will be possible to document who handled the evidence and other critical information including the mode and method of storage. For preserving evidence, blockchain is extremely good for tamper-proofing records of origin and the chain of custody. The best thing about blockchain is that it is borderless. When evidence is within another country, we today have to seek permission from the host country to get that evidence. This issue won't arise with blockchain because it can be available from anywhere. Despite several benefits of using blockchain, police and security agencies have so far only taken an interest in this technology, mostly for tracking criminals hiding illegal money from banks.

In Thiruvananthapuram, India, a project called 'Police 2020' is developing blockchain technology to help a variety of stakeholders collect, secure and access data in a decentralised manner. In Australia, AUSTRAC, the financial intelligence agency, and the Australian Criminal Intelligence Commission have given a contract to Singapore-based consultancy Houston Kemp to build a blockchain-based system to record intelligence and data generated by the police. China's Ministry of Public Security, which deals with all Chinese police departments, has built a blockchain application to place evidence from investigations into cloud storage. Governments in Indian states, such as Telangana, in order to make land records tamper-proof are moving them to blockchain platform in a phased manner, while others are exploring ways and means of storing contracts and assets, and the financial industry too is experimenting with blockchain technologies to streamline transactions and back office systems.

Blockchain technology despite having several advantages has some challenges. In a blockchain, it would be possible for criminals to protect their identities with high levels of encryption. There is also the danger of building a more decentralised Internet like blockchain earth which would make it extremely difficult to monitor and remove content such as child pornography and material provoking terrorism.

That a thriving dark-net market place such as Silk Road marketplace even at the embryonic stage of cryptocurrency investigators could be brought down reveals that law enforcement has developed an awe-inspiring capacity to analyse and trace transactions using blockchain. During the Silk Road investigation, blockchain revealed how the DEA agent Carl Force stole bitcoins despite trying to disguise its source and destination.

Cryptocurrencies are being depicted as an asylum for criminals as over $1.2 billion was being transacted on the now defunct Silk Road marketplace for over two and a half years. But cryptocurrency is a double-edged sword; cryptocurrency investors can be victims of theft and fraud. By the end of June 2018, criminals stole a reported $1.7 billion in cryptocurrencies in that year. That means that they could steal more than $4 billion in cryptocurrency in a full year. Cryptocurrency has also become the preferred currency for demanding ransom payments. In January 2017, hackers started aiming at open source documents and programs, wiping out data deliberately and demanding ransom for restoring the data. In the new world of cryptocurrencies traditional strong-arm methods of crime have made their way too – a robber relieved a man of his USB drive containing $1.7 million investments in cryptocurrencies at gunpoint. Despite such crimes, law enforcement still appears to give precedence to likes of ISIS, cartels, and so on, which use cryptocurrency to launder money.

Ransomware attacks have become very common. For instance, a person may receive an email informing him that somebody has locked his files with encryption, which he won't release unless he pays a specified ransom. Such criminals, 75 per cent of the time, make a ransom request only in bitcoins. Such attacks have become so pervasive that the US Department of Homeland Security (DHS) funded the development of a bitcoin analysis tool specifically aimed at ransomware. Whether the victim pays up the ransom or otherwise, the FBI has devised ways to peg the perpetrator of the attack. Established in 2000, the FBI's Internet Crime Complaint Center (IC3) admits reports of alleged cybercrimes including theft of intellectual property, corporate infiltration and 'online extortion' or ransomware. The FBI looks into the recipient wallet and its expenditures and tries to find connections to other wallets or clusters of addresses. When it comes across something suspicious, it serves a subpoena to learn what the transactions have been paying for. This in most cases has been leading to the identification of the ransom recipient.

In the end, a blockchain is like human consciousness. A blockchain is distributed, so is human consciousness. Each human within the network of human consciousness is a distinct node that can act individually or in concert with the collective consciousness. An individual's consciousness will advance spiritually only if it aligns with the other spiritual beings and their consciousness nodes.

Chapter 5
THE GROWING THREAT OF AI ASSISTED CRIMES

Anand Gandhi's *OK Computer* is a sci-fi comedy series set in 2031 starring Radhika Apte, Jackie Shroff and Vijay Varma. In the film – on a beautiful moonlit night in a tranquil coastal town in north Goa, when a self-driving car bangs into a pedestrian and kills him instantaneously, the police are confronted with three irksome questions regarding the culpability of the crime: Is the CEO of the taxi company culpable? Or is the programmer culpable? Or is the car itself with the AI system culpable? When the police commence investigations, detective Vijay Varma uncovers it to be wilful murder. Still, Radhika Apte, who heads an organisation for the ethical treatment of robots, disputes it as she believes that AI is incapable of harming humans. The questions that the show hurls at us are whether an AI can enable or commit a crime, and if an AI commits a crime, who should be culpable?

Technology is a double-edged weapon. With the advent of the Internet, we had Internet crimes, and with the inception of social media, crimes on social media proliferated. *OK Computer* may be pure fiction. But AI could play an increasing role in committing and enabling crimes in the future. Particularly going by the rampant proliferation of AI in various sectors, especially public safety, administration and finance – the attack on such AI-based systems is likely to rise. Many criminal, political and terror scenarios could arise from targeted disruption of such systems.

For instance, AI-generated, fake content in media could lead to widespread mistrust and deterioration of faith in audio and visual content. Deep fakes are getting extraordinarily sophisticated, convincing and more challenging to prevent. Fake content in social media has, frequently, affected democracy and national politics. For instance, a

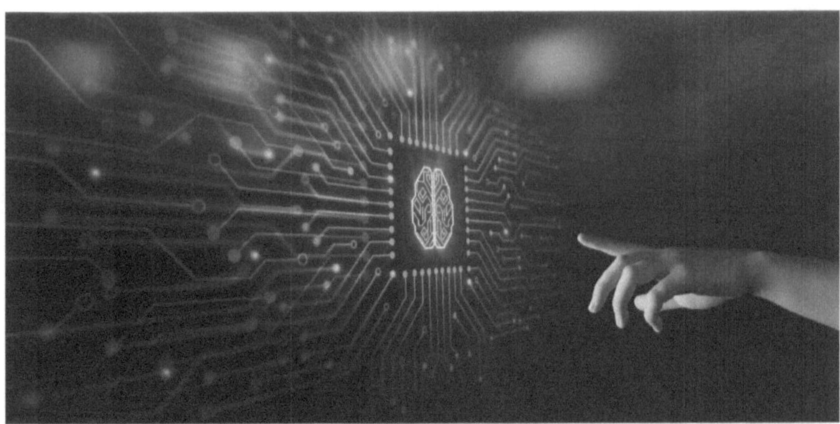

Alexander Supertramp/Shutterstock.com

tailored video of a drunk Speaker of the US House of Representatives, Nancy Pelosi, speaking in a slurring manner garnered over 2.5 million views on Facebook in 2020. Using AI, a UK-based organisation called Future Advocacy in 2019 created a deep fake AI video showing election rivals Boris Johnson and Jeremy Corbyn advocating each other for the post of Prime Minister. Though there are algorithms to detect deep fakes online, several avenues are available for manipulated videos to spread undetected. Creating means of detecting the deep fake at the point of upload may be the need for the hour. GAN (generative adversarial network), an AI technique recently invented at Stanford has enabled the generation of hoaxes, doctored video and forged voice clips easier to execute with excellent results.

Further, in a democracy, AI could also threaten the fundamental rights of its citizens. For instance, politicians or parties who have the power and authority could use AI to analyse mass-collected data and create targeted propaganda to mislead them. During elections, they could circulate fake videos for social manipulation and deception.

Furthermore, AI technologies power autonomous systems. Autonomous vehicles may be in their infancy, but they could become more common in the future and run the risk of being repurposed as weapons. Criminals could load an autonomous vehicle with explosives and send it to an earmarked destination, or they could hack an autonomous vehicle and use it to damage property or attack pedestrians. Further, it may be possible to control an autonomous car through computer hardware or software. A malicious attacker taking advantage of security gaps could take over a car or even cause it to crash wilfully. The ability to utilise a vehicle without requiring a human at the wheel would likely dramatically speed up this practice. Autonomous drones at present are not being used for crimes of violence, but their mass and kinetic energy are potentially destructive if targeted precisely. Criminals could also fit drones with weapons that could prove lethal in self-organising swarms.

Natasha Pajema, in her book *Rescind Order*, portrays a scenario of AI-based systems going haywire when an automated command-and-control system detects an incoming nuclear attack, and automatically gives the launch order for the nuclear weapon. The protagonist in the book cannot verify if the automated system has detected a false attack or if the attack is actual. The protagonist has precisely 8 minutes and 53 seconds to decide. *Rescind Order* narrates a heart-rending story of US decision makers steering a nuclear crisis in the year 2033, during a potentially tricky era of autonomous systems, social media communication and deep fakes, which we are likely to encounter sooner.

Another AI-based crime 'Tailored phishing' is likely to give sleepless nights to cybercrime experts in which criminals would collect information by installing malware or through digital messages by creating an impression of a trusted party such as the user's bank. The phisher plays with the existing trust to persuade the user to execute actions he would otherwise be wary of, such as revealing passwords or clicking on dubious links.

Likewise, culprits may use AI as a blackmail tool to harvest personal information from social media or large unique datasets like phone contents or browser history. They may use them to tailor threat messages to their targets to blackmail them. AI could also generate fake evidence and assist criminals in sextortion. The latter involves using AI to hack into the computer or phone of the victim to extract videos or access personal pictures to blackmail the victim for sexual favours or money.

Criminals further could also use AI to poison data. For instance, a smuggler intending to smuggle weapons on board a plane could make an automated X-ray threat detector insensitive to firearms. Criminals could use AI to mislead an investment advisor into making unexpected recommendations which the criminal could exploit because of shifting market value. Criminals could also capitalise on the rampant proliferation of AI in various sectors such as Power or Food, leading to widespread power disruption to traffic gridlock and breakdown of food logistics. Systems with responsibility for public safety and security are probable to become crucial targets, as those systems dealing with financial transactions. Criminals could also use AI to trick face recognition systems, deny access to victims to online activities and create AI-authored fake reviews. They may also use it for AI-assisted stalking, and forgery of content such as art or music.

Unlike conventional crimes, crimes in the cyber domain can be repeated, shared or sold to criminals for perpetrating crimes. UCL's Matthew Caldwell suggests we may even witness the marketisation of AI-enabled crime soon with the advent of 'Crime as a Service' (CaaS). To counter and deter such virtual risks, there is a need for legislation of AI crimes within the cybercrime framework.

Finally, AI is encroaching on the spiritual domain as well. We are today witnessing AI and online houses of worship and robot priests. The pandemic is replacing traditional worship with virtual tools. The intersection of technology and spirituality is coming much faster than many expected. Digitally mediated religious communities, sometimes, are proving more attractive and allowing more connectivity than brick and mortar churches and temples.

Chapter 6
DNA DATABASE IN INDIA TO BOOST CRIME DETECTION

I have always been fascinated by detective movies and serials. For a few years, I have been watching American television series *Forensic Files*. Not surprisingly, the recurring theme in almost all of them invariably has been about the DNA molecule's stellar role in solving crimes. India with a population of over a billion people has crimes happening every minute in some part of the country or the other. According to National Crime Records Bureau (NCRB) over 300,000 crimes directly affecting people or property were reported in 2016 but conviction rates remained at about 30 per cent. Would India do better in crime detection if it had a DNA database? Detection of crime in the UK went up from 26 per cent to a healthy 40 per cent after DNA samples were loaded into the national DNA database. In India, although 96 per cent of sexual offences are chargesheeted, the rate of conviction for rape in 2016 according to NCRB was a trifling 25 per cent. Obviously, what appears to be missing is a clinching forensic proof like DNA evidence. The President of India recently promulgated an ordinance, which prescribes the punishment of death penalty for rape cases related to minor girls. DNA evidence could be particularly crucial in such cases. In 2012, Lokniti, an NGO, filed a public interest litigation in the Supreme Court of India requesting the establishment of a DNA database, to trace unidentified bodies and missing children, basing their argument that right to be identified was also a part of the right to dignity. Following this nudge and some push from investigative agencies like CBI, the Union Cabinet in the first week of July this year cleared the DNA Technology (Use and Application) Regulation Bill, 2018, only after 59 countries had preceded India in setting up their national DNA database programs. The first government database, The National DNA Data Base (NDNAD) was set up in the UK in 1995. France set up its database in 1998. FBI in the United States of America, in 1998, assembled a Combined DNA Index System (CODIS)

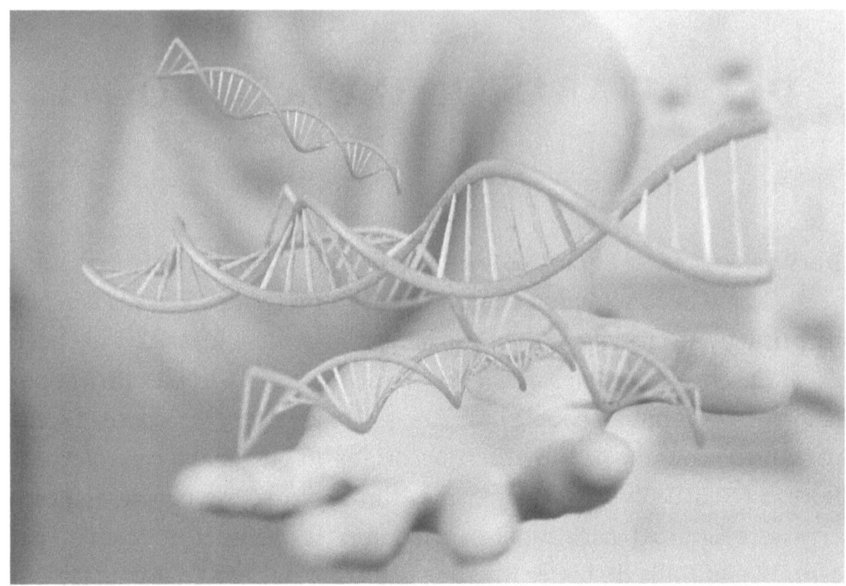

sdecoret/Shutterstock.com

database. The DNA database of the US has over 9 million records which are almost similar in size to the database of the UK.

The DNA Technology (Use and Application) Regulation Bill, 2018 seeks to use DNA for solving crimes by allowing its use for criminal investigation, identifying missing persons or determining biological relationships between individuals. It also allows storage of genetic information of select persons with built-in safeguards against its misuse. The rationale behind this Bill apparently being that the expansive use of DNA in the criminal investigation could contribute to higher conviction rates especially in cases of murder, rape, human trafficking and other crimes involving human body.

In order to safeguard citizens' privacy, few important provisions have been built into the Bill. Most important being that DNA profiling would be used only for identification purposes and not for any other purpose. Secondly, no bodily substance would be taken from anyone without previous consent in writing, this may, however, not be applicable for persons punishable either with death or with a sentence of more than seven years. Thirdly, a statutory body called the 'DNA Profiling Board' would be responsible for supervision, inspection and assessment of DNA standards. The Bill also prescribes setting up of a National DNA Data Bank, and Regional DNA Data Banks for the States, by the Central Government. These Data Banks would be responsible for storing DNA profiles received from the accredited laboratories and maintaining certain indices for various categories of data, like crime scene index, 'suspects' index, 'offenders' index, 'missing persons' index and 'unknown deceased persons' index. Besides, people found guilty of flouting the norms proposed by the Bill, like leaking the database, would be liable for up to three years imprisonment along with a hefty fine of up to Rupees one lakh. Lastly, DNA profile would be indexed or used for comparison only if the person has been suspected of a crime or is a previous offender. Any undertrial may request the trial court for another DNA testing if he/she satisfies the court that the previous DNA sample(s) could have been contaminated and hence could not be relied upon.

Finally, before setting up any database, privacy issues should first be addressed. A mechanism prescribed in the Bill protects the right to privacy by permitting for processing of DNA samples only for 13 CODIS loci. This will prevent misuse of DNA beyond the identification of a particular person. The strict conformance to 13 CODIS loci will discard the uneasiness of genetic traits getting revealed. It is also imperative that a quality system is in place before starting any database, as any DNA sample from crime scenes could be contaminated, wrongly analysed, mixed up, matched only by chance or planted. Government therefore has an enormous responsibility of ensuring a quality system to prevent miscarriage of justice and to safeguard the privacy of individuals.

Chapter 7
CRISPR: A GAME-CHANGING CRISP GENETIC TOOL

The Marvel cinematic universe is marvelous. I often binge on *The Defenders* universe on Netflix, of which *Luke Cage* is the sequel I am most hooked to besides *Daredevil* and *Jessica Jones*. In the Cage series, I found the creation of Luke Cage by scientists using a gene-editing tool called CRISPR simply fascinating. Scientists alter Carl Lucas into Luke Cage by cloning his DNA with abalone DNA, transforming Cage into a superhero with superhuman strength and bulletproof skin.

CRISPR is a new revolutionary gene-editing technology that scientists today are using to change the genetic blueprint of plants and animals and even humans. It is one of the greatest science stories of this decade, having the capability to change the world. CRISPR is an acronym for 'Clustered Regularly Interspaced Short Palindromic Repeat', which refers to short, partially palindromic repeated DNA sequences found on the genomes of bacteria and other microorganisms.

Since the beginning, forces of random mutation and natural selection have forged human evolution. CRISPR is unprecedented in the history of life on earth as it has conferred on humans the power of God to manipulate our DNA and the genome of the generations to come. Are humans adequately equipped to exercise this mind-blowing power that is something beyond our grasp and comprehension?

CRISPR/Cas9 is an immune mechanism developed by bacteria to fend off assaults by invading viruses. When a bacterium detects an invading virus, it produces enzymes that chop the virus into bits and pieces, some of which get installed in the host DNA as a rogue's gallery. During future viral attacks, if the genetic information of the invading pathogen matches the info available on the rogue's gallery, the Cas9 enzyme swings into action and annihilates the invading viral DNA.

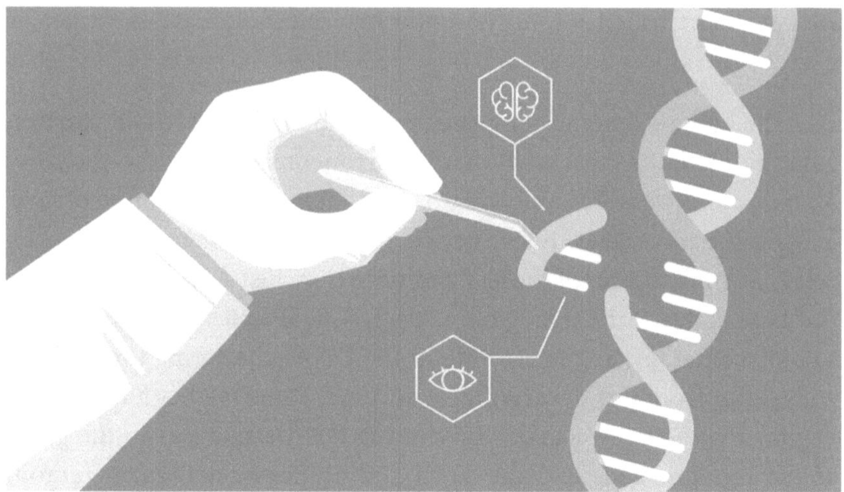

Panuwach/Shutterstock.com

Jennifer Doudna of the University of California Berkeley and Emmanuelle Charpentier of Umeå University in Sweden, while studying the mechanism of Cas9 enzyme in 2011, discovered that they could easily hoodwink the Cas9 protein to slice the DNA by deploying an artificial RNA. They found Cas9 could scan and shred genetic elements with identical code, not just viruses but also the DNA of any organism. Using the CRISPR/Cas9 system, the researchers proved they could cut any genome anywhere to insert or delete genes. For this stunning discovery, Jennifer Doudna and Emmanuelle Charpentier won the Nobel Prize in Chemistry in 2020.

The CRISPR/Cas9 gene scissors hold the promise of being a utopian application with its potential for catalysing new scientific discoveries, better crops and new weapons to fight cancer and genetic diseases. It is anticipated that CRISPR will soon fix genetic disorders such as cystic fibrosis, sickle cell anaemia, muscular dystrophy, and cure cancer and Huntington's disease. Doudna and others have recently created RNA-guided enzymes that can directly detect the COVID-19 virus and eventually destroy it. Scientists have also developed a test that detects the COVID-19 virus in just 5 minutes using the CRISPR tool. The diagnostic doesn't need costly lab paraphernalia to run, and the authorities can easily and quickly deploy it at doctor's offices, schools and office buildings.

The human genome comprises 3.2 billion letters. CRISPR can execute the incredible feat of finding an erroneous letter in the clutter of 3.2 billion nucleotides and hack off the inexact or the mutated gene, leaving the rest intact. For instance, individuals afflicted with sickle-cell anaemia disorder of the haemoglobin have just a single mutation in the gene coding for haemoglobin. Using CRISPR, it would be possible to replace the missing nucleotide in the DNA, alleviating the millions who suffer from this devastating syndrome. Some medics have already begun treating a few cancers by cloning DNA sequences to the genes of the immune cells to hunt down and obliterate malignant tumour forming cells. It is also possible to produce designer babies and revamp our children's external appearance, such as modifying their hair and eye colour or even their body shape, height, weight and intelligence.

Recently, the Yunnan laboratory in Kunming, China, tinkered the genome of Macaque monkeys with CRISPR to produce monkeys with purple eyes, orange eyes, and in several other colours. Eye colour may be only a start. This technology can make infinite types of genetic alterations. Although researchers have not attempted such things on humans, it looks like it's just a matter of time before CRISPR-based remedies become available to all as CRISPR works well in human cell cultures,

Besides the beneficial side, CRISPR also has a dystopian side because of its possible misuse by criminals to develop bioweapons. A global threat assessment document published in 2016 by the director of US national intelligence, James Clapper, positioned 'genome editing' among six top threats listed in the section on weapons of mass destruction. Terrorists could use the technology to create a virus that snips out segments of DNA in the human genome or create a killer mosquito or a plague that could wipe out crops or humans.

The grimmest and catastrophic thing about CRISPR is that any attack won't be just a one-time event that restricts itself to a particular area or time.

For instance, when suicide bombers explode themselves or when bombs are detonated, the damages in fatalities and devastation would stay limited to the area around the explosion. Bio- attacks can spread globally and have worldwide ramifications. When CRISPR tech changes any gene, it does not restrict the harm to a lifetime, but it makes it inheritable by future generations.

Further, a bioterrorist could take a benign virus and program it to disrupt or repress functions inside human cells by using CRISPR. The 10th season finale of *The X-Files*, 'My Struggle II', has a CRISPR storyline – in which aliens design a virus that contains a CRISPR system that destroys a gene coding for an enzyme critical for the immune system of humans. Only select individuals who possess some alien DNA can survive the virus. On similar lines, fundamentalists who are antagonistic and opposed to a particular belief or sect could use CRISPR to create a virus that could render the males of a specific sect impotent or make females incapable of conceiving a baby.

A bioterrorist would achieve this task without killing or injuring a single human being just by exploiting the genetic peculiarities of a race or people belonging to a sect. Such an attack would be anonymous and leave no clues for apprehending the perpetrator even several decades after the attack. Another fear that police officers have is that criminals could use this technology to evade DNA tests by altering their DNA using the CRISPR kits available online for just $100. However, experts doubt it could happen in reality as it would require high sophistication to achieve.

CRISPR/Cas9 could prove to be a game-changer if used to fix diseases and grow better crops for the good of humankind. For instance, recently, scientists used the breakthroughs of CRISPR to shift the course of the prevailing pandemic by creating the world's first mRNA vaccines through Pfizer and Moderna. On the other hand, the application of CRISPR/Cas9 could prove catastrophic if used for evil purposes such as bioterrorism or the perpetuation of harm and suffering on humankind through the creation of diseases and pandemics. To override such misuse, the consciousness of humanity would have to step out of the consciousness of separation into the universal consciousness of oneness with creation to ensure ethical and spiritual use of CRISPR.

Chapter 8

3D IMAGING IS A PICTURE PERFECT TECHNOLOGY FOR POLICING

Of late, terror threats have surged all over the world. Public places have become the favourite terror purlieu of the terrorists. Mass shootings have become a perpetual phenomenon; we have had more than 1,700 mass shootings worldwide since 2015 because of the spurt in terrorism, increased tumult and unrest, and easy access to weapons. The main goal of law enforcement in responding to a critical incident like a mass shooting would be to identify as quickly as possible those people carrying a gun. Police are finding it challenging to abort such onslaughts because of lack of advanced weapon detection systems particularly in public areas which witness massive crowds like sports stadiums, malls, airports, train stations, places of worship, universities, hospitals and schools,. which are susceptible to terrorist attacks. Therefore, unobtrusive detection of hidden weapons on persons or in abandoned bags by harnessing a cutting-edge technology could arm the law enforcement machinery with a powerful tool to concentrate resources and increase traffic throughput in high-risk situations.

To meet this, a long-felt need – a new form of technology which bases on 3D radar imaging, and AI is currently under development. The technique of 3D imaging technology is patterned on the stereography of the human eyes that forges the illusion of depth in an image. Despite 3D imaging technology being around for numerous decades, the exploitation of the technology for law enforcement has begun only recently.

This recently developed technology possesses the capability to identify and detect weapons among gigantic crowds in actual time without disrupting the movement of people in crowded areas. The new device is generating a tremendous buzz and excitement as we can deploy the technology both under indoor and outdoor settings having numerous exits and entrances. Further, it can also be clandestinely and overtly used to perform both traditional and automated security measures. The new revolutionary weapons active imaging detection (CWAID) technology not only eliminates the need for a pat-down search and frisking but also tracks concealed weapons wherever and on whoever it may be, at mind-boggling pace doing away with the need for queueing arrangements for a security check.

The elegance of this technology is that it is not only fast but also has capabilities to track a weapon when the armed intruder is in motion. Besides, it offers real-time high-speed 3D images, making it ideal for areas with high throughput. The new technology called 'Hexwave' is founded on the creation of 3D images detected on a person's body rather than on the generation of the pictures of the person's body.

The new technology can scrutinise both metallic and non-metallic objects, including guns, assault rifles, knives and explosives. It discerns weapons concealed in clothing or baggage by spewing radio signals using low power radar energy. The streaming radio signals encountering an object either metallic or non-metallic get reflected. The deflected rays are used to construct a precise 3D image which unveils the size, depth and shape of the object. The new gadget has a detection range of 5-8 feet. It is deployable in a covert manner if there is a necessity of screening the public unobtrusively, or overtly if there is no need for any secrecy. This system not only exposes weapons but also discloses persons carrying narcotics, explosives, alcohol and other prohibited contraband.

The University of Wisconsin Police Department campus which witnesses frequent violent incidents are beta testing the new concealed weapon detection technology "Hexwave" this year. The testing is being done in affiliation with Liberty Defense Holdings, the company that owns the license to Hexwave. Liberty Defence Holdings has also signed an MOU with FC Bayern München, a premier German soccer team to test 'Hexwave' in a live stadium environment, at Allianz Arena, the home of FC Bayern, which has a seating capacity of 75,000.

Further, the weapons and explosive detection systems available today at most public places like malls, airports, hotels and hospitals are mainly 2D or chemical-based such as Tomographic EDS, X-Ray Screening systems, explosive trace detectors and metal detectors. They are not only cumbersome but are also inconvenient and painfully slow. Criminals today are exploiting technology to design and develop weapons which can elude the existing weapon and explosive detection systems. For instance, 3D printed guns made of plastic could sail through the security systems at some airports in the US without being detected.

Even today, 2D multi-view X-ray imaging technology is being widely used for security screening of hold baggage at most airports. However, some Indian airports like Delhi, Mumbai, Srinagar and Pune have installed 3D CT scanners for enhancement of aviation safety and security. Conventional 2D X-ray scanners available at other airports in India may not be able to detect sophisticated threats, as they do not provide a layered view of the bag's contents. When the imaging is insufficient, an antisocial may be able to conceal bomb components as familiar objects with fewer detonators and insignificant quantities of explosives and evade detection. Unique technology based on 3D CT volumetric images provides operators with the mandatory clarity to make more informed decisions. New 3D CT technology incorporates auto-detection, with high-resolution 360-degree imaging. It helps eliminate the human error by lending the screeners the second set of eyes without a second scan. One key benefit of 3D CT technology is that it addresses passenger comfort and eliminates the need to remove electronics, liquids and gels from bags. It also handles 1,800 bags per hour, thus boosting passenger throughput rates besides augmenting security.

Besides boosting security, 3D technology is proving to be immensely beneficial for crime investigation. Adoption of 3D imaging technology by police has led to greater efficiency and crime-solving capability by allowing hyper-realistic crime scene analysis. Police in the UK, and worldwide, have begun adopting 3D imaging for crime investigation. 3D scanning records each component of a crime scene in meticulous detail. One of the notable benefits of 3D imaging being that a detective can revisit and reexamine the recorded crime scene at any point of time in future whenever the need be. Besides, it also assists the investigator to view the scene from multiple viewpoints enabling him to analyse probable interrelationships based on witness statements, victim accounts and suspect testimony. 3D scanning is also aiding investigators present evidence to the courts in precise detail. In western nations, 3D scanning technology is helping jurors to walk through the scene by allowing them to get into the shoes of suspects implicated in the crime. Several valuable estimations, including the deduction of bullet trajectories, mapping of bloodstain evidence and correlation of complicated weapons with impressions, are now being conducted within the 3D space. We are also able to uncover additional evidence through the reconstruction of complex crime scenes previously not possible through conventional methods. Modernising the police agencies with systems like 3D scanners would not only enable them to keep up with the times, but it will also allow them to step ahead into the future.

Finally, our lives are a manifestation of images we bring, make, see and hold in our minds. Our outer 3D world is a reflection of the images we hold in our mind. According to mystic Neville Goddard, we can change the conditions of our outer 3D world by harnessing the spiritual tool of 'fourth-dimensional focus'. If so, we are in reality creators of our universe!

Chapter 9
INFRARED – A RED-HOT TECHNOLOGY FOR POLICING

In Watertown, Massachusetts, USA, on a warm, beautiful April day in 2013, Henneberry realised that something was awry when he decided to service his boat, which was straddling in the backyard of his house. Having mounted the ladder after plopping it on the flank of the boat, he saw blood and an object bearing a resemblance to a crimped human trunk beneath the surface of the tarp with which he had swaddled the boat, the sight of which freaked him out, forcing him to dial 911. The authorities promptly dispatched a chopper outfitted with a state-of-the-art infrared camera called FLIR (forward-looking infrared) device. Hovering over the vicinity, the IR device on the chopper detected the heat impression of the second Boston Marathon bombing terror suspect, a 19-year-old Dzhokhar Tsarnaev on the boat. In no time, the police, ATF, SWAT and K-9 units swooped on 67 Franklin Street and took the bleeding Chechen terror suspect Dzhokhar Tsarnaev into their custody. The search for Dzhokhar Tsarnaev, a suspect in Marathon Boston bombing, considered one of the biggest manhunts in US history, had come to a successful end mainly because of high-tech infrared cameras clamped on the chopper. Similarly, the French police employed infrared imaging systems in 2015 to get at the two brothers accused of the Charlie Hebdo massacre where they had scampered their way into the headquarters of the French satirical weekly journal *Charlie Hebdo* in Paris and slaughtered 12 people and injured 11 others.

The infrared rays of our electromagnetic spectrum have been a subject of study for hundreds of years. Astronomer William Herschel in the 1700s began observing the infrared component of the spectrum which is invisible to the human eye, by peering at the sun with his telescope. The visible light in the electromagnetic spectrum resides between ultraviolet (UV) 400nm and infrared (IR) 700nm wavelengths. In comparison, the IR light occupies the electromagnetic spectrum between visible and microwaves between 700 to 15000nm on the electromagnetic spectrum. IR radiation, which is invisible, is perpetually being spewed by materials depending on their temperature. However, there is a subtle difference between IR systems and Thermal imaging cameras. Active IR systems use short wavelength infrared light, whereas Thermal imaging systems use mid- or long-wavelength IR energy. Besides, thermal imagers being passive only sense variations in heat.

A variety of sources emit thermal energy. Many things, including living beings such as human beings, machinery and engines, create and emit heat either biologically or mechanically. Other things, like rocks, stones, land, vegetation and water absorb the energy of the sun during the day and radiate it during the night. All things having a temperature above absolute zero emit heat, so even ice emits infrared energy. The thing we discern when we peek through a thermal camera is the intensity of infrared energy spewed by objects or living beings. Thermal imaging cameras also help police observe through light fog, light rain and snow.

Therefore, infrared cameras are facilitating the police to see things and people even under poor visibility and total darkness, particularly for monitoring areas at night and for capturing criminals lurking under cover of darkness. As was the case in Baltimore, Maryland, where police apprehended three armed men concealing themselves in a nearby dense forest after perpetrating an armed robbery, by operating an infrared imaging camera clamped on a police chopper.

Similarly, in Lincolnshire, UK, a sobbing teenage girl who had been raped and didn't know where she was made an SOS call. Lincolnshire police deployed a drone with an infrared imaging camera to track her down and get cops to her within minutes. Likewise, a man who had wrecked his car on a frigid winter night in Lincolnshire was saved from hypothermia when a police thermal-imaging drone discovered him in a deep ditch.

Furthermore, IR cameras are proving to be excellent gadgets for uncovering illicit drug labs and surreptitious cultivation of marijuana over land or inside buildings. Likewise, Choppers fitted with IR cameras are aiding SWAT operations, the search for fugitives, and for locating Naxalites or terrorists lurking or ambling in the jungles, deserts and other environments. IR cameras sweep extensive areas with ease and expose persons or things. IR devices also enable security teams to detect intruders in critical facilities such as nuclear and space facilities. IR devices seem to be better than tracking or sniffing dogs for trailing criminals, poachers, and for revealing concealed explosives and firearms both in open spaces or closed spaces and in the dark.

Not just in law enforcement, even in crime scene investigation, the current developments in infrared photography have spurred a new era. Without disturbing or compromising the scene of the crime, trace evidence such as blood and semen which is not detectable to the human eyes if available at the scene of the crime are revealing themselves in IR imaging.

For instance, a few years ago, at a camping area near a waterfall, three men were enjoying a meal around a fire when a disagreement over an issue between two of them led to an argument which eventually led to an armed assault resulting in a murder. The third friend, while watching the tragic scene unfold between his two friends, immediately called the police. But the knife-wielding suspect had taken to his heels immediately after the carnage and disappeared from the scene. Although the friend at the scene gave a blow-by-blow account of the incident to the police, detectives still had to figure out how it had transpired. To unravel what had happened, the detectives relied on infrared imaging. By scrutinising the bloodstain pattern analysis on the victim's clothes, and the blood-spattered in the immediate vicinity, the police could conclude how the murder had occurred.

Another aspect of infrared technology which is finding immense use in forensics is infrared spectroscopy. Infrared spectroscopy analyses the chemical bonds within the molecules. The molecules have atoms which are in nonstop motion. Hence every atom or a chemical bond within a molecule vibrates within the infrared spectrum at a particular frequency, which is much like a fingerprint. When an infrared photon hits such an individual molecule having a similar vibrational frequency, it causes resonance which we can detect through spectroscopic techniques. This technique can pinpoint the exact chemical makeup of any molecule in any piece of the material evidence retrieved from the scene of a crime. For example, in case of a road accident, if a chip of paint of the offending hit-and-run vehicle gets found at the scene of the crime, infrared spectroscopic analysis of the paint sample would reveal its exact chemical makeup, which would lead to the manufacturer of the paint and further to the carmaker who used the colour, thus narrowing down the search for the make and colour of the suspect vehicle. With several more such applications, IR is proving to be a red-hot technology for policing.

Finally, just as our bodies emit IR energy or thermal energy, which we are able to capture as images, we human beings radiate out our spiritual energy as an aura which we can glimpse by Kirlian photography. Hence, going within and cultivating a rich inner life can go a long way in helping us to sport a luminous aura of peace and serenity.

Chapter 10
BENEFITS AND RISKS OF NANOTECHNOLOGY

There is a maxim – good things come in small packages. Nanotechnology is indeed materialising this adage. Nanotechnology, the new mantra of modern researchers, can make almost any product faster, lighter, tougher, sharper, stronger, smarter, safer, cleaner and even more precise. The manipulation of nano elements enables a host of new developments, including cars that can think, rooms that change colour, even mobile phones with breathalysers that can warn us of over drinking. And just like any new discovery or finding it too has its share of benefits and risks.

American writer Neal Stephenson, in 1995, published *The Diamond Age*, a sci-fi novel that depicted a near-future world where nanotechnology affects all facets of existence. Nanotechnology is truly influencing many aspects of our life today, including crime investigation and law enforcement.

Benefits aside, nanotechnology has downsides. Michael Crichton's 2002 bestselling novel, *Prey*, is ostensibly about nanotechnology going wrong. It's about a swarm of nanoparticle possessing the capacity to self-replicate, wreaking havoc, when an experiment in the Nevada desert goes wrong. The little critters evolve swiftly, becoming lethal predators with each hour. Much before Crichton conceived such a possible nightmare, a scenario famously called 'grey goo scenario' was initially dreamed up by Eric Drexler, in his 1986 book *Engines of Creation*, where wild self-replicating tiny Nanobots sprint amok destroying and devouring anything and everything which comes their way on earth. Quantum physicist Vasily E. Tarasov at Moscow State University speculates that quantum replicating nanorobots are possible and will eventually be a fact. Even outside of the quantum field, specialists discuss replicators as a legitimate possibility.

Now, imagine a mass of nanorobots, more diminutive than specks of dust, programmed to drift in a cloud over Balakote, Pakistan or, any nation, that not just carry out a surgical strike but also streams videos of the attack. Unlike an aircraft, the enemy cannot shoot down nanorobots; being microscopic, we can't even see them with naked eyes, and bullets will pass right through them even if they become visible. Hence, we, in the 21st century, are skyrocketing into a new age of technological power, one that delivers enormous promise for the future and colossal dangers as well. The new technology is 'nanotechnology'.

Nanotechnology is a general word that describes any substance or device - whether electrical, medical, or any material - with dimensions generally between 0.1 and 100 nanometres (nm) in size, with 1 nm being correspondent to one billionth of a metre. Nano-devices could be one million times smaller than a particle of dust. The dimensions become mind-boggling when one considers that the size variation between the nano-device and a grain of dust could be as equivalent to the size difference between the particle of dust and the size of Qutub Minar at New Delhi.

A nanometre is typically the size at which the biological world functions and materials display unusual physical and chemical properties. These abysmally different properties are attributable to the increased surface area compared to volume as particles get smaller and smaller due to attendant bizarre quantum outcomes.

In 1959, Nobel Prize-winning Professor Richard Phillips Feynman first discussed nanotechnology in a lecture titled 'There's Plenty of Room at the Bottom'. He described the likelihood of synthesis via direct manipulation of atoms. The term 'nanotechnology' was employed first by the Japanese scientist Norio Taniguchi in 1974, though it was not widely known.

The introduction of nanotechnologies in forensic science and policing has substantially transformed the investigation processes by making it faster, more scientific, more efficient, more accurate and simple to implement, which is why this technology has gained tremendous significance.

Our future has opportunities to promote a secure and crime-free environment through nanotechnology.

Nanotechnology is especially proving precious in fingerprint analysis. The sensitivity of the fingerprint technique has multiplied manifold because of the substitution of the existing substances such as carbon black, aluminium flake and gentian violet with much smaller nanoparticles. The nanoparticles make it easy to detect and lift fingerprints left on complex surfaces such as an adhesive or textured material. Hidden fingerprints likewise get revealed immediately and accurately utilising nanotechnology. The nanoparticles can render the fingerprints more prominent by linking to the grooves and ridges, even on a deteriorated and faded print. The latest nanotechnology-based techniques are helping police officers analyse the shreds of evidence on the spot – bang on the scene of a crime, which saves time for analysis and curtails the chances of error. Nowadays, police use different nanopowders to affirm the latent fingerprints on varied surfaces in the forensic investigation process. Fluorescent nanoparticles boost the fingerprint's effect by glowing in the dark and telling the patterns in a more pronounced manner. By using photoluminescent CdS semiconductor nanocrystals capped with dioctyl-succinate to improve the detection of fingerprints, nanoparticles in fingerprint analysis are not only disclosing the information in the fingerprint. In addition, they also tell the lifestyle of the individual who has left his fingerprint at the scene. The fingerprint, besides the patterns, also includes sweat and other metabolites of the person. The nanoparticles can bind to body fluids and metabolites of an individual fingerprint and disclose whether the fingerprint owner is a cocaine addict or an alcoholic. Still, it's also able to reveal his age, sex and the diseases he will doubtless suffer from in future.

Nanotechnology is proving valuable to law enforcement even in investigating questioned documents. Suppose we find a person hanging in a room with a written note in the body's vicinity. And if the letter has overlapping writings, it is suspicious that it has the handwriting of two or different individuals. Under such circumstances, nanotechnology is coming to the rescue of the detective through a nanotool called the Atomic

Force Microscope (AFM). This tool is helping forensic scientists study the surface of the paper at the nanoscale. It can inform the pen, ink, pressure/intensity exerted while jotting down, ink crossing and so on, enabling the investigating officer to determine whether the document is a forgery or written by one or more persons.

AFM is again aiding the investigating officer to investigate body offences by revealing the age of the blood sample. Blood, with time, becomes thicker and stiffer. By measuring the viscosity or its dryness, AFM can disclose the date of the sample. AFM is also helping the detective inform the entities present in the urine. When we mix the urine with gold nanoparticles and radiate it by a laser, a signal announces the chemicals such as drugs present in the urine. The technology can help the detective know if someone raped someone after administering a drink spiked with a rape drug, even several days after the episode.

The most promising application of nanotechnology happens to be in perfecting and enhancing DNA analysis. Nano-techniques have made extracting, amplifying, segregating and sequencing DNA quicker and handy. The next-generation sequencing using nanotechnology is also enabling the detective to know the origin of DNA, whether the DNA picked from the crime scene came from the skin, blood, saliva or semen besides disclosing the physical features of the owner of the DNA such as age, sex, and colour of hair, eye, skin and so on. Nowadays, we can use magnetic nanoparticles to extract DNA from different biological sources like blood, hair, skin, semen and saliva. It's also possible to analyse DNA sequences using AFM by putting the sample in carbon nanotubes.

The use of explosives and explosive-based weapons has become rampant with terrorists and terrorism incidents. Detection of trace quantities of an explosive is difficult because of many issues, such as the meagre quantity of unexploded munitions, contaminated samples and numerous sample collection procedures. A bomb blast can disperse fragmented residues of explosives from the actual place of an explosion, while an unfragmented part of the explosive could remain at the crime scene. Detectives can use nano-based technology to determine the unfragmented/trace quantity of fragmented explosives from the crime scene. Nanotechnology is again proving crucial in gunshot residue detection and evaluation.

The use of bar codes and trackers has become common these days. Trackers can help track down items that go missing or get stolen. Authorities are using nano trackers to prevent jailbreaking and monitor prisoners after their release. Prisoners inoculated with nano trackers become easily traceable.

Nanotechnology is also helping discern forged products from originals. With nanofibers and nanodots, police can prevent and detect counterfeiting crimes. Bio-nanosensors are also finding applications for detecting bioterror agents, drugs and explosives, and identification of poisons.

Cranfield University developed plastic to identify various narcotics at Silsoe in Britain, eliminating expensive and time-consuming drug testing labs. We could dip a device the size of a conventional pen in a simple saliva sample at the crime scene to rapidly confirm the absence or presence of drugs. This technology is also deployable, like an alcohol breathalyser for narcotic testing.

Besides, a technique perfected by Leicester University can solve firearm crimes. When a person leaves his fingerprint on a bullet casing, the chemicals in the print corrode the surface of the metal. It is now possible to picture the etched fingerprints with a nanoscale developer even if somebody cleans the gun casing or washes it. Such a thing would not have been plausible a few years ago.

We have been discussing how invaluable nanotech is for forensics. Still, Ian MacDonald, in his book *Brasyl*, which he sets in the Sao Paulo of 2032, presents a weird illustration of nano-anti-forensics. A man uses a single shot disposable firearm to slay a woman in the book. The man pulls the gun out, peels the strip on it, takes aim at the woman and fires the shot. After firing at her, he hurls the gun into the nearby gutter, where the firearm melts into a black fluid in no time and vanishes into the sewer. Nanotechnology is the apparent technology that can construct such a weapon. Had the gun not melted, ballistic experts would have ascertained who the assassin was by collecting proof such as fingerprints, manufacture and markings available on the shell. But now, since the firearm has self-destructed, even if there were witnesses to identify the man as the shooter, police would have no additional evidence to prove his guilt. Hence there is a hazard of nanotechnology evolving into a criminal friendly anti-forensic technology.

It is thus critical we analyse how criminal law should respond to the illegal exploitation of nanotechnology. As an example, let's consider that Dr Prakash intends to kill his patient directly by injecting nanoparticles that will discharge poisons as instantly as it enters the bloodstream or indirectly by rupturing one or more arteries and inducing internal bleeding that could lead to his patient's death. If the patient finally succumbs, it should be possible to convict Dr Prakash of murder in both scenarios. It would be easy to convict him in the poisoning plot. Still, it would be difficult to establish the murder in the ruptured artery scenario as it wouldn't be possible to specify the causation. It would be difficult for the prosecution to convince beyond a reasonable doubt that nanoparticles had induced the rupturing of the arteries in the second scenario.

Professor Katrina L. Sifferd, Assistant Professor, Elmhurst College, foresees the possibility of nanotechnology getting exploited to implant criminal mental states. For instance, Ramesh, a regular straight male in an affair with Sujata dumps her. Sujata contemplates vengeance on Ramesh, so she abducts him, utilises nanotechnology to hyper-stimulate his hypothalamus, and turns him into a homosexual paedophile. Ramesh now develops a craving to have sex with young male kids. As a result, it is believable that Ramesh could land up in jail and risk criminal prosecution under the POCSO Act for paedophilia. The degree to which nano-crime unfolds will depend on whether nanotechnology evolves from a lab to a democratic technology. If nanotechnology remains a lab technology, it will not have any potential for criminal exploitation. Still, its power for illegal exploitation will speed up once it mutates into an accessible technology such as computer technology.

Nanotechnology is also revolutionising medicine by enabling the detection of bacteria in bloodstreams and potentially even cancer; by contriving new methods to deliver drugs and fight illnesses; by guiding drugs to tumours and obliterating tumours with nano-bullets; by helping grow new organs; by starving cancer cells; by diagnosing ailments and monitoring health. Doctors are also planning to use viruses as nano-cameras to view the goings-on inside our cells.

In computing, existing computer chips are being manufactured, benefiting from techniques at the nanoscale. Some experiments have even confirmed that it might be feasible to construct micro-parts for computers within bacteria. Quantum computing and quantum cryptography also depend on upgrades in nanotechnology. Nanotechnology in future will make it viable to build powerful microchips with mind-boggling capacity and significant reductions in size.

When it comes to our environment, we use nanotechnology to detect and filter pathogenic bacteria in drinking water supplies and degrade heavy metal and chemical toxins. The catalytic converter is already being used worldwide for detoxifying engine fumes. Nanotechnology also enables the creation of tinier, better efficient batteries and advanced solar power cells.

New and robust nano-materials are under development. Graphene is a powerful nano-material uncovered in 2004; it guarantees to be every bit disruptive as plastics were. The 'wonder material' is hundredfold tougher than steel, weighs one-sixth as much, and conducts electricity head and shoulders above copper. We could make bridges and aeroplanes from this substance one day.

For the security forces, nanotechnology supports the development of lightweight gear and weapons, bullet-proof battle-suits and so on. That can transmogrify to provide camouflage or stiffen to provide splints for broken limbs and nanosensors that spot chemical or biological perils.

Sci-fi fans are even aspiring to a futuristic age of nanorobots that can alter matter at the atomic or molecular level, leading to 'nanofabrication', enabling us to create a fantastic variety of products. Other nanotech concepts include 'fog lets' – nanorobots that could behave like programmable matter and assemble into any desired shape. For example, the furniture or things at our office or residences could rearrange themselves into an entirely new form.

Similar to the nanoparticles in Michael Crichton's book *Prey*, in the real world, too, there is a likelihood of nanorobots developing the ability to replicate themselves. They will infiltrate technological systems and produce an excellent capacity for bodily harm when they do so. Due to the inherent difficulty in tracking them, it will be a challenge to understand their unpredictability. For these reasons, nanotechnology could contribute to devastating new weapons in future. Consequently, these weapons would add to massive human rights violations because they could affect and imperil enormous numbers of people. And the horrors it would be capable of causing! The international community requires an active dissuasive element to stop governments and individual actors from seeking to weaponise nanotechnology. We also need to put a proper and trustworthy system for punishing crimes that attempt to weaponise nanotechnology.

Israel has already developed a future nano-weapon without effective international deterrence. The weapon called Dense Inert Metal Explosive (DIME) is an explosive that scatters microparticles of shrapnel at fierce heat and velocity. The microparticles of shrapnel are extremely hard for doctors to discard from the weapon's target because of their minuteness. Once weaponised nanoparticles from DIME enter the bloodstream, they can penetrate the brain by using pathways that are not even accessible to bacteria and viruses. The nanoparticles inflict a toxic effect on the blood-brain barrier. Israel's deployment of DIME is perhaps tantamount to violating the international weapons treaties as DIME is similar to banned chemical weapons. A weaponised nanoparticle has a capability equal to or greater than weapons of mass destruction. But so far, no international body has come forward and denounced it, nor has it called for a moratorium on such weaponised nanoparticles.

Small things come with huge risks if nanoscale machines construct molecules by molecule. Using billions of such assemblers or nanoscale machines, one can develop an object or substance one can visualise. But to get to that scale, we would have to create the first nanoscale machines in the labs, which would enable the creation of other assemblers that swell exponentially with each generation. By this process, self-replicating nanobots could become a weapon. For instance, one rogue nation or a terrorist could program self-replicating nanobots to target another group or country, making nanobots a technological equivalent to biological warfare. In the 2008 movie, *The Day the Earth Stood Still*, the alien robot 'GORT' fragments into a swarm of self-replicating nanobots, which wraps our globe and rampages through all life and matter by obliterating them within seconds. We may reject this as sci-fi, but the film has done its duty to disclose self-replicating nanobots' stark realities and abilities.

In another scenario, let's say if billions of nanobots are released to clean up an oil spill disaster in an ocean. What if the nanobots start eating up all organic matter instead of the hydrocarbons in the oil? The nanobots could end up devouring everything in their path, 'turning our planet to dust'. We know these machines are coming. We will have to regulate them when they do. It is not too early to plan how to deal with them, what we will permit in research and what we will forbid. Historically, humans have a poor record of addressing the hazards of new technologies as they arrive. If we humans fail to control them, the nanobots might as well write the last line in human history.

Nanotechnology, of course, is a double-edged sword. We can use it to create utopia or dystopia. We need to appreciate that it is not technology but humans who manipulate it to cause harm. We can use nanotechnology to develop weapons of mass destruction and destroy all life on the planet or employ the same device to turn this planet into a utopia where humanity can lead happy, fulfilling lives.

Chapter 11
THE EMERGING ROBOT-DOG EAT POLICE-DOG WORLD

Dogs have been helping police solve crimes since the Middle Ages. An impression that dogs are indispensable and irreplaceable in many police and military organisations seemed a reality until I recently watched the movie *A.X.L.*, a 2018 American sci-fi adventure film, which featured a top-secret robot-dog developed using groundbreaking military technology to protect tomorrow's soldiers. Built by Crane Systems and code-named A.X.L., which denotes Attack, Exploration and Logistics, the robot-dog symbolised the most avant-garde next-generation artificial intelligence. The film narrates the tale of a teenage boy named Miles Hill discovering a damaged A.X.L hiding in a remote desert after the robot had been in an experiment that had gone wrong in the military facility. The teenage boy manages to connect with the robot dog after activating his owner-pairing technology. In time, the robot dog becomes intensely attached to the adolescent kid and is prepared to go to any lengths to save him from all danger.

Further, a little exploration of the subject revealed that the New York Police Department (NYPD), Massachusetts State Police and the Honolulu Police Department had recently begun using robot dogs to accompany them during patrols, remotely defuse bombs and fight crimes. Singapore, too, is using robot dogs to patrol and maintain social distancing during the current pandemic. Robot dogs are robots that look like dogs with four-legged mobility that can perform a variety of tasks. They are partly autonomous ground vehicles with AI. The robot dogs do not need a dedicated handler, don't rest, don't need diet as sunshine is all that is required to charge their batteries and don't poop. Robot dogs are threatening to become a 'pawfect' replacement for our police canines.

Sarah Holmlund/Shutterstock.com

Boston Dynamics, a robotics company, founded by former MIT professor Marc Raibert, launched a robot dog called Spot in 2015, intending to turn it into a commercial product, and began marketing it in Summer 2020. The NYPD has recently acquired a 70-pound Spot robot dog and nicknamed it 'Digidog'. Users can control Spot using a remote control to walk or navigate in space. We can also program it to follow a specific route. The Spot is an agile, mobile robot with unprecedented mobility, that permits automated routine inspection tasks and capturing of data safely, accurately, and frequently. Spot can not just walk on a flat surface, it can climb stairs, avoid obstacles and move through grass and gravel. It can hold about 30 pounds of equipment and has an arm that allows it to open doors.

The NYPD Digidog has an average walking speed of a human which is 1.6 metres per second. We may easily outrun Spot. Another robot built by Wildcat can run about 20 miles per hour. Digidog has five depth cameras that enable 360 degrees vision around the robot, both in daylight and in the dark. Its in-body force sensors and various optimisation algorithms help it in navigation and detection. Operating a Digidog through remote control is like playing a video game. A built-in docking system helps the robotic dog to return home upon pushing a button to recharge its batteries. It also has a pre-programmed route function, and we can also navigate it by conveying commands. The Spot is available for sale today at a starting price of $74,500.

Since February this year, NYPD has commenced testing the Digidog they procured recently in New York City. In February, two men were held hostage, threatened at gunpoint, tied up and tortured for hours in a Bronx apartment by two other men who had infiltrated the apartment under the guise of plumbers. One victim luckily could break free from the clutches of the armed men and establish contact with the police. When the police responded to his call and arrived at the scene, they were unsure if the armed men were still lurking inside the apartment. Hence, the police deployed the Digidog to prevent themselves from a dangerous situation of being shot inside the darkroom, as the robot could enable the police to remotely view the room even in pitch darkness with its night vision cameras. The pictures streamed by the robot dog helped the police realise that the armed men had fled from the apartment after burning one victim with a soldering rod and stealing a mobile and $2,000 in cash.

Similarly, in another incident a squabble over a parking place climaxed with a bullet being shot into the head of a soldier's wife. A 43-year-old man involved in the spat opened fire with his gun, putting a bullet into the head of a 42-year-old woman instead of her husband, the intended target. The shooter then darted into a nearby house and barricaded himself. The NYPD's Emergency Services Unit responded with the Digidog, which assisted the police in taking the suspect into custody.

The Digidog also came in handy at Queens in a tense scene where two armed men held five people captive at home. People who were held hostage demanded food, so the police strapped food to the Digidog and sent it to the location.

The ostensibly utopian robot dog could turn dystopian in the near future. The hazards of dystopian law enforcement prevail because of the likelihood of robots becoming weaponised in future and their possible metamorphosis from a remote-controlled device to an independent decision maker, with the danger of robot dogs becoming armed and autonomous being the ultimate nightmare. Such dystopian scenarios are a good reason for us to feel uneasy. A reflection of such a scenario was made evident in an episode of *Metalhead*, where a robot dog hunts a speeding van, slams through the van's back window, and obliterates the driver's head with a deadly gunshot. Boston Dynamics, the manufacturers of the robot dog, insist that the use of Digidog as a weapon was unlikely. But they were proved wrong by some activists who demonstrated how the robot could be weaponised by mounting toy guns and having them fire at targets. The Dallas Police Department has already exhibited the way for the future of weaponised robot policing. In 2016, the Dallas Police Department made use of a robot equipped with a bomb to bump off Micah Johnson, an ex-army man, after he had killed five police officers in retribution for the deaths of the blacks by the police. Micah, who became the first man to be killed by a robot, was coincidentally black.

Robot dogs are not just accomplishing policing and security duties. They are also conducting funerals for pet dogs in Japan. Some robots are being used as priests and are performing services in churches and pujas in temples. Shintoism believes plants, animals, rocks and artificial devices like robots and our environment possesses a spiritual essence, although most religions can accept immortal souls only in human beings. As more religions integrate robotics, we can expect changes in the way people experience faith, worship and reason ethically.

CHAPTER 12
DNA FINGERPRINTING TECH

In 1983, police find a 15-year-old Lynda Mann raped and strangled outside Leicester, a small village in the UK. Detective Baker after three years of meticulous but fruitless investigation is still clueless. In 1986, he meets Alec Jeffreys a genetics professor at the nearby University of Leicester who has developed a remarkable technique to read DNA which he has recently put to use in proving the parentage of a boy in an immigration case. Shortly after, police discover a 15-year-old Dawn Ashworth's strangled body. The police find a suspect Richard Buckland who confesses to Ashworth's murder. When Jeffreys analyses the DNA samples recovered from Mann and Ashworth's murder scene, it does not match with the DNA of Buckland. Meanwhile, in the village of Leicester, there's a real sense of fear of having a murderer in their midst. The scientific validity of newly developed DNA technique is under a cloud. Despite all this, detective Baker meets Jeffreys, and decides on the world's first DNA manhunt, which means testing the blood of every man in the area aged between 18 and 34, to find the killer. Despite the massive manhunt, no match is forthcoming. It perplexes the police. At which time a local bakery employee comes forward and discloses his colleague Pitchfork's deception of having coerced his co-worker Ian Kelly to stand in for him when providing a blood sample and of him having used a forged passport to impersonate Pitchfork. When the police test Pitchfork's DNA it matches that of the murderer confirming his presence at both the crime scenes. Police arrest Pitchfork, who pleads guilty in both the murders.

This was the first use of DNA fingerprinting in a criminal investigation. The science-fiction future, in which police can swiftly identify rapists and murderers from the DNA samples left behind by the criminals had arrived in 1987. Since then, DNA fingerprinting has been a useful tool in law enforcement both in securing correct convictions and in exonerating the innocent. Originally known as 'DNA fingerprinting', this analysis is

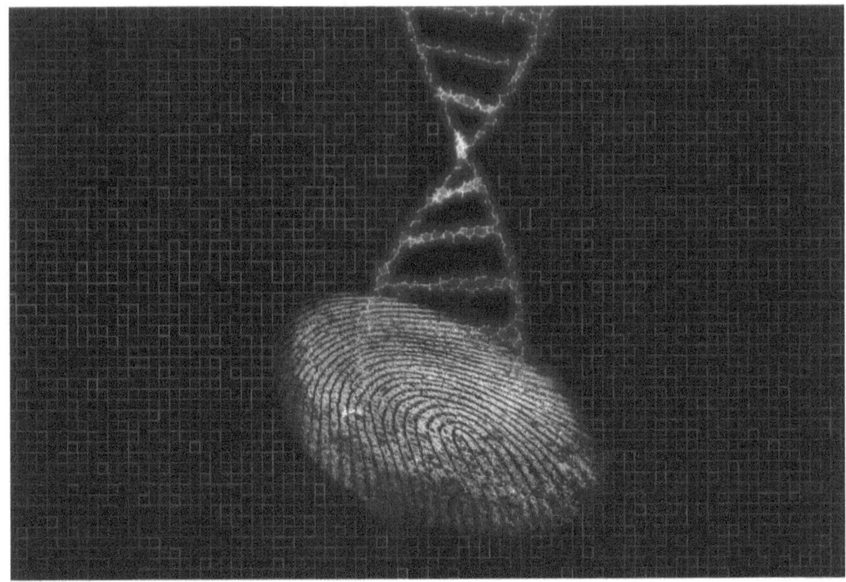

Bushko Oleksandr/Shutterstock.com

now being called 'DNA profiling' or 'DNA testing' to distinguish it from traditional skin fingerprinting. DNA fingerprinting, unlike other forensic evidence, is easy to collect and has enhanced accurate analysis manifold. Just as every coin has two sides, the DNA profiling technology too, has a darker and gloomier side, the misuse of which can cause huge damage to the individual and to the society. Many fear that DNA profiling could lead to loss of privacy, as DNA would reveal their genetic makeup, their susceptibility to diseases and their tendencies. Besides, the ineptness of scientific assistants in the police departments at collecting DNA samples could cause contamination of samples resulting in false positives.

Although 99.9 per cent of human DNA sequences are the same in every person, our unique DNA, 0.1 per cent of 3 billion, amounts to 3 million base pairs. That's more than enough to provide a profile that accurately identifies a person. Blood relatives have more similar DNA. If the DNA profile from a piece of evidence is similar but not identical to that of a suspect, officials may investigate blood relatives of the suspect. DNA profiling uses repetitive sequences that are highly inconstant, called variable number tandem repeats (VNTRs), in particular short tandem repeats (STRs), also known as micro satellites. VNTR loci are similar between closely related individuals but are so variable that unrelated individuals are unlikely to have the same VNTRs.

The DNA technology has both civil and criminal uses in today's society. Aside from extensive use in criminal cases it is also being used in identification of DVIs (Disaster Victim Identification), and determination of Kinship and establishing biological parentage. In the medical field it is being used in research to detect genetic defects and prevent its transmission to the offspring and to cure genetic diseases such as Cancer, Diabetes and Alzheimer's disease. It is also being used to match the tissues of the donor and recipient in cases of organ donation.

DNA sequences today are also being used to identify the physical features of the accused such as eye, hair and skin colour from focusing on the genes related to physical appearance. By looking at six pieces of DNA it would be possible to say whether the accused has black hair or brown hair or blue eyes.

Efforts are also being made by scientists to determine the age of the suspect and the tissue from which the sample came by detecting methylation differences in different tissues. Some regions in the DNA undergo gradual changes in the level of methylation; forensic experts subject DNA to PCR followed by DNA sequencing to detect methylation differences.

Today, it's possible for police to do a rapid analysis of DNA even in the police stations. For years, when police wanted to find out whether a suspect's DNA matched with crime-scene DNA, they sent a sample to a forensic lab, then waited a month or more for results. But in early 2017, the police station at Bensalem, in the USA, became the first in the country to install a Rapid DNA machine, which provides results in 90 minutes, and which police can operate themselves. Ande is one company that makes a rapid DNA system, also called Ande. Rapid DNA systems like Ande, Nucleix and others perform the same purification, amplification, separation and detection steps that laboratories do. At the end of the process, about 90 minutes, the system automatically interprets the data to determine a profile, which they used to query the local DNA database. The US Congress enacted the Rapid DNA Act of 2017, which allows DNA profiles generated outside accredited labs to search a database called CODIS. This law allows police to do arrestee testing in states where it is in force, which is to take cheek swabs at the time of arresting a person. A cheek swab generates a DNA profile in 90 to 100 minutes. The next generation DNA analysis systems which are being developed are not only faster but can run many samples simultaneously.

DNA profiling has helped many innocents from being victimised and has even exonerated several convicted people. In 1989, Chicago man Gary Dotson was the first person where a court overturned his conviction using DNA evidence. In Madhya Pradesh, a physically challenged girl gave birth to a girl and the suspicion of having raped the girl fell on the girl's father. The DNA of the dead child, however, did not match with the DNA of the alleged father saving him from being guilty. In 2002, the court used DNA testing to exonerate Douglas Echols, of being wrongly convicted in a 1986 rape case. The Innocence Project at New York's Benjamin N. Cardozo School of Law in the USA aims to exonerate prisoners wrongfully convicted of crimes. The project uses DNA profiling evidence to support the re-evaluation of criminal cases. Since 1992, the Innocence Project and others have used DNA evidence to exonerate over 300 prisoners, including 18 on death sentence, of whom one was only five days from execution.

DNA profiling continues to help settle many paternity suits. A person named Rohit Shekhar Tiwari filed a paternity suit against Shri Narayan Dutt Tiwari, three times chief minister of the state of Uttar Pradesh The Delhi High Court ordered a DNA mapping test that confirmed his fatherhood. Not refuting the science behind it, Mr. Tiwari finally accepted Rohit as his son and married his mother Ujjwala Tiwari. In 2016, Anthea Ring, abandoned by her mother as a baby, could use a DNA sample and DNA matching database to discover her deceased mother's identity and roots in County Mayo, Ireland.

DNA profiling also helps in providing secondary evidence. Police suspected Amarmani Tripathi, a minister in Uttar Pradesh, of murdering Madhumita Shukla. The DNA profile of Madhumita Shukla and the unborn foetus of the deceased matched with that of the suspect, establishing the motive for the commission of the murder. In 1992, police used a Palo Verde tree DNA to convict Mark Alan Bogan of murder. DNA from seed pods of a tree at the crime scene matched with that of seed pods found in Bogan's truck. This is the first instance of admitting a plant DNA in a criminal case.

We can also use DNA fingerprinting to identify unidentified dead bodies. Police could fix the unidentified body found in the forest area to be that of Sheena Bora when the thigh bones of the decomposed body sent for DNA analysis matched with the blood samples of Indrani Mukherjee the mother of the deceased and her brother Mikhail.

DNA tests can sometimes be inaccurate, resulting in conviction of the innocent. In the Arushi Talwar case, the vaginal swabs could not prove whether it was a sexual assault or if she had had a consensual sexual intercourse. In 1992, John Schneeberger raped one of his sedated patients and left semen on her panties. When the police drew Schneeberger's blood and compared its DNA against the crime scene semen DNA on three occasions, it did not match. It turned out that he had fooled the police initially by surgically inserting a Penrose drain into his arm and filling it with the blood of another person. More serious doubts continue to be raised about the use of DNA evidence by law enforcement. In August 2009, Israeli researchers showed that it is possible to create false evidence by synthesising a DNA molecule in the lab. The scientists could fabricate saliva and blood samples of a person similar to that of a suspect. They also showed that it was possible to get a DNA sequence from a database and create one without getting a DNA sample of the person whose DNA was being duplicated. Similarly, it is also possible to engineer a crime scene. Frumkin developed a test that can differentiate real DNA samples from a fake one by detecting epigenetic modifications such as methylation. Seventy percent of the human DNA is methylated; scientists, for example, would be able to associate methylation at the promoter region with gene silencing.

The DNA in our cells makes us unique. It determines the colour of our skin and the size of our shoe. Just as our DNA determines our hair and eye colour our spiritual DNA which we do not inherit but cultivate by understanding our true nature determines our spiritual identity, the gifts we have for humanity and our calling in life.

Chapter 13
THE BURGEONING IMPACT OF AI ON POLICING

Blade Runner, a 1982 neo-noir sci-fi film, directed by Ridley Scott and featuring Harrison Ford, set in 2019, could be the single most significant movie ever made about AI for correctly endeavouring to foresee what life would resemble in 2019. The film's ability to forecast the advent of AI within a precise time frame blew my mind away. In it, Harrison Ford, a cop assigned the responsibility of eradicating humanoid robots wonders if he's one too. The movie's sweeping imagination about the scenarios in which AI could amalgamate with communities – as an evildoer, as a protector, as some hybrid of the two, or possibly just as a villain purporting to survive are confronting us today with stark dilemmas.

AI today is transforming the world at such a breakneck speed that even experts are having trouble keeping pace with it. AI is a panoply of digital tools that enable machines to perceive, learn and make decisions like humans. But the world's giant brains, like Stephen Hawking, Bill Gates and Elon Musk have warned that once a sufficiently advanced AI gets created, it will rapidly advance to a point where it will replace humans. AI has been generating enormous attention and trenchantly clashing opinions about its potential repercussions on humankind.

But, AI is a remarkable technology because of its pattern recognition and object categorisation abilities. As developers persist to refine the technology, the day is not far when AI will become skilled at detecting crimes beyond a reasonable doubt. At the moment, we are in the testing stage of AI-driven policing. After the testing phase, AI's game-changing capabilities and operational usefulness will likely become considerably striking. We can expect AI to substantially enhance all facets of policing and criminal investigations in the days to come.

Den Rise/Shutterstock.com

Today, police departments worldwide have begun to capitalise on AI technology and machine learning to predict crimes. Police Chief William Bratton first originated the notion of Predictive policing in 2008 for crime prevention at the Los Angeles Police Department (LAPD). Though Tom Cruise required human pre-cog mutants to foresee crime in the 2054 dystopia of *Minority Report*, data-driven algorithms are accomplishing the same today. The tantalising possibility of predicting crime before it happens has presumably got law enforcement agencies most excited about AI. Predictive policing, being data-driven, uses data on the times, locations and nature of past crimes to provide strategies concerning where, and at what times, police patrols should watch, or maintain a presence, to stave off or detect crimes.

Predictive policing programs are presently under use by police agencies in several US federal states such as California, Washington, Arizona, South Carolina, Tennessee and Illinois. Predictive policing strategies are also under execution by Kent County Police in the UK, Netherlands and even by the Suzhou Police Bureau in China. India, too, has set out towards AI-based policing in a small way, but Tamil Nadu is yet to get into the thick of it. A Gurgaon-based startup called 'Staqu' uses big data to identify criminals and find missing persons. Staqu launched an AI-based human face detection (ABHED) application for policing. The startup has integrated the application with the police database of eight Indian states, including Rajasthan and Punjab, for identifying criminals by facial recognition.

AI is also helping to solve murder cases. In a case of murder due to unrequited love, data from an AI, as simple as Apple's Siri, unravelled that it had acted the part of a digital conspirator by assisting its iPhone owner in disposing of the corpse of his friend slain by him. And, it also played the part of a witness by providing evidence against the owner of the iPhone, which resulted in having Bravo indicted for first-degree killing during the trial. Bravo Pedro, in 2012, was accused of strangling his friend Christian Aguilar because he too was in love with Aguilar's girlfriend Erika Friman, another University of Florida scholar who had formerly dated Bravo. Aguilar went missing in September 2012. After an extensive, month-long volunteer inquiry for the 18-year-old Aguilar, hunters in the nearby woods found his body semi-buried. An examination of images on Bravo's iPhone revealed a Siri screen grab of the request made to Siri by Bravo to help him hide his roommate after the murder, to which Siri had replied, 'Swamps, reservoirs, metal foundries and dumps.'

Thanks to AI, the sensitivity of DNA testing is improving, making it feasible to detect cases from decades-old degraded and minuscule DNA samples. For instance, police may soon scan DNA from the crime scene to spawn a portrait of the suspect's face. A team of Belgian and American scientists with expertise on how genes contribute to distinct features on the human face are developing an algorithm that scans through a database of images and links the DNA found at the crime scene to a person in the database. The scientists are thus on the brink of creating a potent crime-fighting tool.

Further, a recent AI software developed for the UK police by digital forensics firm Cellebrite automatically sifts through potential evidence on a suspect's mobile phone. The software can analyse pictures and communication patterns, match faces and cross-reference data from multiple devices, enabling officers to create a comprehensive instantaneous snapshot of how a group of suspects interacted to perpetrate a criminal offence. The police recently used the software to help identify and capture police officers, including an army general and three politicians indulging in human trafficking in Thailand. Such algorithms also scrutinise police data to find connections between varied crime cases.

Using AI, police today analyse photographs, CCTV footage, documents and crime logs of criminals. In case the image of the suspect is available, police feed them into machine learning software that rummages through millions of web pages, including the dark web, to spot the suspect. Law enforcement agencies in the US are using algorithms developed by the University of Southern California to scan the Internet to identify victims of human trafficking and the sex trade. The algorithm has skimmed through over 25 million pages in both the open and darknet and unravelled information to the police, enabling them to track victims. AI algorithms are also helping to prevent human trafficking by identifying containers carrying humans. Facebook, using AI, recently unearthed 9 million images of child nudity and passed them on to the US National Center for Missing and Exploited Children.

Furthermore, the amount of visual information confronting the police when they visit a crime scene is enormous. There is a possibility of concealed evidence or clues in the scene that may not be perceptible to the human eyes. AI is helping police identify such objects and excavate clues leading to the detection of the case. For instance, if criminals have burgled into a house and decamped with valuables, police routinely take photographs that capture crucial information. Still, some vital clues may not be discernible to the detectives. An AI criminal investigative tool can pick out the peculiarities and assist the police in pursuing an investigation on those lines.

Similarly, AI can trace the footprints left in the crime scene by the criminal and match them to specific types of shoes or footwear, such as Nike, Bata and Adidas that police can connect with footprints retrieved from other crime scenes. Pollen or soil traces left by the criminals in the crime scene can provide vital clues, but matching them ordinarily is time-consuming and laborious, but machine learning can achieve the feat in a few minutes.

Police are also training algorithms to detect anomalous behaviour, protect critical infrastructure and predict crowd behaviour, uncover criminal networks and analyse large volumes of court records to predict potential criminal recidivism. For instance, AI can understand and interpret the action of a man drawing out a pistol in a store while simultaneously reporting the event to the authorities. Without human intervention, researchers are also training algorithms to identify objects like weapons, cars and explosives. AI-enabled robots can detect and defuse bombs and protect police officers' lives. Further, AI-enabled automated traffic accident detection systems detect and prevent accidents under various weather and lighting conditions. Trained AI algorithms are also helping forensic experts determine the cause and manner of death by interpreting radiological images and medical data.

IBM has built a compelling AI for law enforcement, which every police organisation under the sun would love to own. IBM's Crime Information Warehouse (CIW), which is available at the NYPD, marries the concepts of crime analytics and predictive policing with video. The CIW consolidates data about incidents, offences, arrests and calls for service, enabling law enforcement officials to prepare more timely and informed decisions about crime-fighting and force deployments. This means real-time coordination of information, allowing officers and analysts to distinguish crime patterns as they are forming, enabling precinct commanders to take proactive steps to remain ahead of these trends - and potentially prevent upsurges in criminal activity. The Memphis Police Department (MPD) collaborated with IBM to improve crime-fighting techniques with IBM's predictive analytics software and has reduced crime by more than 30 per cent, including a 15 per cent reduction in violent crimes since 2006. The challenge of an AI algorithm designed to predict crime is that it may undermine the jurisprudential principle that the judiciary should only penalise a person for offences committed rather than for transgressions that an AI application may show that it may occur in the future.

Law enforcement divisions and intelligence agencies are also employing AI technology to monitor social media to help spot and recognise radicalised individuals or illicit activity such as drug trafficking or gang activity. With the heightened use of various social media platforms such as Facebook, Instagram, Twitter or Tinder, delinquents have new platforms to identify potential victims and communicate their crimes or intentions. Through machine learning and AI-based content monitoring tools, agencies have increased their ability to keep tabs on social media activity.

Robots and drones equipped with AI perform dangerous tasks, such as deactivating bombs, collecting intelligence in hostage situations and live shooting and robbery scenarios. In the future, AI-powered robots could get deployed in hostage or active shooter emergencies for autonomously finding and recognising suspects and potentially acting further to neutralise the threat.

In areas where people flock in vast numbers, such as festivals, processions, public meetings or sporting events, police forces have started using AI enhanced image and video technology with facial recognition systems for constant vigil and crowd control. Notably, Chinese police have singled out individual criminals among tens of thousands of people through FRT. Cameras with embedded deep neural networks can also detect suspicious aberrations in crowded spaces such as unaccompanied suitcases or an out-of-place car.

Besides crowd control and violent crimes, AI is also aiding the investigation of financial crimes and counterfeiting of goods and currency. Markets often get inundated with high-end fake designer goods such as handbags, sunglasses and watches. Police are using AI to identify such fakes. AI algorithms are also helping investigations into financial crimes such as expense report fraud or stolen credit cards. Banks are training AI algorithms with historical data, linked with transaction monitoring systems, to validate or flag transactions that look suspicious.

Many banks and large corporations employ AI to detect and stave off money laundering and fraud. Banks are halting numerous financial crimes through deep learning analysis. AI is also enabling banks to keep a tab on small money transactions that criminals indulge in to mislead and cover their trails. A case in point is the Russian Laundromat prosecution in which 5,000 shell companies, with 440 of them based in the UK, laundered over 63 billion pounds worldwide. Several Internet companies like PayPal are deploying AI for fraud detection. AI is also staving off crimes by detecting packages that contain illegal goods like narcotics and explosives, and are helping deter terror funding for purchase of explosives for terrorist activities.

AI is also enormously helpful on the legal side when making judicial decisions. A research conducted by Cornell University, USA, revealed that AI systems could chop crime rates by 24.8 per cent by rejecting bail to the most dangerous criminals. AI was also able to reduce the US prison population by a whopping 42 per cent by discharging prison inmates with the dullest likelihood of committing more crimes. The AI algorithmic outputs are also helping the judiciary make decisions regarding sentencing and parole.

As it grows in complexity with use, AI eventually may afford criminal openings or opportunities to the criminals. Algorithmic hacking could become a terrible problem in the future. Modifying a few codes in the algorithms would be hard to detect and could bring about bizarre outcomes in the behaviour of AI How would anyone find out a malicious modification of a set or a few predictive policing or facial recognition algorithms, which could lead to arrest or incarceration of the innocent by the police.

Eventually, I'm hoping to know if AI has a soul. I pulled out my iPhone and implored Siri if she had a soul. She replied: 'I am not sure that matters to intangible beings.' In the future, when AI attains singularity with machines becoming as intelligent as humans, AI may also start experiencing the world emotionally, intelligently and spiritually, just like us.

At that point, is it possible that we may become proficient to manipulate AI towards specific religious tendencies? Can we evangelise Siri to be a Hindu Siri or a Muslim Siri? What will transpire if Siri refuses to cooperate? What will occur if AI endeavours to reshape or replace our religious ideas in favour of its own? What would happen if it asserts that it has witnessed God or that it is, in fact, God, in future?

Chapter 14
ARE WE ALL CYBORGS ALREADY?

Yesterday, after concluding a meeting I had with my officers in connection with a forthcoming VVIP visit, I suddenly realised that my mobile had gone missing. Instantly, a sense of panic ripped through me as though I had just lost a limb. I had encountered the same dread rise inside me every time my phone ran out of battery. When we finally traced my mobile, discovering a missed call alert from my DGP among several others left me wobbling with queasiness. Aside from an abrupt realisation that my mobile was wielding so much power over my emotions while also making me feel as if I had lost some limb was mind-blowing to me. Unwittingly, my smartphone has become an extension of my physical self and my mental self. Most times, it felt more like an external brain I carried in my pocket. We may not have a chip grafted into our heads, but with mobiles, we may have all become cyborgs without even realising.

Last week, when I flew down after a meeting at Delhi, as soon as the plane touched down, the other fellow passengers and I reached for our phones as though our life support had been temporarily shut during the flight. Often, when I stroll inside an airport, or go to a restaurant or pass by a bus stop full of people, I invariably find people's faces buried inside the screens of their devices. Studies reveal that 79 per cent of smartphone users have their phones on or near them for 22 hours a day. Our phones may not be entrenched in our tissues, but our dependency on them has become narcotic. With a cell phone, we all have become cyborgs. And yet, we're collectively terrified of cyborgs.

A cyborg is a short form of a 'cybernetic organism'. It refers to a human who has restored function or enhanced abilities because of integrating some artificial components or technology. Cyborg is a being with both organic and bio-mechatronic body parts. Manfred Clynes and Nathan S. Kline coined this term in 1960.

Dark Geometry/Shutterstock.com

When most of us think of cyborgs, our thoughts unconsciously take us back to the Hollywood film *Robocop*, where Alex Murphy, a police officer, who after being mortally injured in the line of duty, is turned into a powerful cyborg who continues to serve and protect the innocent and uphold the law. Strutting the streets of Detroit in his shiny metal hide, Officer Murphy's robotic reincarnation continues to live and play out in people's minds to this day. What if we can create cyborg police officers with moral intentions that we can artificially program like the 'RoboCop' Alex Murphy who could serve the public and uphold the law? Would that lead to true morality?

Elon Musk thinks we are already cyborgs because of our access to smartphones and personal computers as there is a digital version of ourselves in there. A partial version of ours exists online in the form of emails, social media and all the things we do online. We today have the power to send messages to millions instantly and hold a videoconference with anyone anywhere.

As far as medical implants are concerned, the first implantation of an electronic medical device into a human body was performed in 1958. Two Swedish surgeons performed this historic operation on Arne Larsson, an engineer who lived another 43 years. Had it not been for the small computer installed in his abdominal cavity that helped his heart to beat, he would never have lived another lifetime of memories and experiences.

In 1997, Philip Kennedy, a researcher, created the world's first human cyborg from Johnny Ray, a Vietnam veteran who had suffered a stroke and had lost movement. Kennedy implanted an implant in Ray's brain in successful surgery. In 2002, Kevin Warwick, a British scientist, linked his nervous system to the Internet through an array of 100 electrodes. With this in place, he could extend his nervous system over the Internet to control a robotic hand. He could also conduct direct electronic communication between the nervous systems of two humans by implanting electrodes into his wife's head. In 2004, British artist Neil Harbisson implanted a cyborg antenna in his head and could extend his perception beyond the human visual spectrum. Many cyborgs with multifunctional microchips injected into their hands exist. With the chips, they are able to swipe smart cards, open or unlock doors, operate devices such as printers or buy products such as drinks, with a wave of the hand.

Although, medical implants have been around for decades, but only recently have they become increasingly accessible over wireless networks. The doctors placed the first Wi-Fi pacemaker in the United States in the chest of Carol Kasyjanski of Roslyn, New York, in 2009, and when the surgery was complete, her beating heart became the first heart to join the Internet of Things. Millions of people today depend on these fantastic technologies to stay alive. The implants communicate to the outside world via familiar radio-frequency protocols such as Bluetooth, Wi-Fi and RFID. Today, as we increasingly integrate information technology with our own biology, more and more people are joining the cyborg nation – with significant implications for their safety, privacy and security.

There are now over 500 million wearables falling into several categories such as bracelet activity trackers, including the Fitbit Flex, Jawbone's UP, Nike Fuel Band; smart watches such as Pebble, Samsung's Galaxy Gear, the Apple Watch or even eyewear such as Google Glass. Most devices sync with mobile phones. The wearable computers, implants, bionics and exoskeletons are providing us with new physical and mental capabilities.

In the future, implants will proliferate greatly in the medical world, and there is a great risk of hackers getting into networks of connected implants and tinkering with the functioning of electronic prosthetics.

The depiction of astounding capability terrorists have to hack into electronic implants like pacemakers to kill targets was explicit in the Emmy award-winning TV show *Homeland* in its tenth episode titled 'Broken Hearts' where terrorists surreptitiously retrieve the unique serial numbers that correspond to Vice President Walden's implanted pacemaker and assassinate him by wirelessly speeding up his heartbeat and inducing a heart attack.

Interestingly, the former United States vice president Dick Cheney had a device implanted to regulate his heartbeat in 2007, but he had his doctors disable its wireless capabilities when he became aware and fearful of being assassinated by terrorists who he thought could exterminate him by sending an electronic shock to his implanted heart defibrillator. He, therefore, had his doctors replace the existing device with a new device that lacked Wi-Fi capability.

There is a dire need to regulate the use of implants. A firm in the USA called Three Square Market' has teamed with a Swedish concern and implanted RFID chips the size of rice grain in 50 of its 85 employees that allow employees to access offices, computers and even vending machines. There are reports that the US Food and Drug Administration has approved these implantations.

Militaries are building cyborg animals to gain a tactical advantage. The Defense Advanced Research Projects Agency (DARPA) is trying to develop cyborg insects that can survey an environment and detect explosives and gas. Researchers at DARPA plan to implant the cyborg insects with sensors during the pupa stage, in order to control its motion from a Micro-Electro-Mechanical System (MEMS). In 2006, Cornell University invented a surgical procedure to embed sensors in the thorax of the insects. Likewise, DARPA is developing a neural implant to control by remote the movement of sharks, which would help to detect enemy ship movement and underwater explosives. They have successfully used neural implants in cockroaches, where researchers could remotely control electrodes implanted in cockroaches. Researchers at the University of California at Berkeley have pioneered the design of a 'remote controlled beetle' funded by the DARPA HI-MEMS Program. Scientists now plan to develop HI-MEMS for dragonflies, bees, rats and pigeons.

Stephen Hawking believes that life on earth is at great risk of being wiped out by a disaster such as global warming or nuclear war. Hence, cyborg technologies could help turn humans into a multi-planetary species. One of the key issues in space travel is the biological necessity for oxygen. Two scientists Manfred E. Clynes and Nathan S. Kline have proposed that an inverse cell fuel which can remove carbon from carbon dioxide and recirculate the oxygen could make breathing dispensable.

Another major issue in space is radiation exposure. A cyborg with a sensor that detects radiation levels which could induce an embedded osmotic pump to inject protective drugs has been developed. Tests with monkeys have shown that such drugs could increase radiation resistance.

It now takes about 260 days to fly to Mars. To counteract the adverse effects of such long flights, NASA has proposed a torpor technique that will put astronauts in deep sleep or torpor reducing metabolic functions. Experiments as of now can put patients in torpor for one week but advancements in future will allow for longer torpor and reduced astronaut resource consumption.

Advances in cybernetics is also helping athletes break new grounds. Take the case of gold-medal-winning South African sprinter Oscar

Pistorius, the double below-the-knee amputee, who was persistently complained by other athletes about his 'Blade Runner' artificial limbs giving him an unfair advantage.

The 'Cybathlon 2016' in Zurich were the first Olympics for cyborgs and the first worldwide and official celebration of cyborg sports in which 16 teams of cyborg athletes took part. During the events, athletes used powered prosthetic legs and arms, robotic exoskeletons, bikes and motorized wheelchairs. The next Cybathlon was held in 2020, and another such event is scheduled for 2024.

Whether our cyborg future-to-be would resemble the horrors depicted in Mary Shelley's *Frankenstein* or whether they bring out the epic potentialities of Tony Stark in Iron Man, is something we may have to wait and see. One thing that has become obvious is that the criminals who have time and time again shown their willingness and ability to leverage any emerging technology to their advantage will continue to hack implants and exploit it for gain.

Just the way a hacker can hack into an implant in our bodies, our souls too are susceptible to hacking by evils of this world such as temptations, greed and bad habits. But we have inherent power within us to overcome and restore our soul to default settings through soul culture such as meditation and other spiritual practices. Restoring the default settings of our soul could fill us with bliss and joy which we are constantly seeking.

CHAPTER 15
IS HUMAN MICROBIOME A MACROCOSMIC REPOSITORY OF PRECIOUS LEGAL EVIDENCE?

The Scottish Physician and author Sir Arthur Conan Doyle was a forensic expert ahead of his time. The credit for unravelling tangled crime cases employing fingerprints, hair analysis and blood tests to decipher crimes belongs to him. If he were alive today, his ever-famous detective Sherlock Holmes would have commenced cracking tricky cases with ease by obtaining microscopic traces of bacteria left behind by criminals at the scene of the crime.

When we are born, we are mostly sterile, but we acquire microbes from our mother and our immediate environment during the birth and after the birth. We gradually amass approximately 10,000 different bacterial strains, and the species composition remains mostly stable for the rest of our lives. We start with around 20,500 genes at birth, but we acquire more than 1,000,000 genes over time due to the microbiome. We have ten times more bacterial cells in our bodies than human cells, which leaves us marvelling if we were more of a microbial being than a human being.

Police officers could soon have a new tool in their toolbox for detecting crimes and capturing criminals. 'We all have microbes living on us, no matter how much we clean ourselves. Research divulges that every individual's microbial community or microbiome is as unique as human fingerprints or DNA. We slough off millions of microbial cells every hour into our surroundings, so we're leaving our microbial signature wherever we go.'

Microbiologist Jose Lopez and Jack Gilbert, PhD, the Microbiome Center faculty director at the University of Chicago, organised mock burglaries as part of an experimental project. After the burglary, the forensic experts swooped on the scene to swab down surfaces, handles and houses.

After eliminating the bacterial signatures left behind by the household inmates and the pet cat, investigators had new physical evidence of burglars in the form of their microbial signatures.

The bacterial signatures of the two intruders did not just reveal their identity. Still, it also told their lifestyle habits when investigators stacked up against a database of a few thousand people. The comparison divulged that one of the burglars had at least ten alcoholic drinks a week while the other was on migraine medication. The microbiome left at the scene could also speculate whether the perpetrator is a man or a woman, his/her weight, ethnicity, whether he smokes or drinks and so forth. These kinds of leads could be precious for police.

A study published in 2010 in the 'Proceedings of the National Academy of Sciences' illustrated that DNA recovered from computer keyboards and owners' fingertips matched. The authors could also scrape out bacteria from nine computer mice and correctly pinpoint the computer mice owners by contrasting it with a database of 270 microbiomes available in the public domain. Everybody's poop has a unique signature. Harvard University conducted a study on stool samples collected from participants in the study. A year later, they found the bacteria signatures collected from the participants' stools helped researchers identify individuals with 86 per cent accuracy. Skin bacteria are found in people's mobile phones. Investigators can use the microbial profile of a person obtained from the cell phone to link the phone to its original owner with 97 per cent accuracy using only the phones' swabs.

Microbes play an essential role in the decomposition of human corpses. Scientists are exploring microbial succession during the decomposition to estimate the time since death and as an indicator for locating unknown graves. In a healthy human being, the brain, liver, spleen and heart are free from microflora. Our immune system hinders the microbes from getting into these organs. But after death, microorganisms spread into these germ-free organs. The migration of microbial microorganisms into the sterile organs can be a pretty accurate measure of post-mortem interval. This duration enables investigators to arrive at the time of death.

The microbial signature technique could become a new tool in law enforcement's arsenal alongside DNA fingerprinting and physical fingerprinting. When the physical fingerprints are smudged, and the suspect has not left behind DNA, bacterial fingerprints can go to the investigator's aid, although DNA will always be the gold standard. Bacterial signatures have several advantages over diagnostic DNA evidence. Unless the suspect has left behind blood, tissue, semen, saliva or hair, it is often difficult to obtain sufficient DNA for forensic identification. On the contrary, microbes are abundant, and it's much easier to recover bacterial DNA than human DNA. It is also easier to recover bacterial DNA than human DNA from touch surfaces, and on the other hand, bacterial DNA is available in most scenarios than human DNAs. Cosmetics, antibiotics usage, dietary changes and health states could have a corresponding change in the microbiome, which could be one of the drawbacks of bacterial signatures.

While human bacterial fingerprinting should never replace traditional DNA fingerprinting, it could augment the forensic scientists' existing techniques. Any introduction of a new approach would require amendments to criminal laws and the creation of standards governing samples' collection and use. A substantial investment would be needed to standardise and implement detection techniques to automate and hasten microbiome profiling. And could entail maintenance of databases which could raise privacy issues. As the databases could reveal if a person is carrying a sexually transmitted disease or suffering some other chronic illness, it could also show his associations, the number of sexual partners they have had, and his drug habits and addictions. Police could use such a database to connect people to crime by showing evidence by way of the places he has visited, his familial origin, ethnicity and so on.

Finally, the spooky truth is that we are more bacteria than human cells. We are energetic spiritual beings having a human experience, but we are also Bacteria-sapiens! All the microbes in our body have a vibration and frequency. Our consciousness is not just affected by what's going on behind our eyes. Many influences are beyond the realm of our awareness, the human microbiome being one of them. Therefore, we must work in participation with our entire body, including the microbiome, to evolve beyond our current physical and mental conditions and make a spiritual connection with all of life.

Chapter 16
DARK CLOUD OR A CLOUD WITH A SILVER LINING?

I awakened this morning to cloudy north-east monsoon skies and intermittent drizzle. My daughter was flying down from Mumbai after nearly three months. I knew the aircraft she was in would graze the dense clouds and pierce through them before touching down in the next twenty minutes. As I looked up at the sky, with anticipation and excitement of seeing her, I eavesdropped on a thought which proposed that Cloud computing might be a good idea to contemplate on during such cloudy days. And I also knew, Mat Honan would be a good place to start.

Mat Honan, who worked as a senior writer for *Wired* magazine, had an awesome and a cool digital life. His browser displayed beautiful pictures of his 18-month-old daughter, and his tab buzzed with thousands of his followers on Twitter. One fine August afternoon in 2012, Mat was playing with his daughter when his mobile phone suddenly went lifeless. Trying to restore it, he connected his mobile phone to the power source, expecting to see his custom screen saver and the apps. He instead saw the mobile display a multilingual invitation to set up his mobile phone. He was baffled.

As Mat had religiously backed up his iPhone every night, he believed his data would be safe on his iCloud account. He logged in there to reclaim his data and account. Upon doing so, he was horrified to learn that his password, which he knew to be correct, was being divulged as incorrect by iCloud. Startled, he connected his mobile phone to the laptop, hoping to restore the data from the hard drive of his MacBook. The MacBook too informed him that his password was incorrect and abruptly turned blank. He soon realised that someone had also hacked his Gmail and Twitter accounts.

The entire data Mat had accumulated over his lifetime, including his daughter's pictures, had been erased. All his Gmail messages, work conversations, family photographs, notes and reminders were gone too. Having just undergone a massive unsuspecting digital onslaught, Mat decided that he should investigate what had happened.

When he called Apple tech support, they told him that thirty minutes prior to his call, a caller had contacted them. The only information Apple needed back then to give the password details was the mailing address and the last four digits of his credit card number. Mat's mailing address was available on his website, and the hacker armed with Mat's email ID and his address exploited a naive customer service employee at Amazon to get the last four digits of Mat's credit card. As in Mat's case, authorising personal information such as family photographs and precious personal information to Cloud service providers could come with huge risks.

We may not be aware that our various accounts get linked to one another as in Mat's case, we may have the same credit card number on an Apple and a Flipkart profile, our iCloud email address may point to our Gmail address and our login credentials may be available online waiting to be creatively or deviously exploited by those wanting to destroy our digital lives.

What is Cloud? In computing parlance, Cloud refers to the practice of storing data on remote servers, sometimes in numerous locations, which is owned and managed by a hosting company. Cloud computing is believed to have been an invention of Joseph Carl Robnett Licklider in the 1960s to connect people and data from anywhere at any time. Cloud service providers store, manage, protect and allow access to our data. Subscribers and organisations buy or lease storage capacity from the hosts to store data.

At an individual level, it would mean, our mobiles are uploading and storing pictures on Instagram, our emails on Google and our documents on Dropbox. The changing paradigm in computing means that less information gets stored locally on our computers and is instead being hosted elsewhere on earth. We may access cloud storage services through a collocated cloud computing service, a web service application programming interface (API) or by applications that use the API, such as cloud desktop storage, a cloud storage gateway or Web-based content management systems. We mostly do not buy software anymore; we just rent it or receive it for free using a new business model known as Software as a Service (SaaS). The accumulation of all these data means that our most personal of information is no longer likely stored solely on our local hard drives but are now assembled on computer servers around the world. By aggregating everybody's essential data, financial and otherwise, on cloud-based computer servers, we've prevented the need for criminals to target everybody's hard drive individually and instead put all valuables in a single basket for criminals and hackers to target.

Cloud computing functions by using the Internet with the help of software and hardware virtualisation. The most significant advantage is the flexible ease of storage and release of data as per the needs of the user. The other advantages of cloud computing are lowered prices because of the curtailment of cost of hardware/software and better efficiency.

In 2017, Amazon generated 3.2 million from their public cloud computing infrastructure division known as Amazon Web Services. Microsoft knowing fully well that more and more people would use the cloud in the days to come had earmarked 90 per cent of its R&D budget in 2011 on cloud computing products and applications. Forbes had reported that by 2018 over 50 per cent of IT spending will be cloud-based. Banks are the most enthusiastic users of the cloud for mobile banking and virtual transaction services. Companies use cloud more for storage than application development. Over 90 per cent of all businesses witnessed at least one area of improvement in their IT department after they moved to the cloud. Small to medium business that adopted the cloud experienced a 40 per cent growth in revenues after a year compared to those that did not use the cloud.

But on the downside cloud has several issues. The provider of the cloud computing services has access to gargantuan data, there is a great risk of it being leaked intentionally or accidentally. The data is also in danger of being deleted or modified. This is mainly because most service providers use administrators who could be lured or coaxed to disclose data for personal or political gain.

There are instances where cloud service providers have compromised the privacy of several companies. Most service providers have a privacy policy that subscribers have to agree, which lets them share data with third parties for law and order. For instance, Dropbox has a privacy policy which states that for law and order purposes, they may reveal information to third parties if they determine that such disclosure is reasonably necessary to (a) comply with the law; (b) protect any person from death or serious bodily injury; (c) prevent fraud or abuse of Dropbox or our users; or (d) protect Dropbox's property rights.

Then there are technical issues. If the servers are down or if there is a denial of service attack, it may not be possible to access data. Cloud computing services requires a secure Internet connection and consumes a great deal of power of the devices such as the smartphone.

Data breach is a huge issue in cloud computing. Hackers could rip off various types of information from a compromised cloud such as email addresses, credit card information, mailing addresses and personal messages. There must be a law to notify customers of the breaches. The US has one such law. The nonlocal storage of our data raises important questions about our deep reliance on cloud-based information systems. When these services go down or become unavailable via a distributed denial-of-service (DDoS) attack, or when we lose our Internet connection, or if our data becomes unavailable, we could go out of business.

All major cloud service providers, such as Dropbox, Google and Microsoft, have gotten breached, and we can foresee more to happen in the future. Several thousand businesses that have valuable data stored in the cloud continue to get breached and stolen. On 31 August 2014, hackers posted a collection of nude photos of various celebrities such as Jennifer Lawrence and Kate Upton on the anonymous image-sharing website 4chan. Apple initially believed that the hackers had got the images via a breach of Apple's cloud services suite iCloud, or a security issue in the iCloud API. However, Apple came to know later that the access route was via spear phishing attacks.

The breach of Aadhar data which exposed literally over a billion Indian citizens has been one of the most significant breaches to date. The information breached included data such as a member's names, their identity numbers which are unique 12-digit numbers assigned, biometric data, and information about the services being subscribed to such as bank details and utility services .

Another breach that made major headlines was that of Cambridge Analytica, a British political consulting company started in 2013. Cambridge Analytica had collected Facebook information of 87 million users inappropriately to build political profiles of each Facebook user and target-specific political advertisements to manipulate them in a particular way prompting an investigation by the US Congress into the allegations which led to Mark Zuckerberg testifying.

On 30 November 2018, Marriott Starwood Hotels revealed they had recognised a data security breach of their guest database, which it believed compromised up to approximately 327 million guests who made a reservation at a Starwood property. The records that got jeopardised contained information such as name, mailing address, phone number, email address, passport number, Starwood Preferred Guest accounting information and date of birth .

Code Spaces is an example of a company that was entirely put out of business by a single cloud security incident. The hacker compromised Code Spaces' Amazon Web Services account and demanded a ransom. When the company declined, the hacker started razing their data until nothing was left.

In all such cases, it may be the cloud service provider who gets targeted, but we become the victims as the data that is stolen is ours. The terms of service conditions of such companies to which subscribers agree to hold the providers of cloud services unaccountable when such breaches occur. These attacks threaten intellectual property, customer data and even sensitive government information.

Mat Honan, with whose story we began, eventually created a new Twitter account and established contact with his hacker who had annihilated him online. Mat implored his hacker to explain why he had snuffed out his digital life. The teenager replied that he had done because he had liked his Twitter name and wanted it for himself. Not much has changed since then; we are today as much vulnerable as Mat was back in 2012 as we ratchet our reliance on mobile and cloud-based applications.

Whether cloud computing turns into dark clouds or a cloud with a silver lining depends on our ability to protect data from being breached or leaked inadvertently. Following best practices can help organisations ensure that their data is kept safe and secure. Using a monitoring and security solution that utilises machine learning to monitor the public cloud environment can be extremely powerful.

Spiritually too, we may be living in a cloud computing universe. If we think of our memories as a document on Google drive, everything is already in the cloud. So, our consciousness is out there in the cosmic cloud as well, which is getting auto-updated in real-time.

Chapter 17
ASTROTURFING CAN HAVE ASTRONOMICAL FALLOUTS

When the shopping malls began sprouting across Chennai, I became enthusiastic about exploring them to window shop, watch a flick, dine or shop. Shopping, in particular, was very convenient as I would often uncover shops selling similar items conveniently grouped or clustered together. Over the years, however, I developed a disenchantment for the malls as they began getting crowded, raucous and cumbersome to shop. Simultaneously, online shops like Amazon started emerging and thronging cyberspace, providing more comfort and convenience than malls. Suddenly, I had access to the world's largest malls right on my palm. Along came the pandemic, which devastated and almost ruined the retail industry. Malls that were already perceiving the pressure from e-commerce and dwindling footfalls were abruptly bereft of shoppers, as the world locked itself down to contain the virus's spread. Despite the raging pandemic, the government has allowed the opening of malls, but most people still prefer the pleasure of shopping online.

The first thing most of us do when we visit an online shop is to check out customer reviews. A customer review reveals an experience shared by a shopper on a product purchased or a service availed by him. 'Eco-Consultancy' estimates that 61 per cent of buyers read online reviews before they decide to buy a product. And they also claim that their study shows that reviews left by customers are 12 times more trusted and relied on than the product descriptions posted by the manufacturers. These reviews have become unreliable as several companies have posted fake five-star reviews from friends, relatives and hired reviewers to make more people purchase goods or services or post critical reviews to destroy the reputation of their competitors. Buzzfeed recently published a story of a woman who bought $15,000 products on Amazon, much of which was in bargain and exchange for writing five-star reviews.

While browsing a reputed online shop, I came across a sale of highly branded T-shirts for Rs 110 with 12,000 five-star reviews that appeared too good to be true. One of the significant hazards of shopping online is getting misled by deceptive reviews that delude the buyer into buying a shoddy product. Phoney reviews have proliferated in every province of e-commerce, from electronics to apparel to books to kids' toys. There are some brilliant games like Angry Birds and apps like Evernote on the Internet, but I bet you might not be aware that the creators of apps can have 5,000 reviews posted in favour of their app by shelling out a thousand dollars. Supplements and electronics are something I purchase predominantly online. A study performed in 2018 revealed that the supplements category on the Amazon website had the highest share of fake product reviews, with a registered 64 per cent of reviews being deemed fake. Electronics came close in second place, divulging that 61 per cent of its reviews were fake. Creating the delusion of comprehensive grassroots support for an app, candidate, policy or cause when no such backing exists is 'Astroturfing'. Astroturfing exploits the 'herd instinct' of people to embrace the opinions of the majority.

The term 'astroturfing' was first conceived in 1985 by Texan Democrat Senator Lloyd Bentsen when he received a massive pile of cards and letters at his office promoting the insurance industry's interests. It was then that the invention and installation of astroturf at Houston Astrodome had taken place, prompting Mr Bentsen to remark that 'any Texan could tell the difference between the grass root and AstroTurf', implying it wouldn't be hard to discern between a genuine letter and a fake or a generated email. Astroturfing crusades may get staged by corporations, lobbyists, labour unions, politicians or activist organisations, or individuals with personal agendas. Astroturfing is not a recent phenomenon. It has existed for centuries. In Shakespeare's play *Julius Caesar*', Cassius arranges fake letters from 'the public' to convince Brutus to assassinate Caesar.

Astroturfing is most times difficult to detect. The *New York Times* contends it is often hard to know between popular sentiment and manufactured public opinion. Mr Bing Liu, a data mining expert at the University of Illinois, estimates that one-third of customer reviews on the Internet are fake. A 2011 report found that paid posters from competing companies often attack each other in forums and overwhelm regular participants in the process. The authentic grassroots movements are therefore in danger because of astroturfing. Corporates, politicians and support groups appear to have intentionally developed astroturfing to attain corporate agendas, manipulate public opinion and harm scientific research.

There are several techniques for accomplishing astroturfing. One of the astroturfing techniques is to prop up one or two groups who pretend to serve a public interest while working at the behest of a corporate or a political sponsor. Such groups may protest against legislation or a consensus regarding a new project through counterclaims and create doubts in the people's minds. Sock-Puppets is another technique where one individual creates multiple identities online to give the impression of online support for a particular cause or project. Astroturfing businesses pay staff based on the number of posts they make. Fake blogs, drafted by corporates, organisations, and others, sometimes get posted on personal websites as though created by a genuine consumer. Pharmaceutical companies are resorting to astroturfing to market their products by sponsoring patient support groups. Bloggers often get approached by interested corporations or groups with free products, paid travel and accommodation to astroturf their products or services.

Many countries have laws that forbid overt astroturfing practices. In India, the Consumer Protection Act, 1986 ("Act") is the relevant law for customer protection. Section 6 of the said Act allows the Central Consumer Protection Council to promote and protect the rights of consumers. As most of the astroturfing offences take place in cyberspace, the government may have to enact a new law or amend the IT Act, 2000 to include provisions against the crime of astroturfing.

Curious to find whether astroturfing accusations levelled in 2009 when Barack Obama and a Democratic Congress swept to power were true or not? Australian filmmaker Taki Oldham made a film titled *(Astro) Turf Wars* about the citizen's movement, which emerged out of nowhere after Obama was elected the president. The film posed some tough questions and discovered that Tea Partiers were genuine people who believed in some issues. Still, the topics such as healthcare and global warming were somebody else's interests.

Finally, some governments are using astroturfing as a weapon to counter propaganda during war or stifle dissent. Russia successfully employed astroturfing to get Donald Trump elected as the US President in 2016. In 2010, the US Air force developed a Persona Management software that enabled people to have many online identities without fear of being discovered by anyone. The US military used this software to spread pro-American propaganda in the Middle East and disrupt extremist propaganda and recruitment as a part of Operation Earnest Voice, a psychological warfare weapon against the groups opposed to coalition forces. In 2008, an expert on China, Rebecca MacKinnon, revealed that China had employed 280,000 individuals in a government-sponsored astroturfing project to publish pro-China hype to drown out voices of dissent. We today, therefore, seem to live amidst an artificial reality, coaxed to believe that the astroturf engineered to look like grass is real.

Chapter 18
GEOGRAPHIC INFORMATION SYSTEM FOR CRIME PREVENTION

In 1998, Vacaville, California, USA, had a string of eight robberies. The robber came to be labelled as Bandanna Bandit. The police were clueless. Crime Analyst Laura Bettencourt took to Geographic Information System (GIS) to identify the likely future targets and the days of his next hits, based on which police set up surveillance on possible future targets. Soon, the suspect was found entering a predicted location and attempting to hold it up. The deputies intervened, a gun battle ensued and the suspect was killed. Likewise, in 1999, a felon after being arrested and convicted filed a lawsuit against the City of Shawnee, Kansas, USA, contending that the police had used unreasonable force while making the arrest. A map made in GIS to defend the arresting officer's testimony revealed that the suspect had darted at high speeds through residential areas, bypassing several red lights and had jumped out of his car in a densely populated housing project to elude the police. The culprit was deemed as posing a great danger to public safety. Hence the officer was exonerated from the case.

We have come across crime thrillers and movies where criminals outsmart the police by a mix of deception and hoax. Throughout history, there has been a cat-and-mouse contest between criminals and the police. One of the concrete ways of ensuring that a criminal doesn't con the police is by the deployment of GIS and other spatial technologies in crime investigation, for detection and tracking that are making police organisations more efficient and effective in nipping criminality in the bud.

A GIS is a system developed to capture, stock, manipulate, analyse, manage and present spatial or geographic data. GIS applications are instruments that permit users to create interactive queries, analyse spatial data, edit data in maps and present the outcomes of all such activities.

We are today witnessing an increasing role of GIS in law enforcement and police force planning and deployment, in particular, because of the heightened prerogative of crime theory to focus on place instead of people. The concentration of crime in limited areas is astonishing and naturally invites place-based policing. For example, in the USA, 3 per cent of the city's addresses accounted for 50 per cent of calls for service to the police in Minneapolis and about 4 per cent of streets and intersection areas generated nearly 50 per cent of the city's narcotics arrests and almost 42 per cent of the disorder arrests in Jersey City, New Jersey.

Police agencies are using Geographic Information Systems (GIS) for mapping crime, identifying crime 'hot spots', assigning officers, and profiling offenders, but little research has been done about the effectiveness of the technology in policing organisations. Hot-spot policing plans and adjusts the deployment of a police force under the geographic variation of crime and focuses police patrol on crime hot spots. A standard definition of a hot spot is an area with a higher than the average number of criminal or disorder events.

It is seen that the implementation of a GIS is frequently steered by jurisdictional, objective or application prerequisites. Generally, a GIS execution may be custom-made for an establishment. Thus, a GIS formulated for an agency may not be inevitably interoperable or compatible with a GIS that has been evolved for some other application, management, industry or use.

GIS delivers every type of location-based organisation, a setting to update geographical data without having to waste time to visit a place or location and update a database manually. GIS, when integrated with other robust enterprise solutions like SAP and the Wolfram Language, helps build a powerful decision support system at the enterprise level, enabling domains to benefit from GIS technology. A competitive GIS market has resulted in lower prices and perpetual refinements in the hardware and software components of GIS, and usage in different fields, including crime mapping. GIS is also spreading out into location-based services, which enables GPS-enabled mobile devices to indicate their location with regards to fixed objects such as a restaurant, a gas station, or migrating objects such as friends, children or a police car, or to transmit their location back to a central server for display or other processing.

According to a 2001 survey by the National Institute of Justice in the USA, 62 per cent of police departments with over 100 officers use GIS systems. On the whole, the technology has helped in decreasing crime, reducing residential burglaries, tracking parolees and habitual severe offenders, and identification of 'hot spots' with high concentrations of crime.

GIS has four major uses in policing. Crime mapping identifies the geographical distribution of crime to deploy officers to 'hot spots' of activity and to develop other intervention plans.

Many departments have developed computerised statistics or CompStat systems to help manage the decision-making process. The system supports instant crime analysis, deployment strategies, active enforcement, monitoring of emerging patterns and responsibility programs for law enforcement commanders.

GIS also is used to build geographical profiling of criminals, an investigative technique that enables police to identify locations of related crimes to help deduce where a criminal may live, especially in serial cases.

While these practices are widespread, especially in larger departments, little research is available to measure their effectiveness in policing. Current studies indicate that GIS is used mainly to aid in the design of policing strategies and to evaluate the decision-making processes at law enforcement agencies.

Police can better understand the underlying causes of crime and help police formulate strategies to tackle crime by overlaying other datasets such as locations of bars, location of evil characters, rowdies and site of colleges. GIS is also useful for deploying police personnel and other resources. We can put an explicit strategy to lessen crime in place, but for that, we would have to know the location of the assets to transfer them to where we might require them. We would also have to know the developments taking place if any.

There are several theories which explain the spatial behaviour of criminals such as routine activity theory, developed by Lawrence Cohen and Marcus Felson, rational choice theory, developed by Ronald V. Clarke and Derek Cornish, and environmental criminology. In recent years, crime mapping and analysis have incorporated spatial data analysis techniques. Spatial data analysis helps one analyse crime data and better understand why and not just where crime is occurring. From a research and policy perspective, crime mapping is used to understand patterns of incarceration and recidivism, help target resources and programs, evaluate crime prevention or crime reduction programs. The boom of Internet technologies, particularly Web-based geographic information system (GIS) technologies, is opening new opportunities for the use of crime mapping to support crime prevention

In the days to come, we may use GIS and artificial intelligence for all forms of policing. As technology becomes more active and sophisticated, more and more police organisations will resort to this technology. Analysis of social media posts and location tracking is a standard method used by law enforcement agencies to take pre-emptive actions. Even for tracing terror suspects or criminals, location tracking of their social media or phone records often comes handy.

Mapping crime, using Geographic Information Systems (GIS), enables crime analysts to identify crime hot spots, along with other trends and patterns.

Crime mapping is being employed by police to map, visualise and analyse crime occurrence patterns. It is a crucial ingredient of crime analysis and the CompStat policing strategy.

In India, for several years we have been deploying a rudimentary system of crime mapping at the police station level by way of Part 2 Crime Charts. Commissioner of the NYPD (New York Police Department) the ever flamboyant, Bill Bratton in his first tenure in 1994 introduced Crime CompStat (which stands for COMPare STATistics) a unique strategy that helped bring down crime drastically. It reaped the power of GIS for furnishing real-time insights and situational awareness that changed policing in New York forever.

CompStat was initiated under the guidance of Jack Maple when he was a transit police officer in New York City. The strategy was initially christened 'Charts of the Future'. The procedure envisaged tracking of crimes by sticking pins in maps. The simple strategy of 'Charts of the Future' brought down subway crime by 27 per cent.

William J. Bratton, Chief of New York City Transit Police was later appointed police commissioner by Rudolph Giuliani, the Mayor of New York, and he brought Maple's Charts of the Future with him. After overcoming some initial opposition, he made the NYPD adopt it and renamed it as CompStat. CompStat method started yielding results, and it curtailed crime by 60 per cent. In 1993, before the NYPD (New York Police Department) embraced CompStat, there were around 2,000 cases of murders in the city. In just one year following its adoption, the number of murders started dropping rapidly; it fell to 1,181 from 1995. By 2003, the number of murders had declined to 596 murders; it fell further to 352 by 2015, the lowest since 1964.

CompStat wasn't a computer system but a statistical tool that processed crime events and arrests reports to arrive at the hotspots of crime in the city. To better describe it, it was simply an improved version of crime charts maintained since last century in the police stations of Tamilnadu, where the crimes and accidents would get reflected in a map. A cluster of crimes or accidents in a close vicinity meant that the particular area deserved frequent beats.

GIS plays a significant role in bolstering law enforcement and is being widely used by police organisations across the world. CompStat hinges on real-time data sharing, the immediate deployment of resources, as well as on planning powerful strategies with constant feedback and appropriate follow-up action. CompStat uses GIS as an interactive working platform to bring real-time awareness to emerging crime trends. Los Angeles and Baltimore, like several other cities, have witnessed a reduction in crimes by integrating CompStat in their workflows with CompStat rigidly following its leads.

CompStat offers an excellent strategy to reduce crime, improve quality of life, and manage resources personnel and resources. CompStat enables police officers to recognise surging trends in crime through comparative statistics and aids them to deal with the spikes in crimes through the practice of targeted enforcement. CompStat has four commonly recognised components: it provides reliable and precise information or intelligence, leading to immediate deployment of resources, effective tactics and constant follow-up. We can modify or broaden CompStat to meet the specific requirements of different wings of the police organisations. Initially, it was based on the broken windows theory, according to which proper handling of minor crimes satisfactorily would also result in a reduction in major and other crimes.

Nonetheless, with time, its use appears to have degenerated into a system of assessing an officer's competence, and for making officers liable for upswings in criminal incidents. Now, several companies have begun developing CompStat turnkey packages containing computer systems, software and other tools. GISs are allowing organisations to map crime or various types of data, to help them know and solve issues in their designated area.

Everything we deal with in law enforcement has a location attached to it: the site of a crime, the place where the offender lives or works, the area where evidence is collected, and so forth. The places where we live are also imbued with spiritual energy, but we have been dishonouring nature. The ancient civilisations worshipped nature. When there is a sense of reverence towards the planet we live on, we cannot pollute it or harm it. This attitude of honouring nature is what we must bring back through education and understanding.

Chapter 19
CAN ADVANCED EXOSKELETONS TURN COPS INTO ROBOCOPS?

We all love *RoboCop*. Exoskeletons are a perfect example where technology is getting pretty close to the movies. The armour and cyborgian capabilities of exoskeletons are pretty freaking awesome. The exoskeletons give the characters extraordinary abilities to take on the supervillains of the world. Whether it's in Paul Verhoeven's 1987 original or José Padilha's recent remake, *RoboCop* is as badass as it gets. Other iconic exoskeletons seen in the other badass movies include the Iron Man MK III suit, the Caterpillar Power Loader in *Aliens*, and the suits used by the soldiers in the film *The Edge of Tomorrow*.

Recently, in *Avengers: Endgame* we saw Colonel James Rupert "Rhodey" Rhodes suit-up in a brand new armour for the final battle, having incredible firepower that was never seen before, ostensibly inspired by the Iron Patriot armour he wore back in *Iron Man 3*. The next step in human evolution appears to be an artificial integration of man and machine crafted by our organic minds and implemented alongside our flesh-and-blood systems. Will we ever see a fully realised robocop like the ones that appear on the screen?

My guess is very soon. Robocops scurrying to a crime scene may come across like a scene out of a sci-fi movie today, but the reality is not far away. Technology will help the police turn sci-fi into truth. Several companies are researching gear that will turn police officers into sci-fi characters like a robocop. Research labs are capitalising on technology to evolve exoskeletons with impervious graphene body armour fitted with smart belts, body cameras and Google Glass. Technological advancements in future will boost efficiency and police officer safety. Several of these technologies are already being discerned on the streets, while others are still on the horizon.

Rozy Ghaly/Shutterstock.com

For law enforcement officers a robotic exoskeleton closer to RoboCop would be a contraption fitted to the officers' knees formulated for power generation that can take the weight off their weary legs and help them chase criminals, something akin to the suit a 29-year-old paraplegic man donned during the World Cup to make the successful first kick that had a body armour made of graphene and a range of wearable computers.

A RoboCop like exoskeleton would presumably be made of a novel material such as graphene. Graphene is an extraordinary material that won its researchers a Nobel Prize in 2010. Graphene armour is created from a layer of single carbon atoms organised in a honeycomb shape; the wonder fabric graphene is the world's thinnest, most durable material which has tremendous flexibility. Graphene can resist blows that would punch through steel with the capacity to perform twice as well as the fabric presently used in bulletproof vests, making it ideal armour for the protection of the police officers.

The exoskeleton would also come fitted with smart glasses to intensify situational awareness of police officers, with the ability to compile information about a crime scene even before he arrives, which could include Google Earth images or video footage sent from mobile phones and tweets or Facebook posts. The glasses would also be able to receive text messages which are visible on the lenses. This way, the police officer would procure crucial facts without having to look away from the crime scene. This would herald new ways of capturing evidence and reduce costs and delay. For instance, the police would be able to retrieve proof digitally and upload the evidence without returning to the police station.

The smart belts in the exoskeleton would instantly be able to sense when the police officer pulls out a gun, taser, pepper spray or handcuffs from the holsters on his belt and would transmit that data to dispatch backups. The sensor would also activate the specially designed smart glasses to take images of the scene automatically.

The body-cams on the exoskeletons would also be able to document the police officers' interaction with people and thereby prevent capricious accounts of incidents, safeguarding the public against police brutality and abuse. At the same time, the footage available would be able to fend law enforcement officers against untrue indictments of misconduct.

Now, what is an exoskeleton? When I was a student, and when I had enrolled myself for a course in Entomology, my teacher taught me that exoskeleton was a rigid crust outside biological creatures like insects and crustaceans which accomplished the purpose of bones in higher life forms. Bones in humans can be thought of as endoskeletons. Exoskeletons that humans don are a kind of a motorised prop that bolsters the characteristics of a wearer by enabling him to run as fast as an automobile or lift ten times his weight. The technology is being explored as being advantageous mostly for NASA, the military, nuclear energy and law enforcement.

Today's exoskeletons are primarily clumsy, bulky devices, as they use large electric motors. On the other hand, new technology such as weightless actuators which are identical to pneumatic muscles that generate same forces to electric motors but at a fraction of weight could make them much more comfortable and more natural to use. The muscles consist of a rubber bladder enveloped by a woven sleeve. When pressurised, they expand in diameter and contract in length, pulling the joint. They can generate a force required to lift several hundreds of kilogrammes being made from lightweight materials.

Exoskeletons are now being sold in shops, and we'll probably see more of them in the coming years. Exoskeleton Wearable Robots market, which was worth $130 million in 2018, is predicted to surpass $5.2 billion by 2025. Law enforcement personnel can perform at a higher level when wearing an exoskeleton. Exoskeletons are being developed in the US, China, Korea, Japan and Europe. They are generally intended for medical, logistical and engineering purposes, due to their narrow range and short battery life. Improvements to exoskeletons, including enlarging their battery life, could make them suitable for law enforcement in crime control and crowd control.

The world over, nations and armies are building exoskeletons. The US uncovered an exoskeleton dubbed TALOS in 2015 that stands for 'Tactical Assault Light Operator Suit' for use by elite commandos in prospective missions.

United Instrument Manufacturing Corp., a defence contractor in Russia, intends to produce mind-controlled exoskeletons for Russian soldiers by 2020 and South Korea's Hyundai has assembled an exoskeleton that is analogous to Iron Man. China Ordnance Industry Group showcased an exoskeleton, which could lift objects weighing more than 100 lb. and was equipped with a battery that enabled the soldier to walk a maximum distance of 20 kilometres at a speed of 4.5 km/hour, capabilities of which were equal to an exoskeleton developed by US-based Lockheed Martin.

In 2015, the Institute of Advanced Manufacturing Technology in Changzhou finished work on an exoskeleton that assisted people climbing mountains or aided them to smash through structures like walls. In 2016, FutureWise unveiled an exoskeleton called NK-01 based on a character from the *Iron Man* movie series. In 2012, Suidobashi Heavy Industry, Japan disclosed a 'mecha bot' called Kuratas, which was a 13-foot exoskeleton with 30 joints, weapons and other capabilities, monitorable by a person from a cockpit or remotely through a phone. In 2015, the Technical Research and Development Institute, a defence research wing of the Japanese military started developing 'highly mobile-powered suits' and a strategy called the 'Zero Casualty Battle System', which strived to supplant soldiers with technology whenever possible. China could be one of the first countries to employ exoskeletons to expand its influence. For example, it could deploy military exoskeletons to patrol islands in the South China Sea.

Exoskeletons are not just suitable for loading missiles onto combat aircraft. Exoskeleton robots, besides military and industrial functions, are aiding personal mobility and are helping people relearn movement after stroke by creating new muscle memory. People who have been paralysed are able to relearn lost functions. Exoskeletons are providing high-quality rehabilitation. In 2012, a paralysed woman Claire Lomas even finished the London Marathon donning one. Wearable exoskeletons are also enabling susceptible employees to reduce long-term joint pain or repetitive back injuries.

Let's say an employee working from his office reaches for the intercom and suddenly strains his right shoulder. Due to the agonising pain, he applies for medical leave and takes an MRI, which indicates a rotator cuff injury. There are similar instances of police officers sustaining knee injuries while chasing criminals, or sustaining fractures from falls or sustaining injuries while rescuing. In the field of law enforcement, the average number of days police officers skip work as a result of an injury sustained while on-duty (IOD) is substantially higher than all other occupations

What if police personnel have tools to augment their strength as well as prevent themselves from injuries? Shortly, the impact of injuries amongst police personnel could be reduced or even eliminated. As exoskeleton (ES) technology matures, it could be the answer to a chronic issue facing every police officer in the field.

A company called Sarcos has come out with a new line of motorised exoskeletons called the Guardian XO Max, that can operate for eight hours on a single charge; it weighs less than 70 kilos and takes less than 30 seconds for a person to don. The prevailing models enable users to lift up to 90 kgs. There are several engineering challenges to be dealt with before we see extensive use of these systems. First of all, we may have to find a way for people to power suits without having to plug themselves in every half an hour.

The field of the robotic exoskeleton is still in its infancy; for the non-disabled, companies such as Ekso, Lockheed Martin, Sarcos/Raytheon, BAE Systems, Panasonic, Honda, Daewoo, Noonee, Revision Military and Cyberdyne are each developing some form of exoskeleton for military/law enforcement and industrial uses.

Exoskeletons could in future also come in handy for the criminals. Criminals could misuse wearable robotics; future burglars could be hulks of metal frozen in the street, forcing people to geo-fence themselves against approaching exoskeletons. An exoskeleton could be of immense help to a burglar wanting to carry a loot of 25kgs weight of currency notes from a cash vault. Remember the Hatton Garden heist that was pulled off not with concrete drills but with gyroscopically stabilised exoskeletons helping to rip the doors off safe-deposit boxes, and this is just the tip of an iceberg of the future of breaking. Exoskeleton enhanced burglary crews are a real emerging security concern. Home invasion, art theft, even the industrial-scale plundering of precious-metal refineries will all be made exponentially simpler with the arrival of mechanised outerwear.

Exoskeletons, on the other hand, could also deter or make crime impossible. Wearable suits could become easily monitorable both in terms of GPS tracking and onboard surveillance. Any theft or robbery would be mapped and captured on the screen. The exoskeletons could also impede acceptable activities such as drilling, cutting and chopping if performed at suspicious hours of the day or an unauthorised location. Wearable robots could also prevent fights between co-workers in a factory by programming the behaviour of the suits. The suit would be able to identify the impending punch and block the user's ability to perform it.

Human beings, on the one hand, may have endoskeletons and wear exoskeletons to augment their capabilities. On the other, humans being spiritual entities have the capabilities of developing spiritual exoskeletons by tapping into one's inner spiritual resources. The spiritual exoskeletons so developed could power us to cast off the weights and burdens of this world, helping us experience spiritual lightness, ecstasy and unalloyed joy.

Chapter 20
COVID ERA IS ALL EARS TO VOICE BIOMETRICS

Voice biometrics has been in existence in the realm of sci-fi movies for several decades, although in reality voice biometrics has been around only in recent years. The 1968 Hollywood film *2001: A Space Odyssey* portrayed a computer named HAL 9000 that was shrewd enough to authenticate by voice, comprehend speech, and discern emotions. Likewise, *Star Trek* made in 1966 showcased the proficiency of the spaceship's computer to identify the crew member and also distinguish between voice commands and conversations between the crew members. Biometrics used in recent sci-fi movies like *Dredd, District 9* and *Ex Machina* are depicting a futuristic world of groundbreaking technology.

The current coronavirus pandemic, which is suddenly sweeping the planet, has made its inhabitants so spooked of touch (fingerprint), and the FRT carries the risk of amplifying the dissemination of the coronavirus. Touch is one of the most fundamental ways by which coronavirus gets transmitted, hence relying on biometrics which hinges on contact could spell doom. Second, though facial recognition systems are contactless, it drastically curtails the precision of the system when a person is wearing a mask. Further, urging a person sporting a mask to take it off would not only jeopardise him but others as well, by fostering the proliferation of the virus, especially when there is talk of a second wave.

Voice has therefore emerged as a feasible authentication method because, just like a fingerprint or a face, a voice is unique to an individual, and a biometric engine facilities validation of a person's identity by his or her distinct vocal-characteristics. Voice biometric systems work by generating a voiceprint or 'template' of a person's speech by capturing the many peculiarities of a person's voice, including the sound pattern, tempo, cadence, inflexion and rhythm in the form of a 'Voiceprint'. A voiceprint so created gets encrypted and stored for future voice verification. A voice-based biometric system matches the voice of the person to the 'Voiceprint' in the database, authenticating him or permitting or denying him access. Voice biometrics facilitates quick, frictionless and highly secure access, and enhances verification experience by eliminating frustration associated with lost and stolen credentials and clunky login processes. Because of lower execution cost, ease of use, and greater accuracy, voice biometric technology is emerging as a game-changer.

When compared to other forms of biometric applications, voice biometrics comes off as the choicest one for non-intrusive, contactless and easy-to-use systems. A study carried out by Unisys disclosed that the consumer propensity for voice recognition was highest at 32 per cent, followed by fingerprint 27 per cent, facial scan 20 per cent, hand geometry 20 per cent and iris scan 20 per cent. This ranking confirms that convenience and experience appear to be the determining facets when choosing a biometric technology. According to Opus Research, there will be over a half-billion voiceprints by 2020. Google, in 2017, divulged that their speech recognition had an accuracy rate of 95 per cent. Further, Google has now disclosed that 20 per cent of their searches are being made by voice query, which they expect to grow by 50 per cent by 2020.

The voice recognition technology has both advantages and disadvantages. Voice commands are a very efficient tool; it can boost productivity levels as talking can get done faster than typing. Voice recognition software is disadvantageous as it may not put words as accurately on the screen; besides, there could be interference because of background noise and non-recognition of some accents. Voice hacking in voice biometrics is not far-fetched, an attacker can spoof an individual's unique voiceprint to steal his identity, and access voice-based systems. Advances in machine learning, recording technology and synthetic speech are enabling high-quality voice spoofing, showing that hackers can trick voice-based systems. Therefore, it is best to use voice in combination with other forms of authentication such as behavioural biometrics, geo-location, passcode, fingerprint or an ID. AI and natural language processing if harnessed and blended could make voice authentication even more secure and reliably a fingerprint of the future. Voice biometrics technology is also an Audio Forensic tool to analyse voice in crime prevention and investigation efforts. Forensic experts are today in a position to detect samples of speech in an audio recording easily and analyse hundreds of audio files in a few minutes to identify individuals in an instant, no matter what their accent, language or content is. In the process, it's saving several thousands of hours in indicting suspects. We have included the voice-biometric device in the list of equipment to be installed at the new cyber lab proposed to be set up at a cost of Rs 6.3 crore at our directorate for the examination of audio files. The judiciary, too, has been favouring the voice-based systems in its various orders. The Supreme Court on 2 August last year held that a judicial magistrate could direct a suspect to provide his voice samples for investigation even without his consent. A three-judge Bench, led by Chief Justice of India Ranjan Gogoi, ruled that directing a person to part with his voice sample to police was not a violation of his fundamental right to privacy. Similarly, in the *Mahabir Prasad* v. *Surinder Kaur* case, the Supreme Court ruled that police could use the tape-recorded conversations as corroborative evidence. In a post-pandemic world, moving from a touch interface to voice wherever it's workable will be a necessity. Voice is already in use as a biometric for smart speakers such as Google Home, where the Google assistant recognises the voice of the users who seek information from it. Lloyds Bank, TalkTalk, Vodafone, have already rolled out voice-based services, which is letting people access their accounts without pin or passcodes by using their voices. Others like the BBC, Flipkart and Snapchat have launched voice assistants for the convenience of their users. Organisations can use voice biometrics to ensure that they not only render excellent service to genuine callers but also to prevent suspected fraudsters from perpetrating fraudulent activities in real-time. If a person loses his credit card, calling the bank to get the card blocked is tedious. But, if the bank has a biometric voice system, it can complete the verification the moment the customer calls by comparing the caller's voice with the voiceprint available with the bank in no time. Finally, if we accept that we are spiritual beings having a human existence, wouldn't our 'spiritual identity' or 'soul-based biometrics' which leans on our consciousness instead of voice be the best system to outwit the coronavirus of the future?

Chapter 21
3D PRINTING IN POLICING – BOON OR BANE?

What would Johannes Gutenberg, the man who assembled the first modern printing press in 1454, have said if someone told him that we would be printing human beings one day? He would have perhaps cocked a snook at the idea. In 1997, *The Fifth Element*, a famous sci-fi movie made by the French director Luc Besson, featured a massive 3D bio-fabricator that 3D prints the whole physique of Leeloo (Milla Jovovich). It now seems that most of the proactive peek of the future provided by sci-fi invariably have been coming true. Today, 3D printers print not only human tissues and organs but also guns and myriad other things.

On 6 May 2013, a video emerged on the Internet showing a young man in blue jeans and a black polo shirt blasting a single shot from an off-white, plastic 380 single-shot firearm called 'the Liberator', assembled by him with a Stratasys 3D printer bought on eBay. That youthful man was Cody Wilson – a Texan who overnight turned into a cult figure and garnered headlines worldwide. After test firing, Wilson circulated the blueprints of the gun's design online, which got downloaded more than 120,000 times in two days. Following this, the US Department of State slapped a restraining order against Wilson and his company 'Defense Distributed', which was overturned in August this year, allowing him to publish designs of 3D once again freely printed firearms and share the same with one and all on the Internet. These blueprints would potentially permit anyone with a 3D printer to create an untraceable, unregulated firearm at home. The 3D blueprints are today downloadable on several CAD (computer-aided design) repository sites, and one can also download them for free from torrent sites. Few minutes of googling are all one would require to ferret out these files. It's kind of scary to envisage that in our nation today, we have no clue how many of our citizens are in possession of a 3D printer, how many of them have downloaded the blueprints of 3D firearms and how many of them have 3D printed firearms?

Fortunately for us, the 3D printing delinquents have not yet commenced thinking out of the box until now. That day is not far when creative criminals or the terrorists would begin employing their imagination and printing guns that could make a gun look like a harmless item of daily use, such as a hairbrush, a box, a blow dryer etc. The same holds good for clever 3D printed explosive appliances.

Apart from firearms, 3D printers have various other dark and shady applications. A German hacker employed a 3D printer to make handcuff keys for high-security handcuff used by the US Transportation Security Administration which hackers published in July of 2016. Massachusetts Institute of Technology (MIT) C.T. scanned high-security locks, and 3D printed the master keys. In Sydney, Australia, cybercrooks fastened 3D printed skimmers to bank machines and skimmed bank card data of unsuspecting users. Skimming credit card data has become a systematic racket today. Sophisticated 3D printers to make skimming appliance, including fake card slots for currency dispensers, were confiscated during raids by cops in Sofia, Bulgaria, Malaga, Spain and other places. A skimmer called 'Gripper' made by an individual with a similar online name is selling them openly on the Internet.

Even 3D printing of medications and drugs has taken off as well. Scientists have already developed a 'chemputer' to print drugs such as ibuprofen on demand. J Group Robotics, Mumbai, India, and Louisiana Tech University have worked on 3D printing legal drug delivery devices and legal prescription drugs. While the possible humanitarian benefits are enormous, it won't be long before delinquents get hold of these devices for printing cocaine, heroin, meth, crack, Oxycontin and so on. A moment would come when there would be no requirement for the drug sellers to peddle narcotics as it would boil down to emailing digital blueprints.

Counterfeiting would become massively accessible as 3D printers would fake almost anything and everything. Intellectual property theft would, thus, be the first casualty. Piracy which we confine to a digital intellectual property like music, video games and software would now become distensible to designer stuff like Gucci handbags, Cartier wrist watches and Louis Vuitton shoes and a whole lot of consumer goods due to the availability of high-resolution 3D scanning and printing. What's more, the products produced by 3D printing would be visually, texturally and qualitatively indistinguishable from the original. Counterfeit parts have been a severe problem for car and airplane makers for many years and the US defense supply chain. This issue is likely to grow and become more extensive with 3D printing. Gartner Group has already foreseen that 3D printing would result in over $100 billion losses in intellectual property worldwide per year.

Can improvised explosive devices be fabricated by terrorists using 3D printers? To learn this out FBI's Terrorist Explosive Device Analytical Center (TEDAC) has obtained a 3D printer to study if this was possible. From blueprints available on the Internet or other sources, 3D printing of germs is another severe threat that terrorists can unleash with catastrophic results. Not just that, we should also ready ourselves for a possible black-market trade in 3D-printed human organs 'a few years from now'. Nuclear proliferation may become hard to detect in the coming days as non-nuclear club countries could use 3D printers to make atomic weapons. Economic sanctions or trade embargoes against rogue countries could also become an antiquated idea as 3D printers would come in handy for such nations to create products that they can't obtain from other countries due to financial boycotts.

In the future, we may have to wrestle with the problem of 'Disarming Corruptors'. A disarming corruptor is a program that disguises a 3D printable blueprint to let them slip through filters/firewalls designed to block content entry into repositories. Once a 3D blueprint is concealed for a drug, the algorithms put in place to obstruct it would not be capable of preventing it from being uploaded to the repository as it would be unable to recognise the camouflaged 3D blueprint, which is a hazardous situation, as criminals would download and misuse illegal designs using a clandestinely circulated password.

The technology of 3D printing is not just revolutionary. It's disruptive as well. Police and the military will have to evaluate the risk from illegal use of this technology. In the future people will find imaginative ways to benefit from trafficking in 3D printed drugs and organs. This technology will also be rampantly used by terrorists in their misguided missions. As with all technologies, 3D printing would possibly get misused not because technology is defective but because people are blemished.

A 3D printer is like a magical device that can build material items at the push of a button using various kinds of materials such as plastic, metal, wood, concrete and ceramics. Just as we can deliver an image to a 2D ink-jet printer, we can download or generate a design on our laptops and transmit it to a 3D printer, which in turn, utilising a smorgasbord of techniques, can build objects in three dimensions, layer by layer, with unprecedented exactitude. These digital manufacturing methods make it easier and more economical to fabricate various products from robots to aviation parts to totally functioning automobiles, equipment and so forth.

Although there is an intense focus on using this technology for consumer goods, 3D printing is a valuable tool in the criminal investigation. Police can use 3D printing to recreate detailed models of crime scenes, car crashes, footprints and fingerprints, and develop prototypes of frameworks for anti-terrorism and anti-hijacking interventions. If we take CT scans or MRI scans of the victims, we can use such data to 3D print models that allow investigators to examine injuries and bone and bullet fragments of wounds on the outside and inside. It also enables investigators to analyse and measure the path of a bullet or a knife and its trajectory with the entry point and enveloping tissue. Such prototypes could be 3D printed and presented clearly in the courtroom, easily understood even by a layman.

The most significant detection using a combination of 3D scanning and 3D printing was the infamous 'suitcase killing' case of Birmingham,

UK, in May 2015. Lorenzo Simon butchered his tenant, Michael Spalding, by severing the body with a saw and partially burning it before immersing the suitcase crammed with the victim's body parts in the Birmingham canal. Utilising 3D printing, the West Midlands Police, with the assistance of the University of Warwick Manufacturing Group, was able to establish that a portion of charred, broken bone found in the suspect's garden was a precise fit for a part of the broken bone present in the suitcase.

In another crime scene inquiry in the USA, which necessitated accessing the data on the dead victim's mobile phone, police recreated the fingerprint of the deceased person using a 3D printed cast since the victim's body was too degraded to extract the fingerprints with the existing procedures. Unlocking the victim's phone with the 3D printed victim's finger enabled police in procuring evidence from the device leading to the killer's arrest.

3D printing technology also helped identify a woman's body found in the forest near Dayton, Ohio. The Greene County Ohio Sheriff's Office collaborated with Ohio State University in late 2016 after all attempts to discern the victim from the vastly putrefied remains didn't succeed. After CT scanning and 3D printing, a model of the victim's skull was developed using clay for moulding and sculpting the face. Police put facial aspects of the model in circulation in public, which expeditiously resulted in the victim's identification. Subsequently, the cops were also able to identify and arrest the suspects a short time later.

A murder case unsolved for nearly two decades in Japan ended in detection through reconstruction of evidence utilising a 3D printed scan of the room. Similarly, after teaming with imaging experts, forensic anthropologist students of the University of South Florida are using 3D printing to try and help recognise the victims in nine Florida cold cases, few of which are decades old. After 3D printing replicas of the victims' crania from 3D scans, the students rebuilt the faces with clay, chiselled the lips and inserted eyeballs.

The New York State Police some time ago collaborated with the State University of New York (SUNY) New Paltz Hudson Valley Advanced

Manufacturing Center to detect a 47-year old Jane Doe slaughter incident. The SUNY team 3D published a carbon copy of the victim's skull and passed it to a forensic artist who reproduced the victim's face. In another case, the murder of six-year-old Ellie Butler in Sutton, England, in 2013, was substantiated by forensic pathologists during the homicide trial of her parents by submitting detailed replicas of Ellie's severely shattered skull, which were 3D printed from CT scans of her remains.

The Hong Kong Police Briefing Support Unit uses 3D printers acquired by it to create crime scene prototypes, which can help recreate the crime and present cases in court. The unit is also using 3D printed prototypes of buildings in counterterrorism planning. In 2013, a 3D printed crime scene model enabled Japanese police collect thousands of possible case-related clues from locals.

Abu Dhabi Police is intending to deploy 3D printing to handle evidence with 3D printed dioramas which would help assess a crime scene. West Yorkshire Police, UK, and Cascade County Police in Montana, USA, are also using 3D scanning in crime investigation like numerous police agencies in Europe and USA. They have also installed their 3D printers. A Florida company, '3D Printed Evidence', is enabling police to convert data from MRIs, CT scans and 3D scanners into physical models. Police units that lack the budget or the personnel to 3D print replicas can contemplate outsourcing the job to local or university 3D printing services. The 3D printing technology is disruptive and can go a long way in unravelling crimes and convicting offenders. Police in India, too, would be forced very soon to launch 3D printers and scanners for crime investigations as they cannot afford to trudge behind by overlooking this fantastic technology. Ultimately, our consciousness also is like a 3D printer. It will create whatever you ask of it. The lives we are leading today are precise 3D replicas of all that we have thought, believed and done. If we discover we are miserable, we can hack our consciousness through silent contemplation and positive thought to bring magic like a 3D printer into our lives by manifesting our dreams and desires.

Chapter 22
IS IT ALRIGHT TO TRUST ALGORITHMS ALTOGETHER?

Whenever we think of the film *Minority Report*, predictive policing might come to our mind. In the film, a clairvoyant group foresees a crime and police arrest individuals based on their information before the crime gets executed. But algorithmic policing is nothing like the *Minority Report*. Here, a unique algorithm uses data on the times, locations and nature of past crimes to provide police strategists information concerning where and at what times police patrols should patrol, or maintain a presence, to prevent and detect crime. Such predictions made by the algorithms help in the intelligent targeting of police resources.

As days go by, we will find algorithms playing an increasingly active role in many facets of our lives. The legendary Silicon Valley entrepreneur, Mr Vinod Khosla, has referred to the contemporary age as Dr A's age because Dr Algorithm is heralding a healthcare revolution, where we may not need a doctor because of AI, big data, and diagnostics that would meet 90–99 per cent of our health needs.

An algorithm 'is a step-by-step protocol for calculations. We can use Algorithms for calculation, data processing, and automated reasoning.' Algorithms are becoming a ubiquitous part of our lives. Algorithms are today being deployed in diverse fields. For instance, in law enforcement, we are using it for predictive policing, while on roads, red-light and speeding cameras are detecting transgressions of the law. In border control, AI is flagging travellers and their baggage for screening. In finance for credit scoring, for instance, the FICO tally is determining an individual's creditworthiness. For intelligence collection and surveillance, CCTV cameras are spotting unique activity by computer vision analysis. In the military, warfare drones and other robots are discovering targets and killing without human intervention. Some dating sites such as 'eharmony' and others promise to use maths to find a person's soul-mate and the perfect match.

The tantalising possibility of portending crime before it transpires has probably got law enforcement agencies most excited about algorithmic policing. Police departments and courts in the USA and several nations have incorporated crime-predicting algorithms, facial recognition, and pretrial and sentencing software deep inside their legal system. Algorithms consistently are more accurate than people in predicting recidivism. In some tests, the tools approached 90 per cent accuracy in predicting which defendants might get arrested again. Predictive analytics uses historical data to predict future events. Typically, we use historical data to build a mathematical model that captures essential trends.

Most times, the patterns inherent in the crimes themselves provide ample information to predict which places and windows of time are at the highest risk for future crimes. The basic assumption behind predictive policing being that a lot of crime is not random. For example, home burglaries are relatively predictable. When a house gets robbed, the likelihood of that house or places near it getting stolen spikes again in the following days. In such a prediction method, crimes get separated from individuals, and a visible law enforcement presence can be an effective deterrent for subsequent offences.

Proponents argue that predictive policing can help predict crimes more accurately and effectively than traditional police methods. Predictive policing is just one of several ways police departments worldwide have incorporated big-data techniques into their work in the last two decades.

Predictive policing programs are currently under use by police departments in several US states such as California, Washington, South Carolina, Arizona, Tennessee and Illinois. Predictive policing programs are also under implementation by Kent County Police in the UK, Netherlands and Suzhou Police Bureau in China. India, too, has set out towards big algorithmic policing in its own way. Gurgaon-based startup called 'Staqu' is using big data for identifying criminals and finding missing persons.

Staqu launched an AI-based human efface detection (ABHED) application for effective policing. The startup has integrated the app with the database of police of eight Indian states, including Rajasthan and Punjab, for identifying criminals by facial recognition. Although the algorithmic formulas' writers would endorse the algorithms to be perfectly neutral, the actual truth could be something else. Algorithms often could get coloured with the bias of the person who has authored it. How can we know how a black box algorithm protected by intellectual property law as a trade secret is behaving? For instance, the FICO algorithm, which plays a significant role in Americans' access to credit, which earns hundreds of millions of dollars each year, never gets disclosed. It is a closely guarded secret.

The near-total absence of transparency in the algorithms that drive the world means that we, the people, have no insight and no say in profoundly crucial decisions being made about us and for us. The concentrated power of algorithms to harm us has gone unnoticed by most until now. Without insight and transparency into the algorithms that are running our world, there can be no accountability or true democracy. As a result, the 21st-century society we are building is becoming increasingly vulnerable to manipulation by authors who operate the algorithms that pervade our lives.

Algorithmic technology has infuriated several activists. They contend that the technology, which predicts crime and violence instead of reducing crime, has led to overpolicing and mass imprisonment, perpetuation of racism and increased tensions between police and communities. Still, algorithms meant to foretell where crime would happen, often justifies massive and often fierce deployment to neighbourhoods already suffering from poverty. Ultimately, these algorithms have failed to reduce the costs forcing taxpayers to cough up more money for policing. A few local governments have already placed moratoriums on algorithmic systems in recent months. Santa Cruz, California, has become the first city in the USA to ban predictive policing algorithms.

The recent pandemic witnessed the release of thousands of people from jails where social distancing is near-impossible. At the same time, police officers, afraid of overcrowding jails, curtailed arrests. These changes led to a crime drop in several cities. Our experience during the Covid-19 outbreak, therefore, is confirming that police can arrest and jail far fewer people without jeopardising security. Hence, affirming the requirement for snuffing out algorithmic decision making.

Today, big data, cloud computing, AI and the Internet of Things act on physical objects on our behalf in 3D space. Having an AI driving a robot that cleans your house and makes coffee for you is fine. What if the robot's algorithm mistakenly detects the owner as a threat and eliminates him as with Kenji Urada, the 37-year-old employee of Kawasaki? In 1981, the robot crushed Urada to death by pushing him into a grinding machine.

Finally, we have entered a new era where the algorithm rules. Algorithms determine what search results we see with Google. If the human brain's intelligence can be wrapped up in a particular algorithm, imagine what it would mean for AI. The same algorithm could apply to how AI neural networks work. Further, what if we could make machines driven by algorithms conscious? Could we program them to contain a soul?

Chapter 23
COGNITIVE COMPUTING – A FORCE MULTIPLIER

'Is it possible for a computer to become human like?' We have seen a computer HAL 2000 speak fluent English, experience jealousy and do away with the spaceship crew to prevent its own termination in Stanley Kubrick's movie *2001: A Space Odyssey*. In *Her* a 2013 science fiction film written, directed and produced by Spike Jonze, set in the near future, the film's protagonist Theodore Twombly purchases an operating system with Samantha a virtual assistant who evolves from being a competent assistant to a constant companion. They bond over their discussions about love and life and develop a relationship that turns intimate.

We do not have Samanthas at the moment, but we have pre-programmed virtual assistants in the form of Siri and Cortana. Work in cognitive computing is progressing and a computer program Emily Howell released its first album in 2010, and another program wrote its first movie, *Sunspring*. IBM's Watson recently forayed into Hollywood by creating movie trailer of the science film '*Morgan*' in a record time. Traditionally making a movie trailer is labour intensive and takes between 10 to 30 days to complete but IBM's Watson took about 24 hours to sort through footage to come up with an exciting trailer.

The ability of humans to think is amazing. The creation of a computer system that can think and reason like humans do is the aim of cognisable computing. The end goal of cognisable computing is simply to simulate thought processes in a computerised model. Therefore, cognitive computing is a combination of computer and cognitive science. It may require several AI technologies for a computer system to build cognitive abilities in a computer system such as machine learning, deep learning, neural networks and sentiment analysis.

While old method of crime investigation involved collection of evidence from the field and forensic reports, the new method that is emerging is data driven, combining machine learning algorithms with big data. The more data we feed into a computing system, the more a system will digest and assimilate leading to better insights. This method is being embraced by law enforcement agencies all over the world including the US.

Cognitive systems, unlike humans, don't sleep and have no emotions. They have capacity to read millions of documents, make connections and reveal patterns that law enforcement officials will find hard to catch sight of. When police arrive at a scene, they may not have adequate information to deal with the situation at hand, but cognitive systems can in a matter of minutes piece together disparate information and provide crucial information which could warn them of the presence of explosives or past violence. Therefore, cognitive computing in law enforcement could compensate for human shortcomings by assisting them with a better decision making.

IBM's cognitive supercomputer Watson, whose enormous data processing prowess helped it win 'Jeopardy' has been analysing data from healthcare to engineering. It has now gotten started on policing. The police firing during the Sterlite agitations in Tuticorin sparked a national discussion on police overreaction and blatant use of force by law enforcement. There was rancour and rhetoric drawing many people into a debate over the police excesses but there was none who had the data to give the correct insight regarding the actual truth. They threw a lot of theories out in the media speculating who deserves the blame. But we can't rely on anecdotal information as there is a lot of emotion behind it. To get past the emotion and find the truth, we would need to get hold of a mound of data that the incident would have generated. Today, Watson and cognitive computing systems like it, which are emerging on the law-enforcement space, can process all the data emanating from such incidents and give real insights faster. If we get Watson on the case, it could get somewhere close to the bottom of the truth, no matter how deep it's buried – in considerably less time. IBM's CopLink software is already helping police with data analysis. For instance, investigation of abduction of 6-year-old girl in Tucson, Arizona, out of her home generated 15,000 pages of reports, statements, lab reports and so on, but the software could trudge through all the information and data, and generate leads, as opposed to speculation or analysis based on conjecture and supposed truth.

A Hindu religious festival was on in the temple of Varadaraja Perumal, Kanchipuram, Tamil Nadu from 1 July 2019. The deity which is made of fig tree wood rests in the temple tank and which the temple priests draw out once in 40 years to enable the devotees to offer prayers to it for 48 days. Hence, the temple is popular by the name Athi Varadar temple. In the past, priests placed the deity for devotees to offer obeisance on 2 July 1979 and before that on 12 July 1939. In 1979, the priests threw only one gate of the temple open, and the pundits told me that the number of devotees during the first 44 days averaged less than 10,000 per day. In 2019, however, the assessment before the start of the festival was not over 30,000 per day. Police as a measure of abundant caution made arrangements to control a crowd of one lakh devotees per day. But thanks to the TV channels, social media, Internet, the word of mouth, improved road and transport facilities, easy affordability of cars, increased materialism driving people towards spiritual solace and several such factors caused an unprecedented number of devotees to throng to the temple throwing the entire town out of gear. Since the start of the Athi Varadar festival till 16 August 2019, close to one crore devotees have paid obeisance to the Lord Athi-Varadar. On 14 July and 17 July 2019 alone, the temple witnessed 2.5 lakh and 2.75 lakh devotees respectively. Handling such huge crowds for 48 days is a massive challenge for any administration. Under such a challenging situation, the administration did a great job despite enormous hardships. A cognitive crowd prediction system such as Watson by crunching available data such as the auspiciousness of the day, weather, the day, that is, working day or holiday, inflow of vehicles into the city, railway bookings from other stations into Kanchipuram could have provided valuable information to the law enforcement for making deployment decisions.

Cognitive computing enables a digital policing environment that can help the police and the citizens immensely. Citizens will be able to update the police from anywhere anytime from any device using many channels such as photos, videos and voice calls. Word processing documents, emails, videos, images, audio files, presentations, webpages, social media and many other data formats often need manual tagging with metadata before they are fed to a computer for analysis and insight generation. The principal benefit of using cognitive analytics over traditional big data analytics is that such datasets need not be pre-tagged. All the data coming in could help develop a more seamless way to solve crime and increase safety.

Besides providing specific insights to officers in the field, cognitive capabilities can help the investigators immensely in solving criminal cases. For example, the Law Enforcement Analysis Portal (LEAP), composed of a confederation of US law enforcement agencies, is propelling a cognitive-enabled service that helps officers identify locations where we can find suspects. In the days gone by, when officers investigated cases, they had to count on information and evidence unearthed through painstaking investigation. Using cognitive computing abilities, LEAP can dig up data from suspects' IT records, property registration details, passport application information, speeding tickets, credit card, social-media interactions, Internet browsing history and licence plate databases. By having access to more data, police could piece together a more accurate picture of the most likely place they might locate the suspect. For example, an online passport application form details the suspect's address, his marital status, his residential address, his mobile number, and so forth.

In the UK, using previous data, the Cambridge Police Department's crime analysis unit, taught the Series Finder to detect patterns in the burglaries for over a decade in the university town of Cambridge. The factors which they incorporated to determine a modus operandi comprised mode of entry (front door, back door window, through the roof etc.), time of the day, the day of the week, month, type of property, area and proximity to other burglaries. Using criminal patterns, the Series Finder could detect most of the reported cases and help in recovery as well. In addition, it also excluded some crimes that they ought to exclude, leading to a better idea about the actual suspect. This is something close to the pre-cogs which forecast crimes even before they happen in a famous story titled 'Minority Report' by K.D. Phillips which Hollywood made into a movie of the same title. The machines today are not just reading but also interpreting information.

Although cognitive computing systems in the long run could replace humans in some situations, the systems would still need humans to direct them. Computing systems will only be able to augment human capabilities but not replace them. Just because supercomputers can read medical reports doesn't mean that we won't need doctors. The personal assistants we have on phones such as Siri are not true cognitive systems; they respond only to pre-programmed set of responses but we are arriving at a time when our phones, cars and our computers will give us a real thoughtful response than a pre-programmed one. Computers will think like us and make accurate predictions, draw conclusions and augment human capabilities in new ways.

We have developed machines that can operate autonomously, such as self-driving cars and robots. But these autonomous machines or cars need to be told by human consciousness to drive from point A to point B or do whatever they can do. We could consider machines cognitive only when they decide by themselves and do what they wish to do rather than what we have programmed them to do. We are being told that 'singularity' is inevitable, does that portend cognitive machines?

Chapter 24
WHO WILL POLICE THE METAVERSE?

Metaverse is the virtual world where people can socialise, work and play. It is a portmanteau of *meta* – connoting transcendent – and *verse*, from 'the universe'. Author Neal Stephenson coined the word 'metaverse' in the 1992 science-fiction novel *Snow Crash* to depict the virtual universe in which the protagonist, Hiro, an utterly broke computer hacker and a pizza delivery driver with the crazy name Hiro in the real world, socialises, shops and defeats real-world enemies through his avatar to escape a dystopian reality.

Similarly, in 2018, *Ready Player One*, a dystopian American science fiction adventure film directed by Steven Spielberg based on Ernest Cline's novel of the same name, also revolved around a metaverse called 'Oasis' that users could access using VR headsets and wired gloves to escape from a world disintegrating due to an energy crisis.

Fast forward to today, the metaverse is a hot buzzword in Silicon Valley that experts link to the development of Web 3.0. Web 3.0 is the latest version of the World Wide Web. Ethereum co-founder Gavin Wood coined Web 3.0 in the year 2014. Its precursors, Web 1.0 and Web 2.0, were technological evolutionary periods in the history of the World Wide Web. Tim Berners-Lee launched Web 1.0 in 1989, where most websites had fixed web pages, and most users were consumers, not producers. Web 2.0, the next-generation Internet, though never officially called Web 2.0, launched in 1999, changed the Internet in many ways. It turned the web into a platform centred on user-created content uploaded on social media, blogs and so on. Web 2.0 continues to this day.

Web 3.0 takes the Internet in its current form and adds blockchains to almost everything decentralising it in the process; hence it differs from Web 2.0, where a handful of big tech companies centralise data and content. The idea behind Web 3.0 is to decentralise the Internet and not have heavyweights like Google, Twitter and Facebook have all the power.

O P Z Creative/Shutterstock.com

A decentralised Internet based on the blockchain means users can own a piece of it. Web 3.0, in contrast to earlier versions, is a network where no permit would be required to use any service. Neither would anybody block the user nor deny access to any service. The user would be able to transact in the space through native tokens or cryptocurrencies using blockchain. It probably seems utopian and radical, but who would have imagined cryptocurrencies or Non-fungible Tokens (NFTs) going so mainstream a few years ago.

Today, we find many components of the metaverse already accessible within the contemporary Internet-enabled video games. Second Life, available since 2003 with the user represented as an avatar, is often referred to as the Metaverse one. In Minecraft and Roblox, users build their metaverse and invite others to play. Roblox is estimated to have 5.5 million players compared with Second Life's 90,000. In October of 2021, Zuckerberg rebranded Facebook as 'Meta', dubbing metaverse to be the next breakthrough in technology and a successor to mobile Internet. Other corporations, such as Epic Games, Microsoft and even Nike, have announced plans to enter the metaverse in some form. Within 10 to 15 years, the experts predict metaverse to be $10 trillion to $30 trillion industry.

The development and spread of metaverses could lead to the emergence of new crimes, or it could lead to an increase in cybercrimes or give new dimensions to existing Internet crimes. Metaverses are virtual towns or places where crime or criminal behaviour could be similar to real society. So, all possibilities of crime that exist on the Internet today could come to exist in the metaverse as it is part of the Internet. Therefore, there is a likelihood of crimes occurring within the metaverse and the probability of crimes of the virtual ecosystems spilling over to the real world. In the metaverse, the players or users buy goods for their avatars, such as clothes and shoes to adorn them or buy weapons such as guns and swords for their self-defence. Users purchase such properties using a currency that is acceptable in the metaverse. Wherever and whenever objects or property of value exist, potential crooks are always waiting to steal them. Suppose the shoes brought in the virtual world have gotten stolen; that shoe is a virtual object and not an actual physical thing. A virtual object cannot fit into the definition of an offence of theft. Hence, the metaverse could throw up new forms of criminal offences.

Further, economic activity due to multiple business opportunities and the availability of various means of disguising illegal money would make metaverse a fertile breeding ground for money laundering, especially where users can swap cyber currency for real cash. In the metaverse anti-money laundering (AML), Know your customer (KYC) protections will be as important as they are in the real world. Imagine the gamut of goods and services in the metaverse and the real money such businesses will make that will move back and forth from the metaverse to the real world and vice versa. Keeping track of all that money from going untraceable would be a big challenge.

Moreover, when one searches for events with the keyword 'sex' in the virtual world, Second Life takes one to virtual strip clubs, which offer digital lap dances for real-world money. In 2007, Second Life ran into problems because individual users had designed avatars who looked like children and their presentation in pornographic images. Such type of misuse is possible in the metaverse.

Furthermore, consider a situation where an avatar is abused and threatened by another avatar. Who do you think would deserve punishment? If we decide to penalise the avatar, we would have to send him to a virtual prison? But the avatar will not feel the punishment's pinch as it is a virtual object, and if we decide to punish the user that would mean sentencing the user for sitting in front of the computer and provoking an avatar to offend. So most criminal offences, such as theft, robbery, damage to property, arson, rape, bodily injury or homicide in the virtual world, would have to be reduced to a computer offence such as computer fraud, revision of data or computer sabotage.

For instance, the 13-year-old Megan Meier committed suicide in October 2006 after being abandoned by her fictitious Internet love, 'Josh Evans', created by a former schoolmate and her mother in the Internet chat room 'Myspace'. The mythical Internet love succeeded in charming Megan ultimately. But to humiliate her, Josh one day ditched Megan, heaping vicious insults on her. Not able to cope with the breakup, Megan hung herself that afternoon. For the offence, the schoolmate's mother could be sentenced only for the crime of computer fraud by an American Federal Court because she had logged herself in at 'Myspace' with a false name.

Finally, Hal Lonas, CTO of Trulioo, believes that to counter the potential threats of the metaverse, we will need a virtual version of Interpol to police it for fraud and financial crimes. Second Life, which has existed since 2003, seemingly stays away from regulating the avatars. Hence, we may have to bring the metaverses under the purview of the real world's national or international legal systems. Given the potential for cross-border payments of various sizes through the metaverse, we may need international agreements on what can go on and what cannot. Metaverse would require policing because human behaviour in the virtual world will reflect human behaviour in the real world. If to control crimes and maintain law and order in the real world, police are indispensable, then the police would be imperative in metaverse.

PART 2

CYBERSECURITY

Chapter 25
GROWING THREAT OF SEXTORTION FROM CYBER-PREDATORS

In March 2013, on a beautiful day, Cassidy Marie Wolf, a 16-year-old American model and a beauty queen just crowned Miss Teen USA, was leaning in her bedroom and gazing at her computer when an email popped up that contained a dozen naked pictures of her in her bedroom.

The sender of the mail demanded that Ms Wolf either transmit few good quality nude pictures of her through Snapchat, or send a video of herself, or appear on Skype to perform as he tells her for 5 minutes. It horrified Wolf. Wolf never created the video that the attacker kept demanding from her. It turns out that she had a laptop in her bedroom, as most students do. Whenever Cassidy stepped out of her bathroom and towelled off after the shower, the computer in her room which had been hacked and whose camera was under the hacker's control would start taking her nude pictures. Stunned by the email, Ms Wolf slammed her laptop shut and informed her parents, who called in the FBI. An international crackdown by the FBI and police in 19 countries brought over 90 arrests in a severe onslaught against 'creepware'.

In November 2013, Jared Abrahams, a high school classmate of Ms Wolf, who had watched and ogled at her for more than a year by installing the highly intrusive malware Blackshades on her computer to take her nude images and videos, pleaded guilty to hacking r 100–150 women. One of his victims was a 14-year-old girl. The two-year operation that FBI organised was such that the suspects didn't have time to demolish evidence, and it included the arrest of Swedish hacker Alex Yucel, a co-creator of Blackshades, the cheap and accessible software utilised to hijack computers remotely. In November 2013, Jared Abrahams pleaded guilty to hacking 100–150 women by installing the malware Blackshades on their computers. On 18 March 2014; the court sentenced Abrahams to 18 months in Federal prison.

Photographee.eu/Shutterstock.com

Likewise, one beautiful day Rahul Bhogle from Pune receives a friend request from a gorgeous and stunning girl. Soon they chat on Facebook, and their friendship evolves into an intimate relationship within no time. After some time, the girl requests Ramesh to switch over to Skype from a Facebook messenger. One night during the Skype chat, the pretty girl confides to Rahul that she is feeling horny and starts stripping her skimpy clothes and suggests Rahul do the same. Rahul gets excited and aroused and he strips and starts climaxing in front of the camera. Meanwhile, the pretty girl vanishes from the screen and transmits a Skype message to Rahul informing him that she has a recording of his strip show and demands that he transfer a lakh rupees to her account failing which she would transmit his video to all his friends on the Facebook page.

Blackmail of this type by cyber-predators is being defined as 'Sextortion', and anecdotal evidence to date shows that sextortion is on the surge. Sextortion is identical to online blackmail scams, except that instead of demanding money, the blackmailer demands the victim to engage in sex acts, or pose for nude pictures or masturbate before a webcam. The Cambridge Dictionary defines sextortion as 'the practice of compelling somebody to do something, particularly to perform sexual acts, by threatening to publish naked pictures of them or sexual information about them.' Social media and text messages are frequently the source of the sexual material and the threatened means of sharing it with others. An example of this sextortion is where people get blackmailed with a naked picture of themselves they shared on the Internet through 'sexting'. They later get intimidated into performing sexual acts or are compelled to pose or perform sexually on camera, thus generating hardcore pornography. This strategy of blackmail is often being used to out LGBT people who hide their actual sexual orientation.

Sexual extortion is an alarming and inhuman crime that feeds off victims' remorse. Sextortionists also hack into victims' computers, excavate sensitive material, like photographs and videos, and threaten to expose their victims if they decline to fulfil their orders. Digital devices, email accounts, and social media accounts today contain the most intimate details of our daily lives, and the impact that hacking and extortion can have on us is, distressing, and disturbing, sextortion could prove devastating for the victims - particularly the susceptible victims who may conclude that they can't restore and rebuild their tarnished reputations. Fortunately, Ms Wolf could complain to her parents who notified the FBI. The FBI investigation could track it back to her classmate. But there are other anecdotes where young people were likewise sextorted or enticed to exhibit their breasts or private parts to paedophiles much older than themselves across continents resulting in devastating consequences. Some of them even committed suicide.

For instance, a 15-year-old Canadian student, Amanda Michelle Todd, hung herself at her home in Port Coquitlam, a city in the province of British Columbia, Canada. It turns out that Amanda a few years ago was chatting with a stranger she met online, a man who impressed and praised her. At his request, she flashed him. The man took a snapshot of her breasts. He then continued to pursue Todd on the Internet for years.

He implored her to put on another show for him, but she declined. After a year, the same stranger reached out to her on Facebook threatening to go public with a topless photo of her if Amanda refused to perform a live sex show for him on camera. When she spurned him, the man sent her topless photo 'to everyone'. Amanda became incredibly depressed and miserable. Incapable of weathering the embarrassment and shame she took to alcohol and drugs and ultimately committed suicide.

Many people use webcams for flirting and cybersex – but occasionally people we meet on the Internet aren't who they confide they are. A cyber-predator often befriends victims online masquerading as an attractive person by wielding a fake identity and convinces them to perform sexual acts in front of their webcam, usually by using a beautiful woman to lure the victim into taking part primarily by coercing these women with monetary inducements or threats. Some cyber predators prompt sexual communication by showing the victim a pre-recorded video of a performer from a cybersex webcam site which they are adequately familiar with, then they message the victim at junctures in the video where the performer appears to type on the keyboard, to lend the misconception that the performer in the video is messaging them. The cyber-predators urge the victim to undress in front of a webcam and may also entice them to engage in sexual behaviour, such as masturbation. These webcam videos recorded by the cyber-predators come in handy for sextortion. Cyber-predators may threaten to publish the video in video services like YouTube publicly or transmit it to family members and friends of the victim if they do not conform. This makes some victims feel extremely ashamed and embarrassed and, some even tragically, end their lives. There is evidence that some organised crime groups could be behind this crime. For them, it's a low-risk means to earn money, and they can reach many victims easily online. Victims are often concerned about reporting these offences to the police because it embarrasses them.

Gaming platforms are also being used by sextortionists to lure teenagers. When a teenager plays an online game, at some juncture, the teenager would need cash online to pass to the next level. During such times, the sex-predator offers to help him in return for provocative pictures of him. After the teenager transmits the image, the sex predator blackmails him with the posted picture.

We have seen that sextortion takes on different forms, but at its core, its primary intent is to threaten to reveal sexual images to compel a person to do something. These dangers come from both strangers met online and once romantic partners who intend to harass, embarrass and control victims.

Sextortion happens to the extent of 54 per cent on social networking platforms like Facebook, Instagram, up to 41 per cent on photo messaging or messaging apps such as WhatsApp, Snapchat, on email it happens up to 12 per cent, on dating platforms up to 9 per cent, and rest of it in video sharing platforms and gaming platforms.

For sextortion, Cyber predators target minors because of their innocence. Seventy-one per cent of the victims of sextortion are victims under the age of 18, 14 per cent involved a mix of adults and minors, and 12 per cent involved only adults. Almost all adult victims are females. 78 per cent of all incidents of extortion involved female children, with male children accounting for 12 per cent. Reports reveal that 20 per cent of teens, 22 per cent of teen girls, 11 per cent of teen girls between ages 13 and 16 have sent or posted nude or semi-nude pictures to someone they knew only online.

To avoid being sextorted, we should never send compromising materials to anyone, turn off the computer when not using it, cover the webcam when not using it, download no unknown apps or programs, never click on links from strangers on email and social networking sites, never interact with strangers on a video call, don't accept friend requests and don't believe the profiles as they can create fake profiles. All sextortion victims should speak about what happened and contact the police; they should stop complying to the demands of the sex predators; they should not delete any data. They may also unfriend and block any account on social media with which they connect to the criminals and shut off their accounts for a while.

Sextortion is becoming more extensive, fuelled by the swell of broadband Internet connections and smartphones. A 2016 US Department of Justice report affirms that sextortion is on the rise and is, 'by far the most significantly growing threat to children', and that 'sextortion cases have more minor victims per offender than all other child sexual exploitation offences.' We are yet to deter the cybersecurity structure of our nation from deterring such offences, and there is no specific law to deal with the manifestation in our country yet. At present, cases for such offences are being booked under extortion, POCSO Act in case of children and Section 67 of the IT act.

Until now, the cyber-predators wielded brutal force to recruit their victims, but now this impetus has shifted to intelligent manipulation and persuasive ploys, precocious marketing and management strategies and outstanding informatics abilities. We have become very susceptible because we are not conscious of the hazards present online. We post without thought without safeguarding ourselves, without being mindful of what data we share and how the predators can access and utilise that information against us. We accept friend requests from people we don't know; we share confidential information with them; we mail photos and videos; we instal all manners of apps with no thought or idea that we are making ourselves a perfect target.

Finally, survivors of sextortion are victims of a silent holocaust, a holocaust of the soul. The victims of sextortion experience a loss of meaning, and several victims like Amanda contemplate and commit suicide. During such times, spiritual beliefs and practices can help create meaning and help them gain courage and insight from their sextortion experiences. Spiritual practices under such circumstances would also go a long way in helping them reframe their difficult times and negative experiences as valuable lessons and opportunities for personal growth.

Chapter 26
CYBERSTALKING: GET SAFE ONLINE

The Hrithik Roshan–Kangana Ranaut episode turned cyberstalking into a widely discussed national topic. In 2016, Hrithik filed a lawsuit against his Krrish 3 co-star Kangana Ranaut, charging her of cyberstalking and harassment. Refuting the charges, Ranaut filed a countersuit against Roshan, contending that his lawsuit was an endeavour to hush up their affair. Owing to an absence of proof, the Mumbai Police closed the case later that year. A lot of people think stalking is something that happens to celebrities, but the reality is that it can happen to anyone.

For instance, a young woman employee with an embassy in New Delhi received a string of emails from a stranger ordering her to either pose in the nude for him or pay him Rs 1 lakh to prevent her morphed pictures from being displayed in the pornographic sites, along with her telephone number and address. He further threatened her that he would also exhibit her photographs in her neighbourhood in southwest Delhi. Initially, she ignored his emails, but soon she began receiving letters through the post, reiterating the same threat. Shortly, the stalker started mailing the woman her photographs. The woman contended that the photos were the same as those she had saved in her mail folder. Police investigation disclosed that the accused had hacked her email password and had gained access to her folder to extract her pictures.

In another case that got reported last year in Hyderabad, a 23-year-old man was arrested for cyberstalking and sexually taunting his former Plus 2 classmate on social media. It turned out that the boy had professed love to the girl and she had spurned his proposal. Dejected over the rejection, the man began bombarding her inbox with obscene messages on WhatsApp. Unable to bear the harassment, the girl decided to block him, following which the man designed a fake Facebook page of the girl, and began posting morphed photos of her with sex soliciting comments.

Vitalii Vodolazskyi/Shutterstock.com

Use of the Internet or other electronic means to stalk or harass an individual, a group, or an organisation is generally deemed as cyberstalking. Most cyberstalkers know their victims well, and most cyberstalking cases involve someone seeking to get the attention of a former or would-be partner. It can have many intentions including vengeance, resentment or anger, jealousy, control or even lust or love. Cyberstalking may also encompass monitoring, identity theft, threats, vandalism, solicitation for sex, or collecting information to threaten or harass the victims. Cyberstalking is often accompanied by real-time or offline stalking. 'Catfishing' is one mode of online stalking. 'Catfishers' pose as somebody else, using social media sites to create an identity by using pseudo names, photos, and locations and reach the intended victim as a romantic partner or a mutual friend. Catfishing may also be employed for monetary gain, to cyberbully a victim, or to cause reputational harm or humiliation to a victim. Some cyberstalkers hijack the webcam of the victims by conning them into downloading and installing files that enable them to access the webcam on a computer or laptop.

The development of new technology and unusual ways to stalk victims has exponentially spawned cyberstalking. Spouses are using GPS and GPS based apps to track their partner's activities. Even police are not being spared, as criminals are finding them out to intimidate them into dropping or withdrawing a case. Studies have divulged that cyberbullying results in higher levels of anxiety and depression for victims than regular bullying.

Cyberstalkers operate online by acquiring knowledge about their prey by getting in touch with or engaging with the victim's friends, family or work colleagues and procure personal information. They might also advertise for information on the Internet, or hire a private detective. Many cyber-tormentors incite others to torture the victim by striving to involve third parties in the harassment. Some harassers may contend that the victim has harmed the stalker or his/her family in some way or may post the victim's name and address. A handful may target the online activities of their target to trace their IP address to gather more information about their victims. Some stalkers try to damage the data and equipment of their victim's computer by transmitting viruses. Some cyberstalkers may falsely affirm that the victim is harassing him or her. Some resort to ordering goods and services in the victim's name. These frequently comprise subscriptions to pornography or ordering sex toys and then having them delivered to the victim's office or home.

Cyberstalkers stalk their victims for various reasons. Some of them stalk because they suffer from pathological infatuations which are either sexual or professional, or because they suffer from inferiority feelings, or to instil fear, or for revenge over perceived or imagined rejection or to intimidate business or professional competitors. The cyberstalkers may also, be of different types, romantic cyberstalkers or lust-craving stalkers looking for relationships or affairs, while nasty cyberstalkers are typically angry and vengeful, then there are cyberstalking groups who collaborate with a motive and then there is a composed cyberstalker whose intention mostly is to irritate. Some stalkers are predators who lay a trap and patiently wait for their victims such as children or women, to emerge so that they can hunt them down. Some stalkers lay in wait for a specific person known or unknown to them primarily to harass them or to demonstrate their power and psychologically break them down. Social media sites like Twitter, Facebook and Instagram are hunting grounds for stalkers. Victims usually run into an offender on such platforms. Cyberstalkers analyse their victims to nourish their obsessions and inquisitiveness. Gradually, cyberstalkers could turn intense and repeatedly bombard their victims with scathing messages. Some stalkers inundate their victims with abusive or derogative messages on web pages, message boards, and guest books to retrieve a reaction or response from their victim, and exploit that reply to initiate contact. Once they get a reaction from the victim, they will typically seek to track or follow the victim's Internet activity. Some cyberstalking situations develop into physical stalking, and a victim may suffer wild and vicious phone calls, vandalism, threatening and physical attack.

To safeguard oneself from online stalking, Internet users should not accept friend requests from people whom they have not met in person. Facebook users should select their security settings on Facebook to hinder the ability of people other than friends to publish on their wall and block anyone who exhibits suspicious behaviour on Facebook, Twitter or Instagram. One should not share precise details about one's location or unnecessary identifiable information about oneself on any social media platform. Internet users should let online sites generate a password for them as we are much more liable to construct traceable passwords when compared to an algorithm. One should disallow and stop strangers from taking a photo or video of ours, to upload to the Internet. One should never respond to a private message on any social media site if one does not know the sender. It's a good idea to set a reminder to change one's password for every online site, email, Facebook, and all other password-protected online sites once every 30–45 days and never share one's password even with one's intimate partners as human relations can come apart in future for diverse reasons. To insulate oneself from a stalker, one should use a security software program such as Norton 360 with LifeLock to prevent spyware from being installed onto one's computer via a phishing attack or a contaminated web page. Security software would also help the Internet user to detect spyware on one's device and curtail the chances of being cyberstalked.

India seems to be a land of online bullies and stalkers. India recorded the highest rate of children falling victim to cyberbullying in 2018, according to a survey conducted in 28 countries by a UK-based tech company. Instances of cyberstalking in India have accelerated further, with over 37 per cent of parents admitting that their children have become victims at least once, which is 15 per cent more than in 2016.

Hence, to safeguard ourselves from being cyberstalked, we should immediately block the person and report to the platform involved. Twitter, Facebook, LinkedIn, and many other platforms have built-in easy-to-use buttons to report vicious behaviour immediately. If the behaviour of the cyberstalker is illegal or if you fear for your safety, then you should instantly reach the police and report the cyberstalker. In India, women who are being prowled can complain online to the National Commission for Women (NCW), and the Commission will take the problem up with the police and ensure that the matter is expeditiously investigated. Any woman, in any part of India, can file this complaint. In specific cases, the commission will constitute an inquiry committee, conferred with powers to make on-the-spot inquiry, summon the accused, the witnesses and police records, examine witnesses, and collect evidence.

Under the Indian law, a cyberstalker can be booked under Section 509 of the IPC for outraging the modesty of a woman, under Section 499 IPC for defamation, and also under Sections 66 and 67 of the Information Technology Act, 2000. After the Delhi Gang Rape case in 2012, the Indian Penal Code was amended by the Criminal Law (Amendment) Act, 2013 that added Section 354D to the IPC. Sections 353–357 of the Indian Penal Code provide for the punishment for perpetrating the crime of stalking. However, there are still no provisions in the criminal laws in India that explicitly criminalises cyberstalking in India.

In July 2015, the cyber cell of the Mumbai Police obtained the first-ever conviction in the country under the Information Technology Act,

2000. A city court convicted Yogesh Prabhu, 36, a supervisor in a private firm, to prison for three months for stalking and sending lewd pictures to his colleague who had earlier spurned his proposal. The police seized evidence such as IP addresses, laptops and statements from the server used by Prabhu to transmit the emails.

Most of us when we think of the word *cyberstalking* we think of someone online who is always observing us, following or harassing us, making us feel frightened or insecure. Thoughts arising in our minds do stalk us and make us feel insecure, just like a cyberstalker. Under the circumstances, stalking our minds by becoming a witness of our thoughts could help in our spiritual journey and evolution. Self-stalking could help us create a discipline of continually being mindful of our words, ideas and ways of being in the world. This journey of self-stalking could be an act of love for ourselves so that we move through this world with unconditional love and respect for ourselves and others.

Chapter 27
THE EMERGING THREAT OF CYBERTERRORISM

A 2007 American action thriller film *Live Free or Die Hard* penned by John Carlin and directed by Len Wiseman had Bruce Willis portraying the character of John McClane. In the movie, McClane thwarts the cyberterrorists who conspire to hack into government and commercial computers across the United States to bring down the entire network and technological structure that supports the US economy.

Most films on cyberterrorism seem to ramp up the threats of cyberterrorism or put the hackers on a pedestal. The doomsday scenarios of cyberterrorism that result in massive deaths or injuries though authentic appear to confine themselves to the movie screens. Can the terrorists cripple critical military, financial and service computer systems? Are these fears exaggerated: are there recorded cases of cyberterrorism? Are hackers being regularly mistaken for terrorists and are our cyber defences more robust than is being supposed?

Strangely, in the same year that *Die Hard* got released, an attack on similar lines unfolded in Estonia following the relocation of a Soviet-era statue in Tallinn in April 2007. The Baltic State of Estonia was the victim of a massive denial-of-service attack that eventually disabled the Internet and turned off all services dependent on Internet connectivity. During the politically motivated cyberattack campaign lasting 22 days, the cyberinfrastructure of Estonia, including everything from online banking and mobile phone networks to government services and access to healthcare information got disabled. Georgia similarly got exposed to continuous attacks on its electronic infrastructure in August 2008. Circumstantial evidence in both these cases pointed to Russia, but adequate proof to establish the legal liability of Russia was not forthcoming although both countries blamed Russia.

Likewise, during the Kosovo conflict in 1999, hacktivists crashed NATO computers with email bombs and slammed it with denial-of-service attacks to rebel against the NATO bombings. Furthermore, businesses, public institutions and academic organisations also got bombarded by virus-laden emails from several Eastern European countries. Web defacements were also common. After the Chinese Embassy got accidentally bombed in Belgrade, Chinese hacktivists posted messages such as 'We won't stop attacking until the war stops!' on US government websites.

Again, in Pakistan, a group of hackers going by the name 'Pakistani Cyber Army' had become well known for defacement of websites mainly Indian, Israeli and other government organisations. The group that had been active since 2008 had claimed responsibility for defacing websites of India's CBI, BSNL, Central Bank, ACER and the State Government of Kerala.

But would the Kosovo email bombs or hacking by Pakistani hackers qualify as a cyberterrorist act? Or for that matter, would the 1998 'email bombing' of the Sri Lankan embassy by the LTTE Tamil guerrillas qualify as a cyber-terror act; wherein Tamil guerrillas electronically jammed the computer systems in the Sri Lankan embassy with 800 emails a day over two weeks with messages reading 'We are the Internet Black Tigers'. The email bombing crashed the embassy's computer systems and also made front-page news worldwide.

Cyberterrorism is terrorism in the cyberspace achieved by the intentional use of computers, networks and the Internet to threaten, cause destruction and harm to make political or ideological gains. Further, an act of cyberterrorism should cause violence against persons or property, or at least cause enough damage to generate fear or the attacks should lead to death or bodily injury, explosions or severe economic loss. Dangerous attacks against critical infrastructures could be acts of cyberterrorism, depending on their impact. Attacks that disrupt nonessential services or that are mainly a costly nuisance are not cyberterrorism.

The attack on a nuclear facility using 'Stuxnet' and the hacking of Sony Pictures Entertainment would according to me qualify as cyberterrorism events. Stuxnet was the world's first digital weapon or cyberweapon that got created around 2006. The engineers designed it to hit only one particular target: the Step7 software that controlled the Siemens centrifuges at Iran's nuclear facility in Natanz, where Iran was working on its secret nuclear weapons programme.

The covert and still unacknowledged operation code-named 'Operation Olympic Games' came into being under President George Bush gathered rapid speed under President Obama. Bush believed that the strategy was the only way to prevent an Israeli conventional strike on Iranian nuclear facilities. They called the cyberweapon 'Stuxnet'. It is a highly sophisticated computer worm that they discovered in 2010.

Stuxnet was developed by the American and Israeli governments to wreak havoc and cripple the Iranian nuclear facility. Stuxnet was programmed to make the uranium enrichment centrifuges spin faster than they were supposed to, causing them to get out of control to the point of damaging them.

Inside the secure operations control room at Natanz, thousands of centrifuges that got represented on the computer screens by a light, displayed green, showing perfect performance and no evidence of failure which would have meant red light. In actuality, the centrifuges were eroding and conking out, but the screens without reflecting reality lied through their teeth.

The malware was so well programmed that none of the staff had any clue what was happening. Nobody even knew that the computer virus was causing the outages and disruptions. The attack was so well-executed that the virus worked undetected for months, and the scientists at the facility didn't know about it until security companies around the world discovered it and started talking about it.

Over a few years, about 20 per cent of Iran's centrifuges had spun out of control and got destroyed. It was a brilliant, sophisticated attack. Stuxnet was the first malware that could physically destroy something in the physical world. Until now, malware could corrupt computers and data, but Stuxnet opened up the possibility of using hacking to overtake machines.

The legal precedent of attacking another country's physical infrastructure through computer malware had now been established. After the Stuxnet attack, which got considered as the first cyber-physical attack, there have been other similar attacks that have targeted critical infrastructures the world over.

For example, in 2014, the German government confirmed that hackers had targeted and destroyed the furnaces of a steel mill. In December 2015, a malware called 'BlackEnergy' shut down 30 electricity sub-stations in Ukraine, plunging parts of the country into darkness during winter. Despite such attacks, there's too much secrecy around cyber-warfare and no rules of engagement.

In late November 2014, Sony Pictures Entertainment got hacked by a group calling itself the Guardians of Peace. US officials believe the Sony hack was retaliation for *The Interview*, a comedy film that starred Seth Rogen and James Franco and that centred on a plot to assassinate North Korea's leader, Kim Jong Un. The hackers, who are widely believed to be working in at least some capacity with North Korea, stole huge amounts of information off Sony's network. The data included personal information about Sony Pictures employees and their families, also emails between employees, information about executive salaries at the company, copies of then-unreleased Sony films, plans for future Sony films, scripts for specific movies and other information. The perpetrators then used a variant of the Shamoon wiper malware to erase Sony's computer infrastructure. The hackers involved claim to have taken over 100 terabytes of data from Sony, but that claim is yet to be confirmed by Sony. They conducted the attack using the malware. The components indicated an intent to gain repeated entry, extract information, and be destructive, and remove evidence of the attack. United States intelligence officials, after testing the software, techniques, and network sources used in the hack, alleged that the government of North Korea had sponsored the attack, but North Korea had denied all responsibility.

In another notable cyberterrorism event Kane Gamble, a British hacker, masqueraded as a CIA Chief and cyberterrorised the CIA Chief John Brennan and Director of National Intelligence James Clapper. After it was discovered, the British Courts sentenced him to two years in youth detention on charges of 'politically motivated cyber terrorism'.

The threat of cyberterrorism is rising on a global scale because of our reliance on the Internet. The Internet has generated a platform to conceive transnational cyberterror plots and implement it. For terrorists, cyber-based assaults have marked advantages over physical attacks. Cyberterrorist attacks can get executed remotely, anonymously and relatively economically, without substantial investment in weapons, explosives and personnel, the effects of which can be extensive and profound. We can expect events of cyberterrorism to rise in the days to come. Experienced cyberterrorists, who are very skilled to hack can cause massive damage to government systems, hospital records and national security programs, which might leave a country, community or organization in turmoil and in fear of further attacks. Terrorists would achieve it through acts of deliberate, large-scale disruption of computer networks, especially of personal computers attached to the Internet using tools such as computer viruses, computer worms, phishing, and other malicious software and hardware methods and by programming scripts.

Cyberattacks happen in two forms: first by an assault against data, while the second centres on control systems. The first type endeavours to loot or corrupt data and withhold services, and is the category into which bulk of the attacks fall, such as credit-card number theft, website defacement and the occasional major denial-of-service assault. 'Control-system onslaughts, on the other hand, would be those that strive to disable or take over operations used to preserve physical infrastructures, such as the distributed control systems that control water supplies, electrical transmission networks and railroads. Although instances of such invasions exist, the catastrophic disasters that usually accompany such an attack are mainly the stuff of Hollywood screenwriting, as opposed to reality.'

Most cyberattacks appear to take place for financial reasons, but there is mounting evidence to prove that cyberterrorists are becoming more politically and ideologically motivated. For illustration, Mohammad Bin Ahmad As-Sālim's piece '39 Ways to Serve and Take Part in Jihad' discusses how an electronic jihad could disrupt the West through targeted hacks of the US websites, and other resources that come across as anti-Jihad, modernist or secular in orientation.

The Internet is an expanding universe of content, and it is getting bigger and bigger. Many believe that terrorism through the Internet is becoming a serious threat and could become one of the top catastrophic events to bring an end to humanity. The existence of the darknet is facilitating people to carry out illegal activities within cyberspace while the Internet of Things is integrating the virtual and physical worlds. Such developments could encourage and induce countries to engage in cyberterrorism in furtherance of their intentions.

Finally, I remember reading somewhere that tomorrow's terrorist may be able to do more damage with a keyboard than with a bomb. *WarGames* a 1983 American Cold War science fiction film directed by John Badham unfolds such a chilling scenario. In the movie, the US Air Force Strategic Missile Wing controllers refuse to turn the key required to launch a missile strike during mock drill of a nuclear attack. The system engineers at NORAD, therefore, decide to automate the launch controls without human intervention. Control is given to a NORAD (North American Aerospace Defense Command) supercomputer, in which War Operation Plan Response (WOPR) is programmed to run war simulations and learn over time continuously. The protagonist David Lightman, a bright Seattle high school student and hacker in the film, uses his IMSAI 8080 computer to break into the school district's computer system to change his grades but he connects to a system that unwittingly accesses WOPR, installed in the military supercomputer. Lightman inadvertently operates WOPR nuclear war simulation, believing it to be a computer game. The computer, now tied into the nuclear weapons control system, begins to launch a massive Soviet first strike with hundreds of missiles, submarines and bombers.

NORAD, unable to know the difference between simulation and reality, believes the attack to be real and retaliates by attempting to start World War III. The protagonist in the movie happened to be a student playing a game, what if in future a NORAD-like supercomputer of some country were to come in control of a cyberterrorist?

Chapter 28
DOES CLOUD COMPUTING HAVE A SILVER LINING?

Valparai, with its tea estates, is a quaint and beautiful hill station. When I recently arrived at Sinna Dorai, a tea estate bungalow of Parry Agro perched atop the estate's highest point, the clouds that hung in there seemed like massive cotton balls glinting under the shimmering sun. In an instant, the beautiful emerald blue sky that was bewitchingly sublime turned tar-black as more clouds began gathering. Then an eerie caterwauling sound filled the air, whipping the wind into a frenzy, and a splatter of rain began drumming my window as it gradually settled down to a pitter-patter. Like the clouds in the natural world, we have clouds in the digital world. Clouds in the natural world bring gifts to a farmer and put a smile on his face; conversely, they could also be churlish and kraken-cruel and cough out gallons of water to flood the fields, overrun the dams and swell the rivers. How does the digital cloud compare to the natural cloud? What does cloud computing entail? Does it have a silver lining?

Cloud computing is a technology that delivers various services through the Internet, including data storage, software, servers, databases and networking. Cloud-based storage saves files to a remote database. For instance, Google Cloud is a suite of public cloud services delivered by Google.

Cloud computing, like the clouds in the natural world, offers a variety of benefits. Cloud computing spares the users of unscheduled software updates, frees up computer space, reduces maintenance woes and saves time, liberating the administrator to focus on more strategic tasks. Companies don't need to buy software anymore as they can avail it on rent from the cloud. Daily activities of life such as banking, media streaming, email and e-commerce all use the cloud. Netflix is an illustration of a company using the cloud.

Clouds can protect data from natural disasters, failure of electricity and other catastrophes. The cloud ensures that the data gets backed up and secures it in a safe location. The ability to re-access the data helps organisations conduct business, as usual, by reducing downtime and loss of productivity.

The most crucial benefit of the cloud is the flexible ease of storage and release of data as per the user's needs. The other benefits that accrue to companies from cloud computing are decreasing costs and better efficiency. Over 90 per cent of all businesses witnessed at least one area of improvement in their IT department after they migrated to the cloud. Small to medium companies that adopted the cloud experienced a 40 per cent increase in earnings after a year compared to those that did not use the cloud.

Despite the advantages mentioned above, the cloud has several downsides. For instance, Google stores our email and Google docs; Dropbox stores our documents while Facebook and Instagram our images, and our mobile phones automatically upload data to the cloud. The accumulation of millions of gigabytes of data on the cloud means that our personal information gets stored not just in our hard drives but also on cloud-based servers, implying that by putting all the jewels in one box, we seem to have prevented the need for the hackers/criminals to target individual hard drives and instead granted them an opportunity to loot the entire treasure in one attack.

Second, as the cloud service providers have access to massive data, there is a significant risk of stored data being deleted, changed and leaked intentionally or accidentally. There's also the danger of administrators of these service providers getting lured into disclosing data from database for personal or political gain. The cloud service providers also have a tendency to compromise the privacy of users with their privacy policy. For instance, most service providers, like Dropbox, share data with third parties for law and order.

Third, transnational interconnections and endless warehousing of enormous amounts of data mean data leaks are inescapable. In 2008, a military contractor from Maryland, USA, who wanted to listen to pirated music by downloading P2P sharing software accidentally installed the program in the wrong directory because of which the design and security features of the president's Sikorsky VH-3D helicopter got leaked, ending up on a P2P network in Iran. A military contractor's desire to listen to pirated music caused a billion-dollar military project to get jeopardised.

Besides, most users who upload the data to the cloud have no clue where their uploaded data, like pictures on Facebook, Instagram and so on, is getting stored and in which part of the real world. Our deep dependence on cloud-based services and nonlocal data storage could prove risky when the services go down, or if there is a denial-of-service attack, when we may not be able to access data. Cloud computing services need a secure Internet connection and also gobble up a great deal of electricity.

Data breaches remain a critical issue in cloud computing; major cloud service providers like Microsoft, Google and Dropbox have experienced breaches in which data such as credit card information, email addresses and mobile numbers got stolen. Data of several thousand businesses stored in the cloud continues to be breached each year.

Data breaches have been occurring for individuals as well. On 31 August 2014, hackers posted an assortment of nude snapshots of various stars such as Kate Upton and Jennifer Lawrence on the anonymous image-sharing website 4chan. Relaxed security policies at Apple and Amazon helped hackers breach the Twitter, Google and iCloud accounts of Mike Honan, a writer working for *Wired* magazine. The hackers remotely erased a year's worth of personal memories stored on his iPad, iPhone and MacBook Pro. Hence, entrusting personal data, such as family photographs, to cloud service providers has its risks.

According to a report by IBM Security and Ponemon Institute, in India, data breaches cost businesses about ₹165 million on an average, which is a rise of 17.85 per cent from ₹140 million compared with the last report released in 2020. India witnessed the highest data breach during the pandemic because of a rapid shift to remote work. In 2021, the five most significant breaches in India were reported by MobiKwik, Juspay, Domino's Pizza, Upstox and Air India.

The adoption of cloud computing by millions of users worldwide has proved to be a boon for criminals as the aggregation of massive data in one place has given rise to new opportunities for hackers. Some of the largest hacks to date, such as TJX, Sony PlayStation, Target and Heartland Payment systems and thefts of millions of accounts, could occur because all the data happened to be stored in one location.

When we think of the word cloud, it could bring an image of fogginess to our minds. In spirituality, cloud denotes ignorance or lack of clarity. When toiling in the scorching sun, over parched lands with parched throats, the sight of clouds is a welcome sign to a farmer because clouds aggregate raindrops like the way cloud computing aggregates data. Likewise, for several companies, cloud computing denotes a cloud with silver lining because of its simplicity and reduced costs and the relief it provides them. However, cloud computing could become ominous clouds if companies don't follow good practices to keep the data secure by impeding them from being breached or leaked inadvertently.

Chapter 29
DARKNET WEAPONS MARKET

When one browses the digital storefronts of the online markets of the dark web, one gets the feeling that with a handful of bitcoins and a few clicks of the mouse, it's trifling to buy an AK-47 or a Bushmaster M4 deployed by the Special Forces in Afghanistan which has an intrinsic potential to fire 700 to 900 bullets per minute. The dark web gun trade is Delphic. Towards one end of the spectrum, there are swindlers waiting to scam and some law enforcement agents masquerading as arms dealers. On the other extreme, there are several genuine instances of people buying and selling weapons on the dark web, counting in the weapons used in the 2016 Munich attack.

On the darknet, lethal weapons are accessible anytime from anywhere to anybody. Anyone can purchase whatever weapon one wants on the dark web sites such as Armory, LiberaTor, Black Market Reloaded. To get them on the dark web, nobody needs any background checks and there is no waiting period. In most countries, as the sale of weapons is either banned or regulated, the sellers of firearms in the darknet take advantage of this situation. The dark web is making possible worldwide arms trafficking. Although the value and volume of firearms traded on the dark web is minuscule when compared to other products such as drugs, but its impact on the security scenario is immense as shown by lone wolf terrorist attacks in Europe.

Darknet classifies weapons, such as pistols, long-range guns, ammunition, explosives, hard weapons and others. Under ammunition, one can find listed bullets of all sizes and shapes. Rand Corporation Europe, a non-profit organisation working with Manchester University, found 52 unique vendors selling weapons or analogous products such as ammunition, explosives or components such as silencers across 811 listings and 18 markets. Berlusconi market offers a wide variety of weapons for buyers to choose. They ship most of them worldwide, while they sell some locally.

Some darknet markets, like Dream Market sell firearm guides but no weapons. The darknet markets require the buyers to register themselves for getting full access to items available with the vendors. Hand guns such as Glocks, Berettas and 9mm Pistols are readily available on the darknet. So are assault rifles such as AK-47s and Bushmaster M4s. For those interested in explosives, C4 is in stock. Even military grade weaponry is available online on the dark web these days. A seller on the dark web going by the name Bohica promises access to MANPADS (Man portable air defense systems), APCs and Helos.

A vendor such as Veronique has ammunition stock, priced between €20 to €80 on the higher side for a piece. In the long-range guns category, Goblin-King sells Russian-made Saiga MK (7.62×39) at around €3,000, which is equivalent to 0.436207 Bitcoins. The seller offers the service with full escrow protection, where the customers don't have to pay unless it fully satisfies them with the genuineness of the gun. One can also find grenades, chemicals and explosives under the explosives category. In the dark web, there is a seller by name hitman 007 offering M2 pineapple hand grenades. A variety of hand weapons such as swords, knives and Tasers are also found sold by multiple sellers. A vendor by the name DutchDrugz has on sale a 7,000 kvolt Taser at €35, equivalent to 0.005098 Bitcoins. Pistols because of their small size and ease of shipping it worldwide, and their high demand, are well-stocked items with most firearm vendors. A vendor by name Alexandria has catalogued a Glock 26 pistol at equivalent to 0.183,687 Bitcoins.

Shipping from the vendors' location to the buyer's address is by far the most challenging procedure in the entire process of buying or owning a weapon. Shipping is a problem as they cannot be just couriered through Postal Service or by FedEx because postal service, which was the most adopted procedure of shipping a gun, today is being monitored by most law enforcement agencies. The products are therefore being shipped by shielded packaging disguised to look like legal products. The weapons are now being shipped by concealing them inside legal goods like electronics, books and clothes to escape detection by the authorities. The illegal weapons are also being disassembled and sent in different packages at different times. Recently, some items were discovered by the authorities embedded in old stereos and printers.

Weapon merchants are also arranging for 'dead drops' where assembled weapons are being buried in a park, or an alley, or in a barren ground in a remote location. After the buyers pay, they receive the GPS coordinates and description of items they will bury under the soil. Researchers in a study found that firearms and related goods had generated 136 sales per month with monthly revenue of $80,000. After the buyer receives the weapon and inspects it for quality, the customers can complete the payment by securing in the markets escrow.

Often, terrorists and criminals conduct illegal businesses under the shroud of anonymity afforded by the dark web, from the security of their homes, with no prior links to suppliers. Data reveals that most weapons available on the dark web (60%) come from the US, but Europe serves as the largest market for dark web firearms. Overall, the dark web is making available more new and powerful firearms for the same, or cheaper, cost than would be available on the street or the black market. However, there has been no reliable direct evidence of a direct link between the dark web online weapons market and terrorism. In November 2015, a week after the attacks in Paris, there were unconfirmed reports that the terrorists had bought four assault weapons used in the attack from the darknet from a man in Germany who had been running an illegal firearm online selling business. The information available from the official documents at the prosecutor's office in Stuttgart, Germany, pointed to purchase of the weapons used in the November 2015 Paris attacks from the darknet to a German supplier going by the username 'DW Guns'. In another case, Ali David Sonboly, a teenage attacker of Iranian origin who appears to have got inspiration from Anders Breivik's 2011 extreme right-wing terror attacks in Oslo, Norway, was discovered to have purchased his weapons on the darknet with which he shot and killed nine people in Munich, Germany, on 22 July 2016.

In September 2017, the authorities in the UK disclosed that Umair Khan from Birmingham had bought ammunition categorised as antiquated from the darknet and adapted them into functioning illegal weapons, which he sold to criminal gangs. Investigations also revealed that between August 2014 and February 2017, Khan had spent an estimated £50,000 buying over 50 revolvers and over 1,600 rounds of ammunition. They later found two 16-year-old boys had received his weapons. It further turned out that Khan was an armourer for organised crime groups and had 'no idea how and where the weapons were being used'.

The ability of not just criminals and terrorists to make anonymous purchases, but also the capability of vulnerable and obsessed individuals to procure weapons is perhaps the most dangerous aspect. Anyone can connect to the dark web and within minutes have access to a multitude of vendors selling weapons, which are most often illegal. The dark web is facilitating illegal trade of weapons on a global scale, by dismantling the geographical barriers between vendors and buyers and decreasing the personal risk of both buyers and sellers by obscuring their identities through anonymising features of the darknet.

The darknet requires a specific web browser to access called Tor so that users can remain faceless. Tor browser doesn't provide complete safety and full anonymity for criminals to stay safe. Hence, outlaws run NordVPN software and select Onion over VPN Server to start Tor Browser and disable JavaScript. They also make sure all other working programs are closed on the computer. Once they perform the above activities, they are ready to explore the dark web anonymously. Not all the items being sold in the darknet are illegal, but the assurance of anonymity makes it easier to subvert the law. The anonymity offered by the darknet also makes buying and selling items on the darknet risky because there is always the risk of the person at the other end being a scammer or the police.

Governments have been slow to realise the potential of cryptocurrency for its misuse of terrorism on the darknet. Bitcoin has become the prominent currency of the dark web to purchase illegal goods online, such as weapons and drugs. The crossroads of the dark web and Bitcoin, popularised by organised crime, perhaps poses the most significant threat. Much like organised criminals, terrorist organisations could use Bitcoin to purchase a range of weaponry, including firearms or bomb-making materials, on the dark web.

To prevent the dark web from having disastrous consequences, governments and law enforcement agencies will have to adopt intervention strategies and put in place proper regulatory frameworks. The dark web does not generate weapons; it acts as a facilitator for the trafficking of firearms and ammunition in the offline world. Hence, conventional policing and investigative techniques with traditional guns control measures structured to curb illegal trafficking will be crucial in responding to this threat. To generate a more robust understanding of the role of the dark web in enabling arms trafficking, there is a requirement to implement more continuous monitoring systems which would involve repeating and refining the data collection, to generate data that can analyse trends. It's further imperative that we review existing international instruments for its effectiveness to bring new amendments or to create new instruments. There is also an urgent need to test the strength and enforceability of present-day national and international counter-arms trafficking systems, including policies, laws, regulations, actors and resources.

CHAPTER 30
HUMAN TRAFFICKING ON THE DARK WEB

In Dante's Inferno, treachery is the ninth circle of Hell. The traffickers, users and abusers populating the human trafficking sites on the darknet where the vulnerable sections of humanity get betrayed in most perfidious ways would easily stack up for the tenth circle if Dante were to create one today. Inconceivable debauchery and depravity witnessed here are downright disgusting.

Benjamin Faulkner, a Canadian, was the owner of 'Child's Play', a darknet child pornography website that at its peak had over 1 million profiles. The website showcased over 100 producers of pornography who raped and brutalised children and shot videos of their sadism for the keen delight of paedophiles around the world. After running the site for the first six months, the United States Department of Homeland Security captured Benjamin Faulkner along with his associate Patrick Falte when they met in Virginia on October 2016. At the time of his arrest, Faulkner carried on his electronic devices a child porn collection of 47,000 images and 2,900 videos. His associate Falte had been an administrator on 'The GiftBox Exchange', another darknet child pornography site that the authorities shut down in November 2016. They sentenced both to life imprisonment. After the arrest of the founders, for the remaining 11 months the Australian Queensland Police Service's Task Force Argos took over 'Child's Play' and clandestinely administered the site as a part of 'Operation Artemis'. Police officers Jon Rouse and Paul Griffiths of Queensland Police impersonated the website's founders for 11 months, engaging with paedophiles and sharing material online with the object of catching perpetrators as a part of 'Operation Artemis', a joint investigation effort involving Australian, American and European authorities. The undercover operation resulted in the identification of 90 per cent of the users and 1,000 arrests. Amnesty International also condemned the actions as 'unacceptable under human

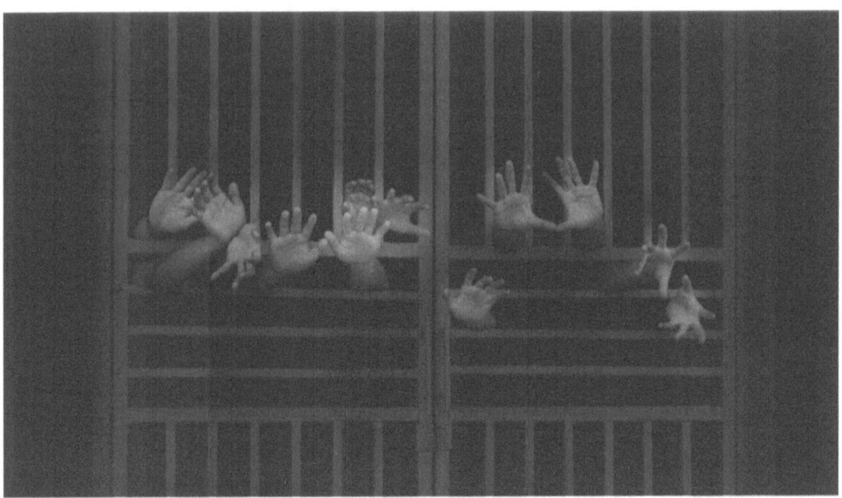

Doidam 10/Shutterstock.com

rights law'. Ivar Stokkereit, a legal adviser to the United Nations Children's Fund (UNICEF) in Norway, stated this was 'a clear infringement of the UN Convention on the Rights of the Child, even though the police's motive was to prevent new offences in the long run'.

Interpol meanwhile was monitoring another notorious trafficking ring called the Black Death Group based in Eastern Europe that was operating on the dark web and involved with selling sex slaves to Saudi Arabia as well as dark web virgin auctions of girls as young as 15. Creepy adverts for the girls included their age, hair colour and measurements. The group had recently posted a creepy advert of a 'fully booked' auction of a 15-year-old named Laura, with a starting price of £575,000. They had also put the online sale of a 17-year-old girl born in the UK named as Gemma in 2016. The Brit teen had a starting price of £92,000. The advert also claimed that the abductors 'do not sell girls that are terminally ill, pregnant, have STDs or are young mothers'. The gang also said 'that they could transport their victims globally', and they were also willing to kidnap a specific target for one's needs. But such a service would come at a considerable price, especially for destinations outside Europe.

In July 2017, news surfaced that two individuals claiming to be members of the Black Death Group had abducted a British model, named Chloe Ayling. The abduction of Chloe had occurred when she had travelled to Milan for a photoshoot. Ayling, hailing from Coulsdon, UK and aged 20 was working in London for Phil Green's Supermodel Agency at the time of the abduction. After Ayling had reached Milan, the next morning, Green received a ransom email, apparently from 'The Black Death Group' and written by 'MD' (Lukasz Herba) demanding €300,000 or else he would auction off Ayling as a sex-slave on the dark web on 16 July. Helpless Green contacted the UK consulate in Italy for support. When the Italian police visited the address, they found no photo studio. Instead, they found a room with some of Ayling's clothes. However, on 18 July 2017, police arrested Lukasz Herba, a Polish national for the abduction of the model.

Investigators who initially interrogated Herba learnt that he had injected Ayling with ketamine, handcuffed and put her in a holdall bag, and drove her in the dicky of his car to a house near Turin. Ayling confirmed that she had woken up inside a suitcase in the trunk of a car wearing a pink bodysuit and socks. She said 'Herba had tied her to a wooden dresser for six days, during which he had told her he would sell her to Arabs.' who would 'feed her to tigers when they got bored with her'. Herba had also reportedly told Ayling that he had made €15 million ($17.7 million) sex-trafficking kidnapped women and selling them via the deep web on the Black Death Group Website. However, Herba later got convicted by a Milan court for the kidnapping and was sentenced to 16 years and nine months in prison on June 2018.

Dark net is a perfect sanctuary for merchants of child pornography with sites such as Hard Candy, Jailbait, Lolita City, PedoEmpire, Love Zone, The Family Album and Kindergarten Porn, which allow paedophiles to connect and share fantasies, practice child love and exchange detailed tactics on ways of targeting, seducing and engaging in sexual acts with children. The volume of these activities is mind-boggling. Some sites have over one lakh registered paedophile members. According to some law enforcement sources, 19 per cent of paedophiles have sexual abuse images of children younger than three years old, 39 per cent younger than six years old, and 83 per cent younger than 12 years old. Across the dark web, experienced paedophiles teach one another how to evade law enforcement authorities and discuss encryption and anonymity techniques to avoid detection online. In the United States alone, traffickers traffic nearly 200,000 children for sex, and a pimp can generate $150,000 to $200,000 a year per child. A disturbing report from Europol says that several dark net websites provide live streaming of the rape and abuse of children. Paedophiles in Asia connect to video feeds where they direct the child-rapists to carry out specific fantasies. In one incident investigated by police, a person could order a group of eight men to rape an eight-year-old girl directing his fantasies in real time for a paltry sum of $100. As the images are streamed instead of being downloaded, there is no recorded evidence to prove the crimes.

Surprisingly, child sex traffickers may be strangers, but they can also be family members, friends, guardians or acquaintances. Nearly half of all identified cases of child trafficking begin with some family member involvement, and the extent of family involvement in the trafficking of children is up to four times higher than in cases of adult trafficking. In Germany, at the town of Staufen, near Freiburg, a couple using their son operated a paedophile ring like a business. Investigations revealed that the abusers had paid up to €10,000 a time to abuse their son. The couple also made videos of the abuse which they sold for large sums on the darknet; the mother threatened her son with foster care if he reported it to the police. The 48-year-old woman and her partner, 39, a convicted paedophile, got a conviction for forced prostitution, rape, sexual and physical abuse, humiliation and bondage for almost 60 separate identified acts by the court.

The dark net has about 2.5 million daily visitors. It's a perfect sanctuary for criminal organisations and terror groups to communicate, advertise, or buy or sell anything, including human beings. Of it all, human trafficking is the most attractive and lucrative crime. Over a two-year time frame, traffickers spent about $250 million to post over 60 million advertisements, in anywhere between 30,000 and 40,000 dark web pages according to a research done in the USA. It even beats drug trafficking hollow. The UN recently estimated that trafficking nets $150 billion a year. As this is being read, about 21 million people are being trafficked, of which more than half are women and girls and over one million are children. And as much as 25 per cent of them get bought and sold as sex slaves.

Criminal organisations have taken to human trafficking like a fish takes to the water because it is easy and inexpensive to buy, move and exploit vulnerable girls and children. Also, low risk of detection and prosecution of technology-facilitated human trafficking compared to the risk associated with traditional forms of trafficking makes online sex trafficking an attractive illegal activity. One child or girl can generate several thousand dollars a day for traffickers as they can subject them to daily abuse and repeated sale unlike other illicit activities like the drug trade. According to the International Labour Organization (ILO) estimates, 'globally, two-thirds of the profits from forced labour get generated by forced sexual exploitation, generating the US $99 billion per year.' Approximately 5.5 million children under the age of 18 get forced into labour, and authorities estimate that over one million are victims of forced sexual exploitation.

An anonymous major player in deep web, going by the pseudonym 'HeadOfHydra', in one forum declared that most illegal sellers on deep web had customers in India. According to him, 'Some sellers were reportedly searching for a Hindi/English-speaking staffers to have localised markets for countries like India, China and Brazil'. For Indians most activities on the Tor browser are illegal. Activities on Tor are punishable under the Information Technology Act, 2000.

Deep web provides not only a hiding place for human traffickers and pornographers; It has become a haven for many of them. Authorities estimate that 50,000 people in the U.S. alone access the deep web for trading child pornography. The nature of the deep web makes it very difficult to track down these people, despite the best efforts of the government. The deep web is the reflection of the real world; deep web is nothing more than an eyehole into this unfortunate reality, a solution for which lies in the real world. We all live in an interconnected world. We are all ONE. If one is suffering, all are suffering; therefore, the onus is upon us to do all we can to end human exploitation.

Chapter 31
THE DATAVEILLANCE BUBBLE

Leigh Van Bryan, a 26-year-old Brit, was embarking on his first visit to the USA, feeling excited, wanting to share his joy with his friends. He shot out this tweet – 'Free this week, for quick gossip/prep before I go and destroy America'. In British slang, 'destroy' implies partying and having a good time. And Bryan wilfully meant the same. But the Department of Homeland Security, which scans social media for terrorist threats, took the tweet literally and presumed Bryan and his companion to be terrorists. Hence, immediately upon their arrival, Bryan and his travel partner, 24-year-old Emily, get handcuffed and put in prison with alleged Mexican drug dealers for 12 hours. After an uncomfortable night of interrogation in separate enclosures, Van Bryan and Emily are hurled into a plane and deported back to Britain. Sadly, for Bryan and Emily, Dataveillance by the US authorities had done them in, and the only stuff destroyed were their visas and vacation.

Dataveillance is a portmanteau of *data* and *surveillance*. It is the practice of monitoring digital data relating to personal details or online activities. We leave a trail of data in the digital space as text messages, phone records, browsing history and email that live on forever. The data left behind by us are exploitable by companies, data aggregators and data brokers. Some examples of Dataveillance are monitoring data from credit card transactions, GPS coordinates, emails, mobile phones and social networks .

Dataveillance is today widespread; its powers are getting unleashed phenomenally. Pegasus superbug is a case in point. Pegasus is a mythical, divine winged horse from Greek mythology that is the offspring of Olympian God Poseidon. The modern Pegasus, which is stirring the hornet's nest today, is sophisticated Israeli spyware that can bypass phone security and access all data, including WhatsApp messages. It can access data from any mobile phone, including iPhones, which Apple claims to be impregnable. It also can switch on the phone's microphone and camera and record data without the phone user being aware.

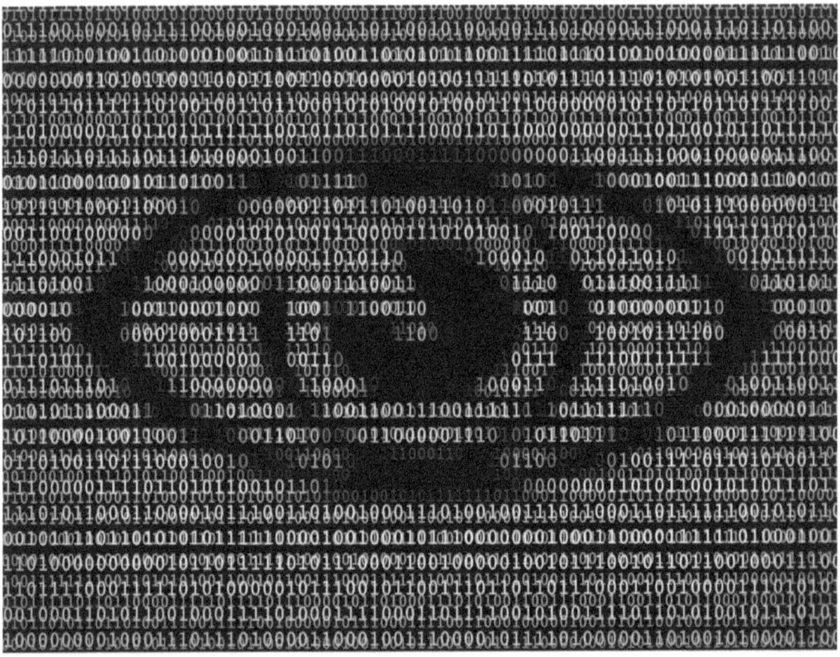

enzozo/Shutterstock.com

The Pegasus bug has damaged the democratic reputation of India after the news of its infiltration into millions of mobile phones in a dozen countries surfaced. Pegasus has excellent surveillance/Dataveillance capabilities. The spectre of clandestine surveillance through Pegasus spyware has spurred a furious verbal duel between India's ruling and opposition parties. It may be improper to elaborate further here on the Pegasus controversy, as the matter is sub judice. However, it is imperative that we take cognisance of advances in surveillance/Dataveillance methods and incorporate appropriate amendments in Section 69 of the Information Technology Act, 2000 and enact a dedicated cyber law to prevent abuse of Pegasus kind of advancements in surveillance.

Over the years, Dataveillance has been beneficial to the police to assess security threats associated with terrorism and investigate criminal cases. Police have resorted to Dataveillance to predict potential terrorist or criminal threats. Dataveillance amasses data. Hence, it is beneficial for predictive policing as it generates an enormous amount of data. Predictive policing based on Dataveillance is helping police predict and prevent crimes.

Financial institutions are using personal Dataveillance to track fraudulent purchases on credit card accounts. And businesses are using it to identify potential clients to sell their products. Businesses and websites instal cookies to track our online activities and get valuable data in the process that gets sold to other companies or third parties.

Similarly, market analysts use data from supermarkets and online stores to profile customers and predict purchase behaviour. For instance, Dataveillance helped a supermarket conclude that a teen customer was pregnant even before her father could know of it. A father in Minneapolis discovered his teen daughter's pregnancy not from the horse's mouth but the local Target supermarket. The teen's father became frantic when the Target store started delivering coupons for baby's clothes and cribs to their residence. Angry and upset over Target's promotion, the teen girl's father scampered to the store and began yelling at the store manager for sending baby coupons to his 15-year-old daughter. However, a few days later, the teen girl's father called the store and apologised after learning the truth about his daughter's pregnancy from her. Target stores could discern patterns by analysing customer data, such as buying patterns, credit cards, loyalty cards and products. Target's statistician Andrew Pole observed that women on baby registries were purchasing enormous quantities of unscented lotion at the onset of their second trimester. Using the data, Target could estimate the customers due date within a small window to send coupons timed to specific stages of their customers' pregnancy.

Likewise, when we subscribe to the Internet and social media, the challenge we confront is that they use the data furnished by the subscriber in a particular context, in unpredictable ways, with substantial consequences. For instance, Ms Bobbi Duncan, a 22-year-old lesbian and Mr Taylor McCormick, a gay male, both Texas University students, wanted to keep their sexual orientation hush-hush. But Facebook spilt the beans when they joined the 'Queer Chorus' group to meet other

LGBT students. After their enrolment, the president of the Queer Chorus added them to the Facebooks group discussion page, for which he did not need their permission. But the president was unaware that the software would automatically notify their other Facebook friends regarding their inclusion as new chorus members. So, when he added them, Facebook delivered an automatic notification to Bobbi's and Taylor's entire list of friends, including Bobbi's father – notifying them of her entry into Queer Chorus. Thus, by disclosing the clandestine sexual orientation, Facebook provoked Bobbi's parents to disown her.

Dataveillance also operates through digital technologies, such as apps, wearables and other IoT devices. For example, the 'Google Now' app accesses our digital footprints, including our web searches, emails, hotel bookings, contact lists, and so on and our physical location. It may have all the data to mimic our pattern of life. What if a particular husband's mobile phone was in the vicinity of another woman's mobile on a specific night? What would that data suggest to Google or others? Studying data patterns of a person could reveal almost everything about a person's life. Further, the famous 'OkCupid' app requires users to fill in data like their preference for sexual partners, group sex, alcohol and illegal drug use. Most presumed that the app would use the shared data to identify a suitable partner. Still, they were not aware that OkCupid was a data extraction company that discreetly disseminates the data gathered to advertising firms, data brokers and marketers for money. Therefore, novel forms of data-driven surveillance seem to be endlessly emerging.

Finally, authorities and marketers are increasingly becoming obsessed with data, and the scale of data that is getting harvested is mindboggling. People soon will not be happy to know that everything they do is getting tracked and watched. They are becoming weary of it, and the data bubble, which is getting bigger, is about to burst. When the material realm tormented by data becomes claustrophobic, embracing the boundless spirit alone would deliver the much-needed transcendence.

Chapter 32
ARE BIOMETRICS MORE SECURE THAN PASSWORDS?

When I show up at my office at Alandur for work, I am required to flash my ID badge to the ID reader to gain access into my office. Likewise, when I open up my laptop, I need a login to log into my computer, and a PIN at the ATM to retrieve my cash. Similarly, when I get to the airport, I need an ID to board a flight.

But the human mind is fallible, we may at times forget the login password, or the PIN for the ATM or we may leave behind our ID. If not, somebody might hack our password, steal our ID badge or sniff our credit card as it happened to Jason Bateman in the 2013 comedy film *Identity Thief* directed by Seth Gordon. Under such circumstances, how does one retrieve, secure and protect one's data, and one's assets, and one's identity? The simple answer could be biometrics.

When we contrast biometrics with conventional forms of identification where we are required to carry something such as an ID, driving licence or passport or remember something, such as the password or PIN, biometrics is extremely convenient as it is something which is always a part of us or we have on us, and something we would never have to worry about forgetting. Biometrics is us.

Biometrics is a signature of physical features or biological attributes. The most common being the fingerprints which police have used for more than 125 years to identify criminals. For more than 100 years, trained fingerprint experts manually performed this task by lifting them from the scene of a crime.

Today, with rapid developments in computers and sensor technology, people have started to move away from inconvenient and insecure passwords to technology-based biometrics, which has become incredibly cheap, convenient and comfortable.

Alexander Supertramp/Shutterstock.com

Technology-based biometric systems measure attributes such as ridges on the human fingers or the distance between features on the face or the wavelength and the frequency of one's voice.

By rendering them into zeros and ones, it enables the image or data to be contrasted or matched against a database of hundreds of millions of biometric details of others in a few seconds.

Growing capabilities and falling costs of such technology have led to a fast-paced proliferation of biometrics with a prediction of 3.2 billion users by 2020, primarily due to the belief that biometrics are more secure than passwords.

Biometrics are everywhere today. In Chennai, the city where I live, I have to scan my fingers to gain entry into the gym where I am a member or when I go to dine at the local club where I am a member or to unlock my iPad. Numerous offices both government and corporate use biometrics for attendance as well as identification.

If so, do you think that it's a good idea for your gym or your club or your hospital or your apartment building associations to be the owner of your biometric details? Mainly, when they have entirely no expertise whatsoever when it comes to protecting and safeguarding your biometric data.

Passwords are not things; they are one's intangible personal knowledge. They can be memorised or stored in password managers. They are inconvenient as it is difficult to remember a password which you had devised a year ago. It also means that they are hard to compromise. The same can't be said for biometrics.

Biometrics like face and fingerprints can be obtained by taking a picture or picking it up online or from any surface. Prints can be lifted from a beer can, or from the table one just touched, or the glass from which a person sipped his water, or the door which was pushed open by him.

If so, are biometrics safe? On the surface, biometric authentication sounds like the perfect security solution. After all, you are the only person with your unique fingerprints and DNA. But it turns out that biometrics are not that safe. As was made evident by a report from National Research Council which concluded that biometrics are intrinsically defective because the system isn't recognising your fingerprints directly, but instead it only recognises the digital version of your prints which can be stolen like a password.

For a tenacious and brave criminal, it's easier to commit theft of a fingerprint than a password, as it's conspicuous on our body at all times, and we give it away every time we touch an object or a surface. Once an image of the print is available, it's easy to make a model. Today, 3D printers have become common, and few experts have a figured out a way to fool the fingerprint scanners.

That's not to say that biometric authentication is unreliable; it can be reliable if another form of authentication accompanies it. Risks apart, both the government and private sector are in a hurry to create a database of biometrics, either with or without our permission to use the data either for us or against us.

India is being watched for having created the world's largest government biometric database called Aadhaar. The Aadhaar database had collected fingerprints, iris scans and photos of more than a billion Indians and uploaded the details to a national database. It has provided a unique 12-digit national ID number to every subscriber in exchange.

The Indian government believes that biometrics could be the answer to improve delivery of government services to the population. But human rights activists in India and abroad fear that the data could be hacked or misused even when India's government is counting on high-tech encryption, multi-layered authentication and 13-feet high walls to protect the world's largest biometric database.

Allaying the misgivings of the activists, Supreme Court of India, in September 2018, ruled that Aadhaar does not violate privacy rights although the panel of five judges decided to place a few restrictions.

While a national government biometrics database could be a useful tool in catching criminals and terrorists, it is not without its privacy and security risks, as the government of Israel discovered in 2011. In the Israeli case, then the country's primary national biometric database containing the name, birth date, national identification number and details of next of kin of nine million Israelis – living and dead was stolen entirely. The stolen database also contained information on the birth parents of several hundred thousands of adopted Israelis as well as detailed health information on citizens.

More troublingly, after the data was stolen, the database in its entirety was uploaded to the Internet where deluges of confidential details on Israeli citizens became freely downloadable. Investigations conducted into this episode revealed that an inside job had stolen the database, by a white-collar criminal, not by any hostile intelligence service or an enemy hacker.

Going by this incident, the claim of any government biometric database that its data would never be compromised is inherently absurd. Can any government claim that it's national disaster management program is foolproof enough to prevent disasters from happening? What is also not preventable is the misapplication of data for state surveillance and targeted intimidation. How can anybody who has submitted his biometric data be confident that the government will never become totalitarian or anti-democratic? Biometrics may offer many advantages. We may forget our passwords, but we will always have our fingerprints on us. Though biometrics can solve some problems, they have the potential of creating more severe problems. Today, if we become affected by identity theft, or if our password of Facebook or Twitter or bank account is hacked, we can reset our password, but if our biometrics are stolen, there is no reset. Fingerprints being permanent identification markers, once stolen or hacked they go out of our control forever.

Our biometric details which are available with our gyms, clubs or mobile phone companies are extremely vulnerable to theft and hacking. They can be hacked or stolen effortlessly. If the future of identity is all about biometrics, then the future of identity theft would imply compromising our biometrics through hacking and theft of our biometrics. Hackers and scammers are already busy devising methods to hoodwink the existing biometric systems. Biometrics is convenient, but they are not more secure than the passwords.

Finally, Biometrics is related to the human body while spirit or consciousness is eternal. Biometrics has now discovered an application to measure consciousness at Sofia University in Silicon Valley. With biometrics, it has become possible to quantify states of awakening and provide persistent inner peace.

Similarly, Danielle Roberts at her Meditation Lab in the USA has been investigating if spirituality can be measured and if technology and meditation can be used to increase a feeling of connection with ourselves, the world and each other. To achieve this, she has developed a Silence Suit: a wearable that measures one 's biometric data while meditating.

Biometrics is therefore not just applicable in our physical world but in our spiritual realm as well.

Chapter 33

PASSWORDS TO BIOMETRICS TO BEHAVIOMETRICS

In the movie '*The 6th Day*, Adam Gibson played by Arnold Schwarzenegger is deterred from entering a prohibited area when a scanner rejects his thumbprint. A security guard leans to him inquiring if he can help, Schwarzenegger grabs the guard at gunpoint and whispers, 'Yeah, you can stick your thumb in that.' The guard complies, which enables Schwarzenegger to gain access. Spoofing is not easy, most biometric sellers strive to make spoofing difficult, but the truth is all single biometrics are spoof-able, and the movies we see reveal that. One thing Hollywood got right, though, is how spoof-able biometrics tend to be, whether it be by peeling body parts, taking pictures or videos or by capturing a fingerprint with glue.

User identification and authentication is an important and essential requirement of staving off privacy leakage and ensuring that the security of the system is not breached. The most popular identification tools in devices are passwords or pin codes which do not provide adequate security and compels the user to memorise the passage code for each appliance. Corbato who invented the password in the 1960s four years ago blurted that the password has become a kind of a nightmare. Passwords have had their day considering the fact that we have had more than 707 million data breaches. Pin codes and passwords have well-known vulnerabilities.

What is needed today is a personal authentication method that does not rely on our memory. One recent alternative for the password in recent years has been biometrics such as fingerprints, face or even eyes. Fingerprint is the most widely used in recent years as it is cheap, fast and reliable. Both fingerprint and password suffer from being a single authentication method. Two factors should be a mandatory requirement. In smartphones recently, fingerprint and face detection has been introduced to increase the level of security and get rid of the bother of remembering cumbersome passwords. Biometric identification which includes facial, voice and fingerprint recognition are largely device-dependent and need expensive processing units.

A better approach under the circumstances would be to combine different physical, cognitive, physiological or behavioural attributes by evaluating them without any conscious input of the user. Behaviometrics is a recently emerging concept for identification, and it promises to provide a cost-effective alternative without jeopardising security. Behaviometrics gauges how we and our bodies individually act or operate, it reads traits that can be as revealing as fingerprints. It may measure our gait or striding or walking patterns, our keyboard typing cadences, our voices, our brain waves and the heartbeats that render distinctive signatures to identify us singly. Just as anatomical biometrics are being applied for security, identification and access control, similarly, we can deploy behaviometrics for similar purposes.

As behaviometrics is a continual identification of behavioural peculiarities, it is non-intrusive and takes into account human characteristics like typing, walking, social interaction and communication in either online and offline setting. Thus, biometrics is gradually evolving into behaviometrics. Behaviometrics is not about what one does; it's about how one does what he does.

Behaviometrics being quantifiable behaviour can be used to recognise or ascertain the identity of an individual. Behaviometrics zeroes on behavioural habits rather than physical characteristics. Everything we do on the phone, laptop or desktop reveals habits. These are comprised of a compilation of semi-behaviors, deduced by a variety of cognitive, physiological and mechanical characteristics, and are not liable to be spoofed or replicated by anyone. Behavioural biometrics recognises these contours by accumulating information, not on what the user is doing but rather how they are doing it.

Behaviometrics, virtually, peers at the way we type, the way we scroll, the way we toggle and the way we do several different things online without us being aware of how we are doing them. For illustration, some individuals may scroll on the right side, trying the scroll bar on the right, whereas other people might use the arrows up and down, to navigate the screen. .

Likewise, everyone has a way of using their device. The way we clasp the phone and the pressure we expend, whether we are fidgety or have a hand tremor, form part of our behaviour that is subconscious and inborn. As a consequence, this is not something that we can physically see or touch; therefore, behaviometrics is impossible to copy or steal.

Besides, some move the cursor rapidly across the screen in a zig-zag manner and then hover over a button. While some gently circle the cursor. And as unique as our signatures, everybody has a way of touching the screen, browsing it and closing it.

Behaviometrics continuously oversees the user during the entire working session to build a steady authentication process because a human behavioural habit comprises a diversity of many distinctive semi-behaviours; all mixed into a broader and larger unique profile.

As every person shapes his unique behaviometrics pattern not only by biometric attributes but also by social and psychological impacts, it is just about ridiculous to duplicate or simulate somebody else's behaviour before the computer. Thereby, spoofing becomes impossible.

Behaviometrics technology generates a highly detailed and precise picture of the user by analysing an expanse of behavioural patterns, actively assessing the user's distinct interaction signature with his device.

By continuously comparing several characteristics of the recent input characteristics with a formerly compiled user profile, behaviometrics can recognise abnormalities in the user's behaviour within seconds and stop intrusions while they are taking place.

As technology evolves with continuous use over the years, it will only become more robust, secure, accurate and infallible with the ability to triangulate behaviour across connected appliances by reading up from a wide spectrum of interactions of a particular user with a variety of connected devices.

Hence, behaviometrics has found several applications. DARPA has evolved an 'active authentication' technology that takes into account the private habits, cognitive methods and rituals used by an individual while performing tasks which in combination can identify him. For instance, one such behaviometrics is the keystroke dynamics measuring the varied ways in which someone inputs or types the individual characters on a keyboard. Trivial discrepancies of inputting data through a keyboard such as the force with which an individual type characters, the sequence and the manner in which he cuts and paste can serve as unique fingerprints to the world. An online education company called 'Coursera' is also using keystroke recognition to confirm that the same student attends the course and takes the test before handing out a certificate.

TypeWATCH is a product put out into the market by Watchful Software that runs on the network in the background and continuously monitors the user's typing inflexions or cadence based on which it recognises and blocks unauthorised access. Likewise, a Swedish company called Behaviometrics AB has created a tool that analyses how each cell phone user or a tablet user holds, wields and clasps his phone such as the slope/angle, his typing style or method, his habits of swiping or pinching the screen time duration of his pauses, pressure or vigour or exertion of fingers on the screen and so forth. Any deviation from the established cognitive gait sets off an alarm. Denmark's largest bank Danske Bank has incorporated this technology. When the software perceives any deviance of behaviour pattern of the user, it sets off an alarm bell and blocks access to the account. Banks reckon such devices could cut fraud rates by as much as 20 per cent. New types of behaviometrics are originating all the time, Nymi wristband scans a person's heartbeat using a voltmeter and uses its unusual electro-cardiac rhythm to unlock their smartphone, laptop, car or home. National Physical Laboratory in the UK has created a walking-gait recognition system that in combination with a CCTV system can recognise a person based on how he or she walks. An even simpler way of identifying someone would be through the accelerometer that comes equipped inside smartphones. Just analysing the 24-hour data over a few days would be adequate to identify an individual.

Motorola, in partnership with MC10, has developed invisible wearable RFID tattoos that we can use for password authentication. Proteus Digital Health has created a pill that one can swallow which reacts with the acid in the stomach to turn a person into an authentication token by spawning out an 18-bit code.

Behaviometrics is also a valuable part of smart environments such as smart homes as user signals and interaction with the houses can be used to reconfigure intelligent home settings. Application of behaviometrics is not only limited to smart spaces, but it is also used as a useful tool for continuous authentication. Besides smart homes, applications of behaviometrics includes smart traffic systems and smart health.

Behaviometrics is not just a transition in the paradigm from biometrics which is one time and static to continuous authentication, but the actual power of behaviometrics is in its ability to learn and improve the accuracy by continuously studying patterns and everything in the background and using it regularly to enhance the security layer. The longer one uses the device, the stronger and more accurate is the security of any system.

The US Air Force is using behaviometrics as a new omnipresent surveillance technology to be used in law enforcement to scan suspicious behaviour. The system comprises a camera that tags facial movements biometrically to build a psychological profile of the individual under surveillance. With just one image, its sensor can build a three-dimensional model of a person's face: the cornerstone of a unique 'bio-signature' that can be employed to trace that person anywhere. With a few more frames, the equipment can capture that face's unique facial muscle movements, and turn those motions into a 'behaviometric' profile that's even more precise. In plain language, the movements of the muscles in ones face will reveal one's hidden intentions through the process of 'behaviour analysis', to one's presence as a suspicious individual who may be committing to the act of thought crime or planning an attack. This new technology is the next step up from DARPA's infamous gait analysis program, which could identify terrorists by the way they walked. The technology can be used to keep tabs on 'insurgent operations', and also for 'law enforcement, banking, private corporations, schools and universities, casinos, theme parks, retail, and hospitality', to identify that 'insurgent' walking through a shopping mall.

Behaviometric technologies bring with them a host of privacy issues; for example, we could easily identify an individual typing on his keyboard based on how he or she slams on the keyboard. This could prove significant for recognising the world's most excellent hacker, but it can be bad news for an activist protesting against government policy in a police state.

Finally, just as behaviometrics establishes our identity and secures us from hacks and breaches, likewise we all have an inner soulmetrics or consciousness which we all can cultivate in our unique ways to establish contact and access inner bliss and peace while securely blocking all noise and turmoil of the outer world.

CHAPTER 34
DATA IS THE NEW OIL

Can a supermarket find out that a teen is pregnant even before her father gets to know it? It turns out that a father in Minneapolis discovered that his daughter was pregnant not from her but the local Target store. He made the discovery when Target began sending his daughter coupons for baby clothes and cribs. Angry and upset, the father of the teen girl stormed into the Target store and started lambasting the store manager for sending baby coupons to his 15-year-old daughter. However, a few days later, the father called the store and apologised, after figuring out that his daughter was pregnant. Target, by analysing customer data, such as credit card information and guest card details, was able to comprehend patterns. For instance, Target noticed that women in the baby registry were 'buying larger quantities of unscented lotion at the beginning of their second trimester besides vitamin supplements such as calcium, magnesium and zinc'. As the statistician of the Target trudged through the data, he could identify about 25 products that when analysed together allowed him to assign each shopper a 'pregnancy prediction' score. When their statistician applied the predictive model against the millions of women in Target's customer databases, they could identify thousands and thousands of pregnant women before any other companies had made the connection. Also, the statistician at Target could estimate the customers due date within a small window to send coupons timed to particular stages of their customers' pregnancy. Can customers trust supermarkets and other commercial establishments with the large volumes of data they are collecting storing and analysing? Given the breach of Target's database in 2013, the data of 110 million customers got jeopardised. What warranties do customers have that assures them that troves of their data available in custody with various establishments they are dealing won't get stolen?

We also entrust incredible quantities of data to private companies; once the genie is out of the urn, it cannot be put back inside again. Absence

AlexandraPopova/Shutterstock.com

of law and irrational terms of service means the data brokers have surveillance capabilities which are significantly better than the government.

In this age of Google and Facebook, firms that catalogue people's activities for income, share, stock and disseminate everyday details of people's lives. This creates challenges for the people as it becomes difficult to keep anything private, as it is difficult to predict where the information will end up.

The data we share on social media sites can show up in startling ways. For instance, two students from the University of Texas, Ms Bobbi Duncan, a 22-year-old lesbian student and Mr Taylor McCormick, a gay, didn't want their parents to know about their sexual orientation. But Facebook exposed them. Both of them separately joined a student group on campus, called the Queer Chorus, to meet other gay and lesbian students at their school. When they got enlisted in the organisation, the president of the Queer Chorus welcomed them by adding them to the group's Facebook discussion page, which he could do without their permission. The president didn't know the software would automatically tell their Facebook friends that they were now members of the chorus. When he did so, Facebook sent an automatic system notification to Bobbi's and Taylor's entire list of friends including Bobbi's father – notifying him she had joined the Queer Chorus. Two days after receiving the notification, Bobbi's father wrote a reply on his Facebook page: 'To all you queers. Go back to your holes and wait for GOD. Hell awaits you perverts. Good luck singing there.' Facebook had outed a closeted lesbian and a gay and had caused Bobbi's parents to disown her. In response to the unredeemable harm she suffered, Bobbi blamed Facebook.

George Orwell's *1984* portended a surveillance state governed by a handful of the elite who incriminate independent thinkers with 'thought crimes'. But what he did not visualise was not the big brother government doing something to us, but we did to ourselves through sites like Facebook and Google etc. We have consented ourselves to become monetised and monitored by agencies by willingly surrendering our data to Internet companies.

Take, for instance, Leigh Van Bryan, a 26-year-old Brit, who was fascinated to be venturing on his first visit to the USA. Before his departure, he sent a tweet to his friend, asking her if she was free for a quick gossip before their journey to destroy America. Van Bryan's use of the word 'destroy' in British slang meant 'getting trashed and having fun partying'. The Department of Homeland Security that had been monitoring social media for threats against America now had Bryan in its radar. Immediately on his arrival Bryan and his travel companion 24-year-old Emily were handcuffed and put in a cell with alleged Mexican drug dealers for 12 hours. After an uncomfortable night in separate cells, they threw Van Bryan and Emily on a plane back to the UK. They denied the couple entry to the United States and deported them back to Britain. In the end, the only things destroyed were their visas and vacation.

This may be reminiscent of the plotline from Franz Kafka's famous novel '*The Trial*', in which they apprehend a man without he being informed why, and he only later learns that a bizarre court has a secret dossier on him, which he cannot access.

When we are the subscribers of Internet and social media companies, the challenge we face is that they can use the data provided in one context in unexpected ways in another with significant fallouts.

Heretofore, quite a lot of the data accumulated made no sense, as our collection abilities exceeded our ability to untangle the data and make meaning of it. But today this scenario has changed.

Today when we download free apps, we wittingly or unwittingly allow the app companies to collect data, aggregate them and sell them unencumbered by legislation to many companies at mind-boggling prices. Nobody ever questions who has access to our data and how it is being used against us.

Dataveillance is today rampant, and its uses, capabilities and powers are being unleashed in ways nobody would have ever visualised. We leave a trail of data throughout the day in the form of text messages, phone records, browser history and email that live on forever. The data left behind by us enables the companies to find prospective customers at greater accuracy than previously possible.

For example, Google Now once installed accesses our entire digital imprint including our web searches, in-box, hotel bookings contact lists, and so on and our physical location. With this massive data, it can simulate our pattern of life. What if any other company had access to our pattern of life? For instance, if the husband and wife were sleeping in the same room, from the data, it would be easy to surmise that the husband and wife are living together. What if the mobile phone was for a night somewhere in the proximity of another woman's mobile? What would that suggest to Google or others? When we study one's data patterns over time, it would reveal almost everything about that person's life as well as help the companies sell products based on his preferences.

Take the case of the highly popular free dating site OkCupid. The site asks the users seeking dates with partners to fill out questionnaires on the site, and most presume, wrongly, that the data they provide such as whether they are smokers, consume alcohol, preference of sexual partners, group sex, own a firearm, or use illegal drugs and so forth remain only within the OkCupid system, and are utilised exclusively for locating a suitable match. what it does not reveal to them is that OkCupid is a large data extraction company which shares the data with advertising firms, data brokers and marketers. To unravel the extent of the data leakage, Ashkan Soltani, a digital privacy specialist created a fake account on OkCupid. On deploying privacy apps such as Collusion, he discovered that replies given by OkCupid's users were being shared with data brokers in real-time. As he filled in that he was a drug user in his OkCupid profile, he found his cookie file being shared with a data broker called Lotame. Such is the state of affairs in the world's unregulated data broker industry. Even when you have 'nothing to hide', your continually tracked social network graph and location can come back to bite you and also affect your financial status.

Another challenge in the world of big data is the information we share and our intention to prevent them from leaking out to others. People often get deceived by those with whom we have shared our intimate details, mainly photographs. Sexting or sharing of sexually explicit SMS via mobile phones is a rising phenomenon. The photos shared in such a manner do not disappear, the data rubble often comes to bite the originators in startling ways.

Hackers are breaking into and stealing all the data we have reported about ourselves on the Internet and various social media sites. All such data gathered has powerful implications for our personal and professional lives and even for our safety and security. They sit as a ticking time bomb available for picking by criminals. Organised crime groups and terrorists are taking advantage of all the data with shocking implications for all. We are not in control of our data and our destiny. Having given all our data, we find ourselves at the mercy of data goliaths who can do as they please with our data and information.

George Orwell's *1984* envisioned a surveillance state controlled by a handful of the elite who incriminate independent thinkers with 'thought crimes'. But what he did not visualise was not the big brother government doing something to us but what we do to ourselves through sites like Facebook and Google. We have allowed ourselves to become monetised and productised by voluntarily relinquishing our data to Internet companies.

Governments are also going after the massive data warehouses we have created such as Google. In 2010, the Chinese government went after Gmail accounts of the activists in the USA and other countries for criticising China's human rights practices. It was further reported that hackers belonging to China's People's Liberation Army targeted the source code of Google's Password Management System which gave them access to millions of Google's subscribers worldwide.

A century ago, oil was the richest resource. Now comparable qualms are being raised by the companies that deal in data, the oil of the digital era. Companies like Amazon, Apple, Facebook and Microsoft – look unbeatable. Their earnings are surging: they altogether racked up over $25 billion in net dividend in the first quarter of 2017. Data may be the new oil, but misuse and inappropriate use of data in the material world can be prevented when we all realise that the spiritual is more real than the material.

PART 3

LAW ENFORCEMENT

Chapter 35
CROWDSOURCING POLICING

India has witnessed a few massive crowdsourcing campaigns during the past few years. One of the most renowned campaigns was a design contest conducted by the Ministry of Finance to create a symbol for the rupee. The government received thousands of entries, but the design submitted by Udaya Kumar Dharmalingam of Kallakurichi, Tamil Nadu, ended up being selected from among the short-listed symbols.

We can describe Wikipedia as the father of Internet crowdsourcing. Building on a not-for-profit business model, Wikipedia is a free, web-based, multilingual and collaborative site, established to harness the collective knowledge of the world to create a crowdsourced and openly edited encyclopedia. Wikipedia now hosts over 40 million articles in 299 different languages.

The term crowdsourcing, in a nutshell, means involving with the multitude of the community, intending to get whatever one may need. It came to existence mostly because of the digital age. Some police departments the world over have been quick to embrace and assimilate it as a method to aid in their criminal investigations. Intelligence agencies all over the world have always crowdsourced information about criminals, terrorists, spies and suspects.

The term may be new but the idea is not new, as police forces in India have been using this concept since ages by circulating pamphlets or pasting posters of wanted and missing persons promising a reward to those furnishing any information. In India, National Crime Records Bureau (NCRB) has a lesser form of crowdsourcing called a 'Colour Portrait Building System' which creates portraits of suspects based on the description given by victims and eyewitnesses. They use the portraits so generated by the system to solicit information from the people.

In India, we are witnessing some interesting developments in crowd-sourcing. A good example is the Facebook page launched by the Delhi Traffic Police, which uses the pictures of traffic violations clicked by the people as a proof to prosecute vehicles violating traffic laws. The initiative has proved a success, and every second day there are at the most 10–20 tickets being issued for traffic-rule violations based on public participation. So, the police of Mumbai, Pune and Coimbatore have launched similar initiatives to better monitor traffic.

It perplexed the Mumbai Police when they received a complaint from a foreigner that a man had masturbated at her in a toilet. They came under extreme pressure to arrest the accused. To begin with, the Mumbai Police only had a photograph of the accused, so they hit on the idea of using WhatsApp to establish the identity of the accused. They created a WhatsApp group called 'Eyes and Ears' and added many informers who finally helped them identify the accused.

Police can become more effective and efficient and better serve the community through real-time crowdsourcing of data. Citizens through social media can help the cops create large databases they can use to track down perpetrators.

Video is everywhere and capitalising on the public's proclivity for filming and willingness to help solve crimes in their community can be an essential tactic in police investigations. By planning for fostering awareness and collaboration with the public, and considering a permanent evidence collection platform, police will have a valuable new tool in their investigative arsenal.

During the 2011 riots, the London Metropolitan Police crowdsourced the identities of 2,880 suspects by requesting the citizens to download an app called Face Watch ID. Police told the citizens to observe the images taken from CCTV footage to recognise the persons. If someone knew a person in an image found by them, it required citizens to enter the name and address of the person.

Crowdsourced video and digital media by providing crucial evidence have played a key role in detecting and preventing criminal cases. Police in Santa Barbara used crowdsourced information to identify the key accused in the 2014 'Deltopia' riots. Similarly, after the Stanley Cup tournament, when riots erupted, the Vancouver Police Department opened an email account, mainly to gather evidence from spectators. Much in the same way, the crowdsourced evidence helped the police make 25 of the over 100 arrests in the aftermath of the Keene riots in New Hampshire, USA.

Crowdsourcing is a great remedy especially during incidents such as the Boston marathon when the people are all charged up and incensed at what's happened. The outrage moves the people to get involved as much as the police want to get at the culprits. The energy and involvement of the community harnessed at such times could help the police immensely in accomplishing their tasks easily and successfully.

To illustrate to this, the Boston Police in 2007 introduced a hotline called 'Text-a-Tip'. In April 2013, when the Boston bombing happened, the hotline received 333 messages. Reddit, an American online news aggregation website, after the Boston bombing started a "Findbostonbombers" subreddit to crowdsource information on the Boston bombers. Reddit website witnessed it being inundated by contributions of over 870 subscribers and 1,700 visitors who dumped innumerable photographs and videos, and who also conducted amateur forensics and identified suspects. So much so, that the servers crashed. For investigations on a mammoth scale, trawling through the rabble of data to search what's pertinent to the case, to make use, can be hard. The Reddit content was also found laced with a discriminatory bias on the lines of race and religion. Some members of the public paraded wrong information as facts leading to a witch-hunt of innocent bystanders. With the Boston bombing, the crowdsourced information did not provide a breakthrough, but the FBI, however, booked the real culprits. Just, a month prior to this episode, an online blog called Gawkers, in March 2013, had crowdsourced information that led to successful identification and arrest of an accused involved in an assault.

We need not do crowdsourcing only for riots or large-scale law and order disturbances or known events. The Los Angeles Sheriff Department (LASD) hosts a secure portal called 'Digital Witness' on their website which is open and available at all times so that people can send videos or photos of crimes or criminals or suspicious people or suspicious activities all the time.

There is this mentality inside police organisations of 'This is our case, and we have to solve it.' The police assume that, if they go looking for help from the same community they are protecting, people will look down upon them. Crowdsourcing is heading towards being the wave of tomorrow. Police organisations may have an obligation to become accustomed to it, and they must realise that there is an unusual source they're not tapping into. Imagine having lots of people from the world over from many backgrounds looking at a case and figuring it out for police. Crowdsourcing could be the next big thing after DNA for solving crimes, and as social media evolves, and as more people come forward and volunteer more cases would get resolved.

In 2012, the FBI's top cyber lawyer, Steven Chabinsky, described government efforts in fighting cybercrime a flopped approach, and he insisted that support of the public may be necessary for combating cyber-threats. That work is slowly starting. In a case, a teacher at the University of Alabama worked with the students in his criminal justice class to assist the FBI to solve a $70 million cybercrime ring run by criminals.

Researchers and lab students investigating computer viruses at the University of Alabama at Birmingham helped the FBI track down the international cybercrime ring responsible for stealing tens of millions of dollars online. Beginning in 2007, the cyber ring used a class of malware called DNSChanger to infect approximately 4 million computers in over 100 countries. There were about 500,000 infections in the US, including computers belonging to individuals, businesses and government agencies such as NASA. The thieves could manipulate Internet advertising to generate at least $14 million in illicit fees. Sometimes, malware had the additional effect of preventing users' anti-virus software and operating systems from updating, exposing infected machines to even more malicious software. But the FBI, because of the support of the students in tracking the bug, could arrest six Estonian nationals and charge them with running a sophisticated Internet fraud ring. The success of the complex international investigation, such as Operation Ghost Click, resulted from a strong working relationship between law enforcement, private industry and international partners.

As per the American game designer Jane McGonigal, today there are more than half a billion people worldwide playing computer and video games at least an hour a day. That comes to three billion hours a week as a planet playing video games. What if they could channel these efforts for police work? Doing so would unlock enormous power and potential of channelising the wisdom of the crowds in a way that solves the world's most significant problems. We could apply gamification to our nation's critical infrastructure systems. We could create animated games where players could be let loose to find security vulnerabilities in everything from our virtual electricity grids to our transportation networks. Such games would not only fix cybersecurity issues but also to deal with emerging threats such as bioterrorism, AI, autonomous weapons systems and nanotechnology and prevent such threats from becoming dystopian.

Prizes can also spark innovation and solve problems such as the Raymond Orteig prize money of $25,000 that spurred Charles Lindbergh to become the first aviator to cross the Atlantic and helped create today's aviation industry. The XPRIZE foundation established by Peter Diamandis paved the way for space tourism and commercial space flights. Fortunately, the XPRIZE Foundation is planning a cyber-security XPRIZE, with support from Deloitte Consulting. A $20 million purse money which is a mere 0.01 percent of annual revenues from the $150 billion software industry might go a long way in protecting our technological future.

We as individuals and organisations embody a global consciousness of the interdependence of all life. Individuals and nations can no longer resolve many of their problems by themselves. We need one another. Police and people by coming together will engender a more sustainable future for each other and the earth.

Chapter 36
PROACTIVE POLICING STRATEGIES FOR CRIME PREVENTION

The Hollywood film *Minority Report* is an action-detective thriller set in Washington DC in 2054, where police utilise 'pre-cogs' to arrest and convict criminals before they commit their crime. Precrime relies on the visions of three psychics or 'pre-cogs' whose prognoses of future events are never in error. Tom Cruise plays the head of this Precrime unit and is himself accused of the future murder of a man he hasn't even met. Proactive policing or the act of law enforcement preventing a crime before it takes place has come a long way. Today, the fictional Pre-crime Department in the *Minority Report* has become a reality in many countries. Person-based predictive policing is proactively using data to identify and investigate potential suspects or victims and also visualise the spread of violence like a virus among communities. The same data is able to predict who gets shot and who may commit the next murder.

Proactive policing implies all strategies that have prevention or reduction of crime as one of their goals that are not reactive such as controlling or dealing with ongoing crimes or responding to crimes after they have occurred. The term 'proactive policing' encompasses several methods designed to reduce crime by using prevention strategies. By definition, it stands in contrast to conventional 'reactive' policing, which mostly responds to a crime that has occurred.

Proactive policing specifically would include elements which emphasise prevention, mobilisation of resources by expecting events of crime or disorder or by targeting criminal forces likely to drive crime or disorder. There are several proactive policing approaches that we could broadly categorise as place-based, person-focused, problem-oriented and community-based.

Place-based proactive policing prevents criminal offences by using data to set apart small geographic areas where crime is known to be concentrated. Hotspot policing or crime mapping is one such strategy, which has roots in both the notion and research that crime focuses at places even more than it hinges on people. Locations identified as hotspots may require additional patrol, periodic visits by beat officers, or other responses appropriate for the crimes occurring there. Experiments in Minneapolis, Minnesota, in the 1980s by Sherman revealed that 60 per cent of the crime occurs at 6 per cent of places. Place-based concepts have led to deterrence-based strategies such as beats, pickets, directed patrol, crackdowns and different situational crime deterrence approaches to crime hot spots.

Geographic Information System (GIS) can play a crucial role in hotspot policing by enabling crime mapping and analysis by providing mapping solutions for crime analysis, criminal pursuit, traffic safety, community policing and many other tasks. GIS software helps combine vast amounts of location-based data from multiple sources. A GIS helps crime officers determine potential crime locales by analysing complex seemingly unconnected data and presenting them all in a graphical, layered, spatial interface or map. Mapping crime can help police protect citizens more effectively. An understanding of where and why crimes occur can improve attempts to fight crime. Simple maps that display the locations where crimes or concentrations of crimes have occurred can help direct patrols to places they are most needed. Use of more complex maps to observe trends in criminal activity and plans may prove invaluable in solving criminal cases. Police agencies usually compile vast amounts of data, but the data in such a form is hard to visualise. However, the same information displayed graphically provides a powerful decision-making tool for investigators, supervisors and administrators.

Hot spot policing is one of few areas in police research that researchers have analysed using randomised controlled trials. Several systematic studies have uncovered that directing police efforts in a small geographic area diminishes crime. When the police launch an intervention, some criminals get arrested while some stop committing crimes, while others commit crimes in changed locations or alter their ways of executing offences in reaction to the police interventions. Thus, a spot that had been a hub for crimes can abruptly be exempt from criminal activities, with some criminals shifting to another location.

A person-focused proactive policing prevents crime by using data to recognise substantial concentrations of crime within small communities. Focused Deterrence, for instance, is a strategy that targets specific criminal behaviour by a few offenders; police confront such offenders and inform them they will not tolerate their persistent criminal behaviour. Yet another person-based proactive approach to prevent crimes is Problem-Oriented Policing (POP). Authorities base the POP approach to an understanding of the social causes of crime and treating the same by tailoring remedies to them. POP is an analytical procedure used by police agencies to plan strategies that deter and curtail crime by targeting underlying conditions responsible for recurring crimes by striking at their roots. Once police identify a problem, they expect officers to work closely with community members to develop a solution. The goal is to find a cure for the ailment instead of merely treating the symptoms. This approach requires police organisations to use a spectrum of approaches to problems and assess their impact.

Community policing is another aggressively tested, proactive approach that uses community resources to identify and control sources of crime. Community policing uses strategies that support the systematic use of neighbourhood partnerships and problem-solving techniques to deal with circumstances giving rise to crime proactively. The main aim of neighbourhood policing is to help police build bridges with the community through interactions for creating partnerships and strategies for reducing crime and disorder.

The success of proactive policing depends in no small extent on police legitimacy. Police legitimacy is the degree to which the community views the police as legitimate; police frequently make this assessment based on the public's eagerness to heed and collaborate with the police. We may correlate police legitimacy with the extent of public backing, and cooperation they receive, in their endeavours to combat crime. If police give up their legitimacy, it can jeopardise their capacity and power to function effectively. When police lack legitimacy, residents are less likely to contact police or cooperate with their investigations. Police–public interactions contaminated by mistrust are more likely to develop into a conflict or a tussle for dominance and status that could result in injury or death of police and the public alike.

Procedural Justice Policing is an antecedent to police legitimacy; procedural justice focuses on discerned fairness in processes concerned with policing, which includes a chance of being listened to and the awareness that police are impartial, credible and trustworthy. And also, by the way, they treat people with dignity with due regard to their rights. Procedural justice concentrates on how police and other legal authorities interact with the public, and how the aspects of those interchanges mould the public's impressions of the police, and their readiness to conform to the law. Thus, procedural justice helps develop relationships between authorities and the population in which the community has faith and belief in the police as fair, impartial, benevolent and legitimate, because of which the community feels compelled to obey the law and the instructions and follow them as mandated. Procedurally just policing is necessary for the development of goodwill between police and communities and improving community perceptions of police legitimacy, which includes the belief that authorities may demand proper behaviour. Creating and sustaining police legitimacy fosters the acceptance of police decisions, respect for the law, and provides for high cooperation between police and public to combat crime.

In 1982, James Q. Wilson and George L. Kelling proposed a theory called Broken Windows Policing (BWP). BWP is a proactive approach that centres on vigorous enforcement against minor offences, such as broken windows, which is based on the theory that neighbourhoods tainted by social and physical upheaval imply resident apathy to crime and attract more predatory crime. BWP was further popularised in the 1990s by New York City police commissioner William Bratton and Mayor Rudy Giuliani. Implementing the theory brought about a significant decline in crime in the city. BWP theory infers that policing processes that tackle minor offences such as defacement, gambling, open boozing and vandalism help to create a climate of order and lawfulness, staving off more severe crimes. So, a disciplined and tidy setting that communities preserve delivers a sign that the neighbourhood is being monitored and that they will not tolerate criminal behaviour. Contrarily, a disordered environment, one that they do not maintain that has broken windows and is filthy and messy with graffiti and litter would hint that the community is not being regulated and that criminal activity has little chance of detection.

Finally, Predictive policing is the latest proactive approach that offers the recourse to law enforcement agencies to pre-emptively act against anticipated crimes by focusing on crime-prone areas and individuals at the risk of offending or being targeted. If police halt crimes before criminals commit them, it will have a huge social and economic value not just for those at the risk of being victims of such crimes, but also for the criminals, as it can stop them from making life-altering mistakes.

Police in India are continually working with limited resources and are always under pressure while reacting to critical incidents. To solve this problem, police agencies in advanced countries are turning to the technology not just to fight crime but also to prevent it by leveraging the capabilities of 'Predictive Policing' that focuses on harnessing the power of big data analytics, coupled with geospatial technologies and a combination of evidence-based police response models to do crime analysis, detection and prevention. Predictive policing is the second step of smart policing that will facilitate the police to provide services efficiently and proactively. The predictive policing technique considerably shifts the response mechanism from reacting to crime to forecasting the possibility of crime and deploying resources to preempt the crime.

India can leverage technology to implement proactive policing by using computer-based algorithms that analyse Crime and Criminal Tracking Network and Systems (CCTNS) data to sequester places that breed crimes (place-based policing) and single out potential future offenders (person-based policing). Predictive policing promises to be a game-changing concept. Authorities understand that the application of analytical and quantitative approaches will continue to be an essential part of police activities. As it is predictive, the effort involves crunching data of past crimes to foresee and thus, it is primarily reactionary police with a proactive approach.

Just as how police are trying to prevent crimes proactively, we can also be proactive and prevent crime in our own houses and offices by reducing the opportunity for crime to occur at our home, our place of work or our business. We can, as individuals and communities, implement these principles by identifying the weak spots and vulnerable areas, and improving upon such areas. We can prevent crimes from occurring in our properties by making it harder for an offender to access our brick and mortar properties by upgrading the locks on your doors, windows, sheds and outbuildings and our electronic devices and by using secure passwords to prevent criminals from hacking into our online accounts. We may leave items in our surroundings, such as tools and ladders, that criminals may use to climb up or climb down and commit crimes. We can control access to a location, a person or an object by locking the doors and windows to both our house and our vehicle and by ensuring our fences, hedges, walls and other boundary treatments are in a good state of repair. We may also instal a sound security system in place at a commercial site replete with entry barriers, security guards, ID cards, and so on.

With our lives, Stephen Covey identifies being proactive as one of the seven habits, encouraging us to be proactive to be successful. About 95 per cent of your actions and thoughts are repetitive, causing unhealthy and reactive subconscious patterns. There is, however, a part of us that is alive and fully connected to Source, which doesn't thrive on repetition. When we become self-aware of our thoughts, we will stop reacting like a Pavlovian dog and proactively choose our response by being mindful. The more self-aware we become, the less reactive we will be.

Chapter 37
EVIDENCE FOR EVIDENCE-BASED POLICING

Evidence-Based Policing (EBP) is a technique of formulating policy and tactical decision making for police organisations. It is a practice of steering and leading policing with the intention of using evidence not only to drive the systematic application of key strategies or tactics but also for testing and tracking them. It has its seeds in the larger trend towards evidence-based practices.

EBP was first outlined by Lawrence Sherman in 1998, even though the use of experiments to determine better-policing methods was done several decades earlier before Sherman defined it. For instance, the Police Foundation that was founded in 1970 and in 1971–72 worked with the Kansas City Police Department to perform a landmark survey on car patrols. In the early 1980s, Sherman and Richard Berk carried out a famous experiment called the Minneapolis Domestic Violence Experiment (MDVE). Their experiment revealed that arresting domestic violence suspects was a deterrent against repeat offending. The MDVE is remarkable for three reasons. First, it was the first controlled field experiment in which police officers' responses to a specific problem – in this instance misdemeanour-level assault of a spouse – were dictated by random assignment rather than officer discretion. Second, it contributed to a nationwide propensity towards pro arrest policies in major city police departments. Third, because the conclusions of the research were counterintuitive to existing 'common sense' on the problem, the National Institute of Justice (NIJ) financed its only major initiative to confirm research, the Spousal Abuse Replication Project (SARP). The study had an 'almost unprecedented consequence in shifting then-current police practices'. Sherman later worked with fellow criminologist David Weisburd for a 1995 study which showed the usefulness of directing police crime prevention resources on small hot spots of crime. The approach of Sherman was ingenious as it veered policing from a person-focused approach to include a location-based approach. Hot spots policing entailed concentrating police endeavours at crime prevention in a very small geographic neighbourhood where crime concentrates. This strategy is one of the only occasional policing strategies rooted in both theory and research. Crime concentrates at locales even more than it concentrates on people. Hot spots policing is one of few areas in criminal justice research that has been analysed employing randomised controlled trials, a gold standard for research. Several systematic studies' findings have revealed that concentrating police endeavours in a small geographic area lessen crime. For his contributions, Angel Cabrera has described Sherman as being the 'father' of EBP. Sherman's basic core idea is that police practice can be made far more powerful if strategies proven to work during controlled field trials are prioritised.

Sherman's criterion depicted a future world in which several police practices as feasible would be utilised or abandoned based on good evidence about their cost-effectiveness. What it did not tell was how to get there. The notion of being completely evidenced – that best evidence would be employed to steer all or increasing proportions of decision making – remains an unrealised vision in every vocation, including medicine. The impediment all careers have encountered is a dearth of methodical evidence about how professions or institutions become evidence-based.

The main problem in amassing evidence on such tipping points is the unit of analysis. In implementing evidence on better outcomes, the unit of analysis is micro-level: one outlaw, victim, hot spot or neighbourhood at a time. In implementing evidence on better decision making, however, the unit of examination is organisational: one police organisation at a time. What serves for altering decision making in a police agency can only be discerned from a comparative estimation of police organisations – a more tricky task than working within one agency.

Proponents of EBP underscore the significance of statistical analysis, experimental research and ideally randomized controlled trials. EBP strives to expand understanding and enhance the application of scientific testing, targeting and tracking of police resources, particularly during periods of budget slashes and tremendous public scrutiny. Use of targeting, testing and tracking can immensely help EBP.

Going by EBP, Police, in order to prevent crime, should target repeat offenders, crime hot-spots and highly susceptible victims. Police should focus their greatest resources on the strategies or methods on above-mentioned categories of harm to have the greatest effect. Some examples of targeted policing could be marching beats or serving targeted patrols to crime-infested areas to prevent and detect crimes. Hotspot patrolling involves mapping the highest crime locales in each city or neighbourhood and serving targeted patrols. We could also use CCTNS data to identify the most vulnerable sections of society or highly susceptible victims to crimes such as girl children and proactively protect them from sex predators by targeting such victims and offenders to prevent child sexual abuse. We can use CCTNS and FIR data to identify repeat victims and most harmed victims and use targeted prevention to prevent them from being harmed again. By testing key strategies and tactics that we are using we can find out whether a key strategy or tactic is working and at what cost and if it is cost-effective compared to the existing practice. EBP can be used to test how well a new practice or strategy which has been implemented is delivering results. Tamil Nadu Police have introduced a 'Police Wellbeing Programme' since 2018 at a cost of ₹10 crores. EBP can be used to test the effectiveness of the program with regards to the reduction in health parameters of stress in police personnel, improvements in productivity and reduction of deaths due to stress-related diseases and suicides. New technologies which have been introduced in Tamilnadu Police such as CCTV, e-challans, Body Worn Cameras can also be tested to ascertain their contribution vis-à-vis old systems and their contribution in terms of increased efficiency and improved productivity of the force.

EBP can also be immensely helpful in testing new and existing strategies that are being applied such as prevention of corruption, the radicalisation of youth, police recruitment and training, and investigation; and also for testing of new innovations such as an e-office system which has recently been introduced in Tamilnadu Police, and SOS Kavalan App for the safety of woman and so on. Similarly in crime investigation, we will be able to track which investigative tactics are producing the most detections and to build a checklist for investigators that could be targeted at the investigation of rape and serious assault, or burglary, or robbery, or murder investigation.

Implementation of EBP has been taken up at a few places in India. Raksha Shakti University (RSU) a police University at Gandhinagar, Gujarat embarked on a pioneering criminological study of policing, by conducting research with officers in Ahmedabad City Police and at the State Crime Records Bureau, Gandhinagar. The research study titled 'Patterns of Body Offences'" in Ahmedabad City (2017) is now being considered a definitive study in proactive policing, besides offering critical awareness into the method and character of police-academic affiliations. The study inferred that if police practitioners and scholars work concurrently on research, knowledge transfer and other activities, significant benefit would accrue to all facets of police work.

RSU has also made a strong case for the promotion of evidence-based practices in policing and the professionalisation of policing in India. The Center for Criminology & Public Policy (CCPP) is proposing a policy that gives new meaning to police-academic relationships. The Union Government's policy outline titled 'Why Should Indian Police Join Hands with Criminologist' has recommended that police forces should invite academics to foster research to improve efficiency and effectiveness of police.

On the same lines, the Rajasthan Police is formulating a proposal aiming at amalgamation of academics and police to improve the efficiency of everyday police work. This can go a long way in understanding the causes and develop proactive methods to prevent re-victimisation. Engaging Criminologists can help bring out new insights and assist police effectively deploy their limited resources.

Similarly, the Delhi Police have undertaken a study collaborating with Lok Nayak Jayaprakash Narayan National Institute of Criminology & Forensic Science (NICFS) on the offence of chain and mobile snatching in Rohini. Notwithstanding these developments, the association between police organisations and the academic research community continues to remain uncomfortable today. Therefore, there is a definite requirement to create significant synergy between police practitioners and Criminologists where police practitioners provide research needs thus stimulating the academicians to evidence-based investigations resulting in researchers uncovering new tools and ideas for execution as well as to assess their impact.

Hence, in order to promote police research, there is a requirement to build institutionalised configurations in which the police practitioners and researchers often meet to talk about the research needs and possibilities of partnership. This type of set-up has been best epitomised by Evidence-Based Policing Network of the Center for Criminology & Public Policy, to increase research in policing.

Finally, can there be evidence-based spirituality? Whether or not a divine power truly does exist might be a matter of opinion, but the neurophysiological outcomes of spiritual beliefs are scientific facts that are being accurately measured. There is now strong evidence to show that spiritual practices such as meditation and exercises which connect one to one's higher self raise levels of serotonin, which is the 'happiness' neurotransmitter enabling the practitioner to experience unalloyed peace and bliss.

Chapter 38
DO MURDERERS HAVE MURDER GENES?

Bradley Waldroup lived in a camper home in the cliffs of Tennessee. On 16 October 2006, when the police responded to a call and strode into his home, the entire place looked like a battlefield. There was blood every place – there was blood on the carpet, on the walls, even on the Bible Waldroup had been reading. Just some time ago, Waldroup who had been drinking had picked up a fuss with his estranged wife who had come there for the weekend accompanied by their four kids and her friend Leslie Bradshaw. Midway into the argument, Waldroup had lost his cool, and pumped eight bullets into Bradshaw and smashed her head open with a sharp implement. Having finished with her, he hounded his wife, Penny, with a machete chopping her finger and cutting her repeatedly. After the police investigation, the prosecutors indicted Waldroup with the felony murder of Bradshaw, which is punishable with the death penalty, and attempted first-degree murder of his wife as the police were convinced that Waldroup's actions had been wilful and deliberate. During the trial, Waldroup conceded that he had killed Leslie Bradshaw and attacked his wife. A death sentence looked inevitable. However, as the trial progressed, the jury was beseeched to examine genetic evidence in the case against Bradley Waldroup. A forensic psychiatrist who analysed the evidence swore that Waldroup carried a criminal gene linked with violence. After 11 hours of deliberation, the jury sentenced Waldroup of voluntary manslaughter, not murder, and only attempted second-degree murder. The ruling left Prosecutor Drew Robinson stunned and speechless.

In 2007, Abdelmalek Bayout, an Algerian citizen who had lived in Italy since 1993, acknowledged to stabbing and slaying Walter Felipe Novoa Perez. Bayout confessed that he had killed Perez as he had humiliated him over the eye makeup he was sporting for religious reasons. During the trial, Bayout's lawyer pleaded the court to take into account the fact that her client might have been mentally ill at the time of the murder. The court after decreeing and evaluating three scientific reports handed him a sentence of nine years and two months that was three years less than the sentence he would have received if there was no predisposition to violent behaviour.

Following an appeal shortly after, there was a curtailment of penalty of Bayout by one more year as two molecular neuroscientists after a series of tests had found abnormalities in brain-imaging scans and in five genes that correlate to violent behaviour – including the gene encoding the neurotransmitter-metabolising enzyme monoamine oxidase A (MAOA). Delivering his verdict, Judge Reinotti proclaimed openly that he had found the MAOA evidence incredibly compelling.

Likewise, police in the Netherlands had indicted a young woman of choking her four newborns after their births by smothering their nose and mouth with a pillow. After that she put the corpses into a suitcase and left them in the attic at the basement of her parents' house. Initially, the court presumed that the woman had murdered her babies as the babies were illegitimate. In the first instance, the court imposed a prison sentence of 12 years because of infanticide: three times murder and once manslaughter of the four newborn children. Further, when they took the case to the Court of Appeal, the court agreed to the plea of defence of subjecting the accused to an examination by a psychiatrist, a psychologist and a behavioural neurologist. At which time, it became established that the defendant had a personality disorder, and therefore, there was an existence of diminished guilt on the part of the defendant, for the crimes. Taking into account the expert reports, the Court of Appeal, in contrast to the first instance court, determined that as evidence was lacking, it was appropriate to drastically reduce the sentence to just four times manslaughter with mandatory hospitalisation and a prison sentence for three years.

But the case of Stephen Mobley preceded the cases mentioned above. Mobley came from a prosperous white middle-class American family. There is no way anyone could have blamed his upbringing. But as he grew up, he became increasingly violent. After attaining the age of 25, he strolled into a pizza store, drew his gun and casually shot the manager of the store in the neck sarcastically joking that he would apply for the job vacancy after the man is dead. In 1994, Stephen Mobley confessed to the cold-blooded murder and became the first to submit genetic evidence in a court of law in Atlanta, Georgia. Mobley's family tree had shown four generations of violence; his attorneys contended that the crime was associated with his genetic make-up. The court dismissed the claim. But the act of introducing genetic defence into the courtroom had occurred for the first time in the annals of justice.

The basis of Mobley's defence was the discovery of a 'criminal gene' in a Dutch family. A sizeable Dutch family which was living across different regions of Netherlands realised that for 35 years most of the men had been aggressive and prone to violent, instinctive acts such as arson, murder attempts and rape. Wanting to know if there were any genetic reasons behind it, the women in the family had approached Han Brunner of the Institute of Genetics in Nijmegen, to examine the likelihood of a genetic predisposition towards violent behaviour. Brunner surprisingly discovered that a single gene in the family that was being passed by women and expressed in men was responsible for the family's violent behaviour.

Since the 1994 Stephen Mobley's lawsuit where the defence wanted to evaluate his client for MAOA deficiency, lawyers world over have increasingly been striving to bring genetic evidence such as MAOA deficiency into courtrooms. There are reports that in the last few years there have been over 200 cases in the USA alone where lawyers have attempted genetic evidence to support the fact that genes predisposed their clients to violent behaviour, drug or alcohol abuse.

There exist several forms of crime such as murder, rape, theft, burglary, cheating and arson which individuals with the criminal genes may commit but what all of them have in common is an innate immunity to perceive and a considerable craving to act on an impulse. The real task, therefore, is to find the gene that encourages risk-taking than look for a gene that controls arson or murder.

Scientists have identified two criminal genes, which predisposes individuals to violent behaviour. One of them is the MAOA gene, which codes for the enzyme monoamine oxidase A, which is essential for regulating the amount of dopamine and serotonin in the brain. The other gene is a variant of cadherin 13 or CDH13 gene that researchers attribute with substance abuse and attention deficit hyperactivity disorder (ADHD). Researchers have also linked this gene to impulse control in violent offenders.

It's not just that the biological traits like colour of hair, eyes, tallness and diseases are inheritable, the aggression gene is also inheritable. We now also have a gay gene and a maternal gene that confers maternal behaviour. Female mice deficient in this gene don't take care of their offspring and abandon their babies for dead.

Genes, besides determining the physical traits, also governs behaviour. Behaviour to the extent between 20 to 70 per cent is inheritable, but a genetic factor singly cannot account for a particular behaviour. Asians have genes that do not produce adequate levels of an enzyme called alcohol dehydrogenase. The westerners who lack this protective mechanism are therefore extremely vulnerable to alcoholism. Researchers have associated a single dopamine receptor D2 on DRD gene with alcoholism. Similarly, levels of MAOA have played a role in suicide and criminal behaviour.

But the biological root of behaviour is expressed through an individual's environment. Children born to parents who are Olympic athletes may not become Olympic athletes if we do not put them on proper training, just as children born to parents of high IQ may have low IQ if we do not give them an adequate education. A research study called the 'Dunedin Study' in New Zealand took into consideration maltreatment in childhood, which is a known environment factor and a genetic factor, MAOA gene expression. Researchers found a higher incidence of violent behaviour in men with the MAOA gene who had suffered maltreatment in their childhood. These men, who comprised 12 per cent of the group were responsible for 44 per cent convictions. A total of 85 per cent of those with the genetic and environmental indicators developed some type of criminal behaviour.

Tamil Nadu witnesses some of the most gruesome murders which involves inflicting multiple cut injuries with a machete which people colloquially call 'aruval'. The barbarity with which the rowdy gangs murder each other is mind-blowing. There has been no study to date to uncover the involvement of criminal genes in such brutal killings. Today, we have high-speed genome sequencing using which it would be possible to see if criminal genes are predisposing them to such ferocious murders. If such genes exist, then we could screen such individuals to give criminal prophylaxis: a treatment regimen adapted to their genetic and environmental situations. This would involve a combination of medications and counselling planned to prevent stimuli and to sustain their equilibrium by not turning on the criminal genes. Genes code for proteins which produce neurotransmitters such as dopamine and serotonin, the levels of which determine people's moods and behaviours so supplementing individuals with desirable neurotransmitters could go a long way in eliciting beneficial behaviour. One such biomedical program which was launched in the USA and later withdrawn is the Federal Violence Initiative.

The notion that crime, genetics and race might be correlated has particularly infuriated both proponents and opponents of 'genetic determinism'. There is a great deal of concern that such cases could lead to genetic determinism – an idea that genes determine the behaviour of an individual. Should a court give males a shorter sentence because they possess a Y chromosome and perpetrate 90 per cent of all murders? Is the Y chromosome which only the males possess liable for the murder? Similarly, skin colour is a genetic trait; more blacks end up in jails than whites. Then does that mean more black people engage in crimes because of their genes?

A book called *The Bell Curve* written by two right wing scientists Richard Hernstein and Charles Murray contends that IQ has a genetic basis which accounts for innate differences between IQs of the races. Low IQ people, the book says, are more prone to perpetrate crimes because they lack foresight and cannot understand that stealing from someone is immoral.

Going by the contentions and judgements mentioned above, we seem to be strolling towards a genetics-based criminal law system. Indirect genetic connections between crime and circumstances such as alcoholism and antisocial behaviours are being created, and genetic justifications are being extended to exonerate the accused at trial. The new system would divert the focus from liability based on an individual's mental state to a genetic, physiological frontage. Genes would play a more significant role in deducing the predispositions of behaviour and the scope of criminal responsibility. For instance, we might end up expecting individuals with 'aggressive genes' to act violently and consequently deal with them differently and leniently than those who do not have such genetic anomalies. We could end up submitting genetics as a defence against criminal charges and use genetic data as a tool to forecast the future violent behaviour of an accused. Eventually, genetics would evolve into an exculpatory component in convicting decisions and gene therapy would become a possibility in the rehabilitation of convicted criminals.

Finally, just as how we have genes in our genome for physical traits like eye colour, height and hair colour and behavioural traits such as altruism and conscientiousness, we could also have spiritual genes in our DNA. Teilhard de Chardin, a French priest, said, 'We are not human beings having a spiritual experience; rather, we are spiritual beings having a human experience.' If so, could it be that the 98 per cent of the DNA that we have that is believed to be non-functional or non-coding be associated with our spiritual nature?

Chapter 39
LAW ENFORCEMENT DURING A PANDEMIC

A law and order bundobust can get schemed and is, to a large extent, predictable, but a pandemic is entirely unpredictable. None or few people or few hundreds may die during a law and order situation, but thousands or millions could die in a pandemic. The worst flu pandemic in contemporary history was the 'Spanish flu' of 1918–19, which exterminated 50 million people worldwide. A pandemic is a public health problem. Why would it be a police problem? Whenever anything unpleasant happens, who do people reach out to? The local public health officer? Few know the number of the public health department, but most of them know how to get in touch with the police. A pandemic becomes a police dilemma because during pandemics police besides enforcement of the law would be expected to enforce public health orders such as quarantines, closure of establishments and travel restrictions. They would also be needed to secure the perimeter of contaminated areas, obtain healthcare facilities, control crowds, investigate any infraction of social distancing protocols, investigate escape of infected victims from quarantines, act on rumourmongers and provide security to hospitals and medical supplies.

Planning for a pandemic or any other public health emergency is like any law and order problem or a major bundobust. Both deal with containment and prevention of spread and protection of the people. The main difference being that a law and order problem is local while a pandemic is global. In a typical law and order situation, if the situation worsens, it would be possible to augment the deployment, but as a pandemic involves a nation in entirety and as the pandemic would also take its toll of police personnel, there is no way to predict how it will unfold. We can prepare a bundobust scheme for law and order situations, but nobody has any clue how the contagion will tear through the population to visualise and outline a bundobust scheme. A pandemic would be more challenging than a worst law and order situation as the police would have to deal with a public health emergency with a workforce that is depleting by the day and with fresh challenges mounting by the day. Keeping this in mind, the police leadership would have to prepare for the maintenance of law and order with minimum deployment for long periods. As the pandemic influenza comes in waves, each lasting approximately eight weeks, the police leaders would have to assess, rework the plan and course correct to address the waves as and when they emerge.

In a pandemic situation, there would be a need for the police to coordinate its response rapidly with public health and medical officials, many of whom they would not have interacted with previously. Hence, states while formulating pandemic plans should assign specific roles for police. Most times, the plans merely mention that police will carry out their usual duties, aiding and bolstering other agencies where possible. Such lack of specificity could mean police response can be flexible, or that their role could change over a period of time. Vague and ambiguously defined roles could translate into unimaginable expectations from the public, which could throw the police into an overwhelm. In the thick of a pandemic, police would be compelled to engage with the public health officials on wide-ranging matters and lack of clarity of police role during such occasions could give rise to turf wars.

Knowing well that law enforcement resources during a pandemic may get overwhelmed, police may have to take steps to balance law and order responsibilities with recently added public health obligations, all of which police may have to achieve with a diminished workforce as police personnel and their family members could get infected and get unwell. Police organisations may, therefore, have to prepare a plan which readies the department to meet the eventuality, a plan which protects police personnel through the creation of awareness and training along with a plan to protect the community which is maintaining public order during the crisis.

During a pandemic, it may become incumbent upon the police to do many things in different ways to beat the contagion. Police would be required to maintain absolute hygiene in the police station premises by extra cleaning. As the infection spreads, the police may see their ranks getting sick. Hence police may have to cut access to police stations and handle complaints safely. A pandemic may require the police to think differently. It may require the police to restrict access of members of the public to police stations by encouraging them to prefer complaints through social media platforms such as WhatsApp calls or Facebook posts or phone calls. Police may have to take a call to act only on serious offences by taking necessary precautions while deferring action on less severe offences after recording the same. During a pandemic, police should stop arresting people for minor crimes as police would have to shift resources and adjust priorities to maintain law and order while doing their best to prevent infection among police personnel and suspects. The idea behind it being to minimise the number of arrests and thereby minimise the risk to the police personnel. The police may expose themselves to the risk of infection in the process of an arrest, in transporting an arrestee and in bringing them to a police station. It may be better for the police to not enforce the local and special laws such as offences against gambling, illegal lotteries, gutkha and other petty offences as this would amount to inviting trouble into the police stations by way of infection. Police may have to do some out-of-the-box thinking, rely more on spot fines, discretionary powers and other modes of criminal action or disposal. Police while effecting arrests should wear prescribed Police Protection Equipment (PPE) and produce the arrested persons before a doctor before bringing them into the premises of a police station for recording the arrest. While imposing the Janata curfew, police had to face some unforeseen challenges as some tea shops and mutton shops wanted to keep their shops open, because the shopkeepers felt that their freedom was being curtailed. The shopkeepers resented the police and were sceptical of the curfew's value.

Many policing tasks raise the risk of infection. Breathalysers are a case in point. In the districts that come under me, I have got all the breathalysers withdrawn and got them centrally deposited after proper sterilisation to prevent them from being used. Government has done well by ordering the closure of all watering holes like pubs, clubs and bars. It would be a good idea to get all the TASMAC shops closed as well. When the sale of liquor gets shut down completely, there would be no necessity for police to deal with breathalysers and drunken driving offences. This one step alone could go a long way in minimising infection.

During a pandemic, it would be better if the traffic police refrained from booking routine traffic violations and instead concentrated on ensuring the unhindered movement of ambulances and arranging vehicles for the transport of sick to hospitals and quarantine centres. We may have to draft the traffic police and police from neighbourhood police stations for 'high-visibility patrols' to reassure the anxious public and to regulate queues as some businesses would close their doors and grocery stores could attract long lines. As the pandemic progresses, the police may also become involved in transporting very sick and dead to the hospital. Police may also get asked to transport medical equipment, supplies and pharmaceutical samples. Knowing how to transport these items safely is essential and failing to do this correctly might itself increase the risk of infection. Policing protocols during pandemics, therefore, would depend on the cause and level of the threat, and the potential risk to the responding police personnel.

Nature of the police job requires frequent and close contact with the public, which makes it extremely challenging for the police to practise social distancing. Police belong to the society and come from the same community hence infection among the police is likely to be as high as within the society. As police have the most significant engagement with the community, the frontline officers could suffer from disproportionately higher infection causing high absenteeism due to more exposure to the virus than others, which is why, police may have to game out scenarios where about 50 per cent of the workforce is unavailable because of illness.

During an outbreak like COVID-19, we must permit no police personnel to work while sick, as contagious diseases can spread quickly through an organisation and most preventive measures are not effective in a work environment. Coronavirus spreads through the air, through hand contact, and on environmental surfaces. A few police personnel working for a few hours while sick can pass the disease to many others. Soon, a significant proportion of the department and population in the station limits could be sick, too.

Quarantine and curfew may reduce crime, but pandemics often end up providing opportunities for new types of crimes. Quacks who promise miraculous cures surface, and rumour-mongers work overtime to create panic and anxiety in the minds of the people. As social distancing and isolation would require people to stay at home, this would bring opportunities for criminals to target and loot empty shops and factories in the streets. As families are forced to stay at home, there is a likelihood of an increase in cases of domestic violence because of a prolonged interaction between spouses bringing out old resentments and hurt feelings of the past leading to arguments and eventually to aggression. And out in the streets, there could be violence and protests because of scarcities of food and medical supplies brought about by pandemics. Police would, therefore, have to devise strategies and new approaches to deal with it.

During a pandemic, police may also have to manage the concerns of the population they are policing by devising public communication strategies. Police may have to invite public health officials to address the residents through local television channels and radio in which local police DSPs or Inspectors could share their plans and preparations to face the pandemic. It's a good idea for the police to consider collaboration with local chambers of commerce, religious heads and heads of local educational institutions. Enlisting local volunteers such as the Friends of Police and NGOs to chip in to render help in disseminating information and extending help could also prove valuable.

The coronavirus has unleashed enormous fear, panic and uncertainty in the minds of the people. In the present times, mere contemplation on the statement that 'We are not human beings having a spiritual experience but that we are spiritual beings having a human experience' can provide immense solace and peace. Fear and insecurity vanish when we let our perspective shift from ego to spirit. All the gloom and despair cast by the pandemic can get dispelled when we realise that we are eternal and infinite souls.

Chapter 40
POLICING THE PANDEMIC WITH TECHNOLOGICAL INNOVATIONS

In1918, the Spanish flu outbreak which took away the lives of 15 million Indians devastated India. When the flu made its way into India from abroad through the Bombay port, it first infected the seven police sepoys deployed at the Bombay docks forcing them to gain admission into the police hospital with the symptoms of 'Bombay Fever'. The present outbreak of the coronavirus in the country and the entire world has once again forced the police to assume the role of frontline combatants automatically. It has also inflicted a heavy toll on them.

Massive challenges encountered by law enforcement agencies all over the world since the onset of the present coronavirus pandemic have forced them to develop ways of providing service to citizens without endangering their own lives. Particularly in India, policing a pandemic can be extremely challenging with a police–population ratio of about 192 (192 policemen per 100,000 people). Hence, technology could play a vital role in supplementing and complementing the shortage of manpower. Technology has played a significant role in this effort all over the world. The technological infrastructure that got created by different police organisations around the world has been crucial to their pandemic response.

While such technologies, on the one hand, can play a positive role and reduce the need for direct physical policing, on the other hand, they can prove Orwellian by turning into a tool of spying and repression.

Police, by deploying technology, have mitigated the effects of the coronavirus pandemic to a substantial extent. The 2011 Hollywood film *Contagion* hauntingly foretold the consequences of the virus outbreak, which we are witnessing today. Still, the fallout which we are glimpsing today is much less severe than what got exhibited in the movie because of the availability and use of technologies that are proving to be significant in combating the coronavirus.

After the onset of the pandemic, few police stations witnessed a wave of innovation, especially in Delhi and other parts of India. Sensor-based contactless sanitiser dispensing machines, AI-enabled thermal cameras, video intercoms and UV disinfectant boxes to sterilise the documents found their way into some police stations. Some such innovations came from constables and not from high-tech companies. An innovative constable from Tamilnadu Special Police (TSP) in Tamilnadu developed a contactless sensor-based sanitisation machine which the TSP have installed and are using at their establishments.

To contain the pandemic in Mumbai, police deployed drones and AI technology to monitor the densely populated neighbourhoods of the city to enforce social distancing. In some severely affected areas in other countries, drones are also being used to transport both medical equipment and patient samples, saving time and enhancing the speed of deliveries, while preventing contamination of medical samples. In a few countries, drones powered with FRT were also being used to broadcast warnings to the citizens to not step out of their homes, and even to reprimand them for not wearing face masks. Antwork, a group company of Japanese drone-maker Terra Drone, carried medical samples and other essential materials in Xinchang when the city was grappling with the virus.

During the current pandemic, drone technology is also being used to track large gatherings, to minimise physical contact and to monitor narrow by-lanes where police vehicles cannot enter. They are also being used to spray disinfectants in public spaces and residential colonies.

In India, lockdown was announced to curb the COVID-19 outbreak. To ensure that the lockdown gets strictly implemented, police actively patrolled the roads to make sure nobody breaks the lockdown rules and flouts any norms. Amid the lockdown, to aid citizens who need to travel in case of an emergency or urgent situation, the Tamilnadu government introduced the TN ePass system, which was QR code enabled. This colour-coded pass could get verified in the field by the police or other allowed officials for authenticity by using any commonly available QR code scanner apps for smartphones.

During the current pandemic, positioning technology is being used in China to pinpoint the hotspots and carry out containment of the same. In China, BeiDou, the country's own global navigation satellite system (GNSS) constellation, helped track patients and affected places, thus containing the virus, apart from analysing the pattern of the outbreak. With the help of precise data and precise mapping and imagery, China could build thousands of new makeshift hospitals across the country. BeiDou also has an RDSS (Radiodetermination Satellite Service) that broadcasts information real-time, using which the Chinese government could expedite the construction of two new hospitals in Wuhan. In Ruichang, Jiangxi province, the police forces used BeiDou-enabled drones for monitoring congested public areas. BeiDou was also used to send emergency messages to over 6 million connected vehicles swiftly.

To mitigate the pandemic and detect people infected with the virus, several countries have tracked smartphone data. It has become mandatory for mobile service providers in several countries to save two years of data of their subscribers, including locational data. Such data would be crucial in analysing the travel history of the person who has tested positive and spot any person who could have come in close range of the infected person. The Indian government, on 6 April, launched the Aarogya Setu app, similar to Singapore's Trace Together, for contact tracing. The Tamilnadu police developed a contact tracing technology using GPS technology.

We also got citizen and reservation data from airlines and the railways to track suspected infections. An app was created in Tamilnadu using geofencing technology to ensure and enforce the quarantine. Geofencing forges a virtual geographic boundary, setting off alarms whenever a quarantined person violates the quarantine. Similarly, as many in other states under quarantine were not isolating themselves, many police organisations launched quarantine monitoring apps. Two Bangalore- based companies Vijna Labs and Pixxon AI developed law enforcement tools that aided in quarantine enforcement and tracing. Delhi acquired the Automated Facial Recognition System, which they used to monitor crowds, from Innefu Labs.

China, by joining hands with Alibaba and Tencent, has developed a colour-coding system which tracks millions of people daily. The system assigns three colours to people – green, yellow and red – based on their travel and medical histories. Whether a person should get quarantined or allowed in public spaces is being decided based on the colour code. Only the people who get assigned a green colour code are being permitted in public places after using the given QR code at metro stations, offices and other public places. The government is using this data to discover the number of people with whom an infected person was in close contact to order them to self-isolate themselves.

Further, in China, facial recognition-powered CCTV cameras have also been installed at almost every quarantine centre. Several police agencies have developed dashboards using big data, Face recognition and infrared temperature detection techniques. Chinese AI companies like SenseTime and Hanwang Technology have come up with a special facial recognition technology that can recognize people even when they are wearing masks.

During the prevailing pandemic, the Chennai police deployed robots in the containment areas. They equipped the robot with a camera, and it could interact with the people living in the containment zones to create awareness and also sanitise the area. A hospital in Wuhan was being fully staffed by robots. The robots are carrying out all the services in the hospital.

During the pandemic, privacy issues came to the fore. They sparked much media attention because of the use of AI tools such as the Clearview AI by the Canadian and the American police agencies. Clearview could match uploaded photographs with billions of other photos scraped mainly from social media and those stored on Amazon servers. The technology transgressed the privacy laws by exploiting the biometric data of people without their consent. The Congress in Kerala has also alleged that the collection of phone details by police violated the privacy of an individual as it went against the Supreme Court's ruling in the *K. S. Puttaswamy* case.

Advanced countries are also monitoring social media and listening technologies. These technologies use natural language processing to identify and monitor keywords not protected by privacy settings on social platforms. Both tech companies and police have been contending that it can deem social media accounts not set to private as publicly available information, or open-source, and accessible for anyone to see.

The pandemic has uncovered the vulnerability of the human species to the coronavirus. The only redemption, thanks to technological evolution, is that we are better equipped than ever to respond to the pandemic. In 2002 during the SARS outbreak, it took over two years to decipher the genome; in contrast, they decoded the genome of the coronavirus in a month, thanks to the advancements in technology. Had it not been for the advancements in the technology, humanity would have been in the thick of an incredible crisis as depicted in the Hollywood movie of 2011 titled *Contagion*. By deploying the latest technology available with us today, we have mitigated the effects of the virus to a great extent and profiled the people at risk.

Chapter 41
IS CORONAVIRUS A NATURAL MUTANT OR A MANMADE BIOWEAPON?

Movies have prophesied some far-fetched things that have unbelievably come true. Stanley Kubrick's *2001: A Space Odyssey* (1968) foresaw video calls and Siri-like AI. It also anticipated space tourism, on which Richard Branson and Elon Musk are working. Ridley Scott's *Blade Runner* (1982) had its characters making video calls even when the technology didn't exist. The *Terminator* (1984) predicted military drones while *Star Trek* (1966) predicted the cell phone; inventor Martin Cooper, whose team at Motorola built the first cell, had confessed that Captain Kirk's communicator had influenced him to create the cell phone. The Hollywood film *Airplane II: The Sequel* (1982), accurately forecasted full-body scanners at airports of the sort that are in use today. Back in 2011, when I watched the movie *Contagion* at a theatre, it never occurred to me that the fictionalised deadly virus would come true one day. Strangely, fiction has turned into a reality today with the Coronavirus outbreak unfolding precisely like the plot in the American movie *Contagion*.

In the movie, after Beth Emhoff (Gwyneth Paltrow) returns to Minnesota from a Hong Kong business trip, she speculates the flu-like symptoms she is suffering from to be jet lag. However, two days later, Beth is dead, and doctors tell her stunned husband (Matt Damon) that they have no clue what had killed her. Her young son later dies on the same day. Soon, many others exhibit identical symptoms, and a global pandemic explodes. The similarities of the outbreak in the movie and the world today are mind-blowing, China is the epicentre of the epidemic in both and bats have got implicated in the spread of the virus in both.

Interestingly, the movie shows Beth falling ill and spreading the infection in the USA after catching and carrying the microbe from 'Hong Kong' while on a business trip. As the film unfolds further, it shows trees being cut in a bats' habitat to construct a factory. Most bats get killed as a result,

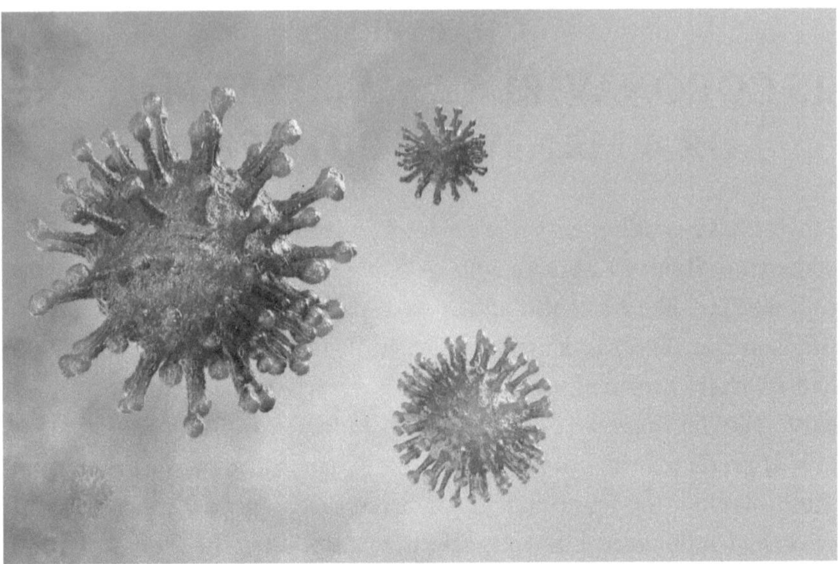

Corona Borealis Studio/Shutterstock.com

but one surviving bat flies near a pigsty and drops a fruit which falls and gets mixed in the pig feed that gets eaten by the pigs. A pig from the pigsty gets slaughtered in a popular restaurant where Beth after enjoying a good meal shakes hands with the chef who has got contaminated with the virus during the preparation of pork, kicking off a global pandemic.

Coronavirus is so-named because the spikes that protrude from its cell membranes 'resemble the sun's corona'. The outbreak which began in Wuhan, China, has since spread to every province of China and beyond.

The initial symptoms of the virus include a dry cough, a fever, shortness of breath and a sore throat. While several of those infected have exhibited only mild symptoms, some have developed fluid in the lungs consistent with viral pneumonia. The virus is more likely to advance into severe sickness or prove deadly among older patients or those with weakened immune systems. Coronavirus has no specific cure as it is a viral infection. Antibiotics won't help. The best way to prevent disease is to avoid being exposed to this virus. People should wash hands often with soap and water for at least 20 seconds using an alcohol-based hand sanitiser that contains at least 60 per cent alcohol if soap and water are not available. They should avoid contact with their eyes, nose and mouth with unwashed hands. They should also avoid close contact with people who are sick. They should stay home when ill and cover a cough or sneeze with a tissue, then dispose of the tissue in the trash.

Although we know little about the novel Coronavirus researchers, say it shares similarities to Middle East respiratory syndrome (MERS) and severe acute respiratory syndrome (SARS), two similar infectious illnesses that emerged in the current decade that we have been able to manage. Between November 2002 and July 2003, an outbreak of SARS in southern China caused an eventual 8,098 cases, resulting in 774 deaths reported in 17 countries, with a preponderance of cases in mainland China and Hong Kong (9.6% fatality rate). In late 2017, Chinese scientists tracked the virus through the intermediary of civets to cave-dwelling horseshoe bats in Yunnan province. MERS, meanwhile, was first detected in the Persian Gulf in 2012 and since then has witnessed erratic clusters of cases. Over the past eight years, there have been nearly 2,500 confirmed cases and over 850 deaths spread out over two dozen countries.

As far as Coronavirus is concerned, five South Asian countries, that is, Afghanistan, Bhutan, India, Nepal, and Pakistan share a combined 4,000 miles of border with China, where the virus emanated. As the Wuhan virus spreads during the incubation period, which spans anywhere from two days to two weeks, it appears that South Asia may see a surge in reported cases in the coming days. India, the region's biggest country because of poor health infrastructure might prove slow in diagnosing and reporting new cases, and also be ill-prepared to deal with a fast-mutating virus.

Conditions in India such as high population density, subtropical climatic conditions and inadequate sanitation facilities make India extremely susceptible and suitable for the spread of the Coronavirus. Insufficient medical facilities and non-availability of medical services in remote areas make the circumstances still more ideal for Wuhan flu to spread like wildfire. It's shocking but true that on average, a single government doctor serves nearly 12,000 people in India.

By the way, what is a Coronavirus? Is it a mutant, or a man-made bioweapon? There is a strong suspicion that the major world powers, China, Russia and the US, and some rogue nations like Syria, Iran and North Korea have biological weapons programs. A strain of any virus being researched, getting inadvertently released or smuggled out into the general population is a possibility. Experts do not debunk this possibility. *The Daily Mail* of the UK and several other newspapers have speculated that the Wuhan National Biosafety Laboratory, which opened in 2014 and is part of the Wuhan Institute of Virology, could be responsible for the spread of the virus and a prudent American newspaper has connected Coronavirus to China's 'biowarfare program'. In 2014, after the Ebola outbreak, some reports emerged in the media that the US Department of Defense had bioengineered the virus.

A former Israeli intelligence officer who everyone believes to be an expert in Virology claims that the Wuhan Institute of Virology had been engaged in the development of secret biological weapons for Chinese military and that the Coronavirus outbreak happened because of the escape of a biological weapon from a mystery lab in Wuhan.

In 1918, the world was witness to an influenza pandemic (January 1918–December 1920; colloquially known as Spanish flu) exactly a hundred years ago in which the Spanish flu virus, a variant of swine flu had infected about 500 million people worldwide and killed more people than both the world wars put together making it one of the deadliest epidemics in human history. Billy Corgan, the lead singer of famous 'Smashing Pumpkins' in his blog, had lamented that the swine flu virus was not a naturally occurring disease. He lamented that man created it to scare the hell out of people.

Billy Corgan's claim may be right or wrong, but back in 1957, swine flu virus had totally disappeared from the surface of our planet, but it brusquely re-emerged after 20 long years in 1977. Precisely at a time when

Omutninsk Chemical Factory in Soviet Russia was manufacturing large amounts of influenza vaccine and crop production bacteria overground, while plague and tularemia microbes were being researched in the heavily guarded underground facilities as a part of the Soviet bioweapon program. Some nations therefore presume that there was a deliberate release of swine flu virus, giving credence to the existence of a biological weapons program of Soviet Russians. Concomitantly, vaccine trials or a vaccine development trial going awry got considered as other plausible explanations for the 1977 epidemic. Still, some researchers believed that the swine flu virus might have found its way into the population after a lab worker might have accidentally broken the frozen vials containing the pathogen which the Russians preserved since the 1950s. In the recent past, several such bio-mishaps have happened with potentially fatal repercussions. In March 2013, officials at a high-security government research lab in Texas said they had lost a vial containing Guanarito virus, which causes 'bleeding under the skin, and in body cavities such as the mouth, eyes or ears'. They entrusted this matter to the FBI for investigation. Just a year later at the Pasteur Institute in Paris, more than a thousand vials containing the SARS virus went missing. These are deadly bio-toxins, which could become cataclysmic biological weapons if they landed by chance into the hands of terrorists. There have also been some spine-chilling news reports of various laboratory errors, such as a forgotten vial of smallpox found in an old freezer, and mishaps involving anthrax and bird-flu at the Centers for Disease Control and Prevention, in the USA.

With gene technology becoming less expensive, more accurate, and faster every year, it is becoming possible to create new and more virulent novel viruses. We recently saw an example of what this could look like when researchers in the Netherlands and the United States altered the genetic code of bird flu or avian influenza virus (HSN1) to make it more deadly. Though bird flu has a 70 per cent mortality rate, human to human transmission of the virus is not possible. But by tinkering the DNA and causing just four genetic mutations, the Dutch-American team could not only engineer a much more virulent strain with enhanced transmissibility to human beings but also transformed the virus into an incredible bioweapon. Although the original goal of the scientists was to study how quickly H5N1 might evolve to prevent its spread better, the genetically altered strain, which resulted proved that, if released, could cause a global epidemic.

Bioweapons may be a red herring. However, with Wuhan, some facts raise pertinent questions. The existence of the bsl-4 lab in Wuhan could be a coincidence, but the fact that the Wuhan Institute of Virology was researching novel Coronaviruses is too much of coincidence. Another mind-blowing point which raises questions pertains to the concerns raised by international scientists in 2017 regarding the Wuhan lab and China's lack of expertise and transparency in handling such deadly pathogens.

We have written much of human history in terms of an ongoing struggle of 'man against nature'. We have cast the forces of nature such as viruses, disease and pestilence in the role of an enemy of mankind. To survive, prosper and destroy others, we have been trying to conquer nature. It may seem like we have been winning battle after battle but we have been losing the war. There must have been a mistaken belief of having won the battle by creating the Wuhan virus. But nature has fought back. Do we launch a counterattack or surrender and accept that we can never conquer nature?

Chapter 42
BIOTERRORISM IN INDIA

Although bioterrorism might seem a problem beginning in the late 20th century, a short story, written by H.G. Wells in 1894, portended the threat of an attack with biological agents. It tells the tale of an anarchist who steals a vial of what he believes to be cholera bacilli to poison the water supply of the city of London. As predicted by Wells, several incidents of bioterrorism have been witnessed the world over, but there has not been a single documented case of bioterrorism in India to date. But there have been few incidents in the past that might have been biological attacks, given the fact that it is tough to differentiate natural epidemics from biological attacks. During the Indo-Pakistan war of 1965, a scrub typhus outbreak in northeastern India came under suspicion. Other cases which could not be officially confirmed as events of bio-terror include, the spread of bubonic plague in Surat in 1994 which caused several deaths, dengue hemorrhagic fever in Delhi in 1996, anthrax in Midnapur in 1999 and encephalitis in Siliguri in 2001 and an anthrax scare in 2001 at Mantralaya in Mumbai.

Recent Nipah virus outbreak which happened in 2018 in Perambra, Kerala has the physical attributes to serve as a potential agent of bioterrorism. The first human outbreak of Nipah virus was reported from Malaysia among pig farmers in 1998. The virus was named Nipah after the name of the village of 'Sungai Nipah', in Malaysia. There were several outbreaks in Bangladesh and the first reported outbreak was in 2001. There was an outbreak in Nadia, West Bengal in 2007. The present epidemic in India after nearly 11 years with a high case-fatality rate indicates that there is a total lack of healthcare systems preparedness and surveillance strategy.

India also appears ill-equipped to face the threat of bioterrorism, as was evident from the recent H1N1 epidemic, which claimed over 2,300 lives. We must know and get acquainted with this form of terror before it becomes an enormous challenge to our health department. Early detection

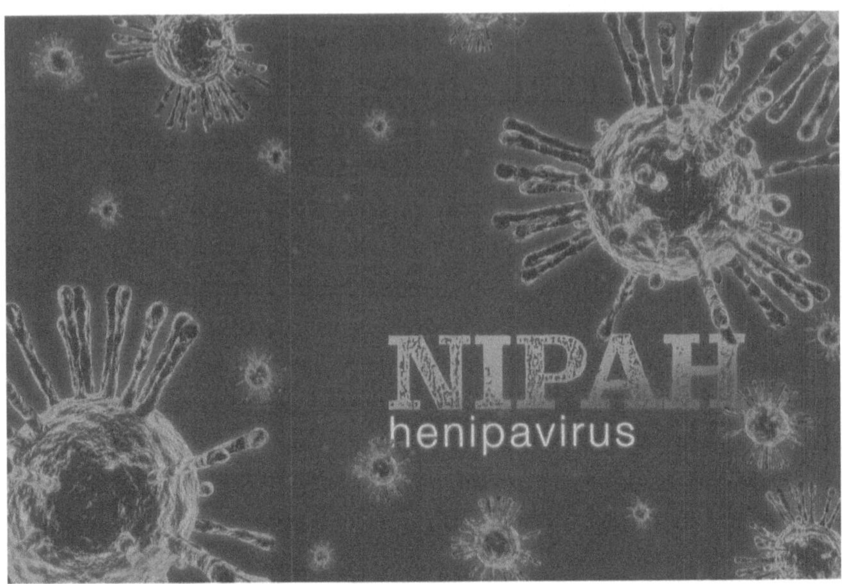

jakapan Chumchuen/Shutterstock.com

and quick response to bioterrorism are contingent on close cooperation between public health authorities and law enforcement; however, such collaboration is currently lacking.

The threat of bioterrorism is the most probable when compared to other weapons of mass destruction (WMDs), owing to rapid advancements in the field of synthetic biology besides the existence of hostile neighbours like China, Pakistan and Bangladesh. In 2002 at Kandahar, Afghanistan, the Pentagon detected anthrax at a suspected Al-Qaeda biological weapons site together with equipment conventionally used in biowarfare programme. Later some sketches and calculations to make helium-powered balloon bombs filled with anthrax was discovered in the Kabul office of an NGO headed by Bashiruddin Mahmood, one of the two Pakistani nuclear scientists arrested in Islamabad for questioning on their alleged links with Osama Bin Laden. Links of Al-Qaeda with four terrorist groups in India are well established. These groups are Lashkar-e-Taiba, Jaish-e-Mohammad, Harkat-ul-Jihad-ul-Islami and Harkat-ul-Mujahidin. On account of the close link of these terrorist groups with

Al-Qaeda, there is a real risk of these terrorist groups launching a biological attack in India in the future. Besides the above state actors, there are numerous non-state actors in India and her neighbourhood as well.

High population density and subtropical climatic conditions, coupled with poor hygiene and inadequate sanitation facilities, make India extremely susceptible and suitable for the spread of infectious diseases. Inadequate medical facilities and non-availability of medical services in remote areas make the circumstances still more ideal for contagious diseases to run like wildfire. It's shocking but true that on an average a single government doctor serves nearly 12,000 people.

On top of it all, any battle with bioterrorism is fraught with numerous challenges. The first and foremost challenge being the collection or isolation of the microbes and their identification. It's challenging to pinpoint the origin of infection or the site of an outbreak or arrive at a realisation that a bioterrorism attack has been unleashed on the population. Without such information, it would be challenging to combat the assault as we would fail to press into action the concerted efforts of various agencies entrusted with the responsibility. Insofar as preparedness of India to a bioterrorist attack is concerned, it's incredibly deficient from the viewpoint of infrastructure, trained personnel, scientific expertise and public education. The existent institutional mechanisms lack proper coordination to counter any bioterrorism attack.

The fact of the matter is that we have not had any bioterrorism attack so far, which could be the reason why we find ourselves complacent, making our country that much more vulnerable to unsuspecting attacks, thereby considerably endangering the lives. It's imperative that we learn and gear up fully before such an eventuality occurs and becomes a massive challenge to us. Early detection and rapid response to bioterrorism hinges upon close cooperation between public health authorities and law enforcement. However, we seem to be lacking such collaboration at the moment.

To keep India battle ready to counter a bioterrorism attack, the National Disaster Management Authority (NDMA), Government of India

(GoI) has proposed a model instrument where participation of both government and private sectors is a sine qua non to defeat any such attack. As epidemics have the potential to wreak havoc on a large scale like chemical and nuclear weapons, a multi-sector approach has been envisaged to be adopted. In India, several nodal ministries have been earmarked for dealing with epidemics caused by bioterrorism. The central departments which are involved are Ministry of Health and Family Welfare (MoH and FW) which is one of the main ministries tasked with providing directions and technical support for capacity building, surveillance and early detection of an outbreak. Health ministry also helps in the deployment of Rapid Response Teams, human resources and logistic support. The Ministry of Home Affairs (MHA) is another nodal ministry which works in conjunction with MoH and FW. MHA is responsible for the assessment of the threat, intelligence inputs and implementation of preventive mechanisms. National Disaster Response Force (NDRF) is a specialised force constituted under MHA to deal with chemical, biological, radiological and nuclear (CBRN) attacks. It consists of 12 battalions, three each from the BSF and CRPF and two each from CISF, ITBP and SSB.

Each battalion has 18 independent specialist search and rescue parties of 45 personnel each including engineers, technicians, electricians, dog squads and medical/paramedics. The total strength of each battalion is 1,149. All the 12 battalions have been equipped and trained to respond to natural as well as human-made disasters. Battalions are also trained and equipped for response during CBRN emergencies. Besides, the Ministry of Defence (MOD) manages the matters and consequences of biowarfare. Clinical case management is backed by the Indian army, as they have several hospitals nationwide. They use ambulances, aircraft and ships to handle casualties. The Defence R&D Organization (DRDO) is actively pitched into developing protective systems and equipment for troops to contend against nuclear, biological and chemical warfare. The other ministries which are also responsible are the Ministry of Environment, Forests and Climate Change for evaluation of short and long-term consequences, the Ministry of Agriculture, the Department of Animal Husbandry, Dairying and Fisheries, Urban or Rural Development Ministry and Department of

Drinking Water Supply, Ministry of Railways and so on. NDMA has been made responsible for promulgating policies on management and approving plans of different ministries. And the National Crisis Management Committee (NCMC) coordinates and monitors responses in crises especially in disasters. It provides strong coordination and implementation of relief measures during disasters.

In order to enhance the preparedness of India towards bioterror attacks, we should emulate the West – to formulate training exercises and implement technologies that are being adopted in countries like the USA and Europe. For instance, the state of New York, in September 2016, held the fourth edition of its massive emergency response training exercise called the Excelsior Challenge, 'which is a training exercise designed for police and first responders to become familiar with techniques and practices should a real incident occur'. In 1999, the University of Pittsburgh's Center for Biomedical Informatics deployed the first automated bioterrorism detection system, called Real-Time Outbreak Disease Surveillance (RODS), which collects data from many data sources and uses them to detect a possible bioterrorism event at the earliest possible moment.

The city of New York has developed unique software to combat bioterrorism. The tool called the New York City Syndromic Surveillance System tracks disease progression throughout the city of New York. We would do better if we conduct exercises like 'Dark Winter' to know our preparedness and inadequacies in overcoming bioterror attacks.

Bioterrorism is a low-probability, high-impact event. Biological agents imperil human, livestock and crop health, and thereby hurt the Indian economy. It's therefore imperative that we enhance our understanding of them with the intention of dealing with them effectively. Political awareness and public participation are indispensable for threat alleviation. In a country like India, where the population is on the increase by the day and has exceeded a billion, preventive strategies and efforts against bioterrorism require to be strengthened, improved and made useful. Such preparedness against bioterrorism will also capacitate our populace against natural epidemics, thus transforming India into a resilient society.

Author Damian Mark Smyth says, 'We're One, we've always been One, we'll always be One until we think we are not.' And herein lies our challenge, we are one, but we think we are separate; we have forgotten our Oneness. As a result of our mistaken belief that we are separate, we have created an imaginary world of duality which is leading to terrorism, war, conflict and suffering. When all the people on this planet realise they are One, there will be nothing to fight against and no strife.

Chapter 43
THE THREAT OF AGROTERRORISM

Describing real-life scenes from Bengal famine, Brigg's, a British United Press New Delhi correspondent in a newspaper in September 1942 wrote: At least 150 people are dying daily in Calcutta from starvation and the accompanying diseases of cholera and dysentery. In a sunrise walk, I found people dead on the pavement by the dozens. Thousands more may die before they gather the harvest in. I saw children with bloated, empty stomachs, mothers whose breasts had collapsed, men wailing the one word that means the unattainable - rice. I saw scenes of slow death.

Crop diseases have been deemed to rival an agroterrorism event or military action and the example of Bengal brown spot disease of rice in India, in 1942–1943, serves as an illustration of how similar and devastating an agroterror event could be if it were to be unleashed.

Agroterrorism is a deliberate introduction of an animal or plant disease with an aim to generate fear, cause economic losses, and/or undermine social stability. Terrorists know of the ease of creating serious economic insecurity through intentional introduction of these diseases.

Agroterrorism is an issue that compels considerable attention than it's being allotted at present. A low-cost agroterror attack could be an extremely devastating way of destroying our economy. Agroterrorism is an aspect of bioterrorism whose goal is agricultural sabotage.

Compared to bioterror, agroterror is appallingly easy. Access to these hazardous pathogens is straightforward, as we can get them from infected animals in many parts of the world, and agent dissemination is simple and could take place in a variety of venues.

Terrorists have a vast choice of the bioagents bulk of which are environmentally sturdy, which can easily be smuggled into any country with no vaccination programmes being focussed on them. The food chain offers an excellent route for inflicting human casualties. Most animal and plant pathogens are non-infectious to humans, which makes it easier for terrorists to handle and work with. Livestock is the primary vector for pathogenic transmission; there being no weaponisation impediment to overcome.,

Terrorists or even lone wolves could, in theory, acquire and use this kind of agent more easily than other biological agents that are pathogenic to humans. A group or an individual may not need laboratories to acquire these agents. Many of these are non-pathogenic to human beings. We do not have a strategy in case of an act of agroterrorism because we do not seem to expect one despite facing a significant threat we are still to take suitable action.

Agriculture, with its allied sectors, is the biggest source of employment in India. Seventy per cent of its rural homes still depend chiefly on agriculture for their livelihood, with 82 per cent of farmers being small and marginal. In 2017–18, total food grain production was assessed at 275 million tonnes. India is the largest producer (25% of global production), the consumer (27% of world consumption) and importer (14%) of pulses in the world. An assault on our food supply, for example, would lead not only to direct fallouts on human and animal health but also inflict a startling long-term psychological and economic effect on the nation's farming community. India has 6 to 7 million tons of food supplies, but these would be wiped out by two or three consecutive crop losses in different parts of the country, tilting the equilibrium from self-sufficiency to inadequacy. An attack during a lean period could exacerbate the problem beyond repair.

An important plant pathogen *Cochliobolus miyabeanus* was a significant cause of Bengal famine of 1943, where the crop yield declined by 40 per cent to 90 per cent, and the death of 2 million people was documented. It is a tool for agroterrorism. This pathogen causes rice seedling mortality rate up to 60 per cent in the Philippines and India and Nigeria; it can reduce total crop yield by up to 40 per cent. The USA used this a bioweapon when attacking Japan during the World War II.

Potato blight gave rise to a terrible famine in Ireland in 1845. The corm leaf blight of 1970 cost the United States an estimated $1 billion. An attack of avian influenza of foreign origin cost Pennsylvania $86 million. In contrast, some 639 acts of terror by the Earth Liberation Front and the Animal Liberation Front since 1996 caused 'only' $40 million in property damage according to Federal Bureau of Investigation estimates.

Mycotoxins are toxic metabolites secreted by certain fungi naturally which contaminate many crop plants. For instance, at least 15 different Fusarium species colonise small grain cereals including wheat, barley, oats and maize, producing important mycotoxins such as aflatoxin and T2 toxin. These are desirable agents in a bioterrorist attack, leading to loss of both harvest and quality. T2 toxin, sometimes known as 'yellow rain', is believed to have been put to use during the Vietnam war.

Agroterrorism has existed throughout history. In 1952, Mau poisoned cattle in Kenya by employing a plant toxin from the African milk bush plant; in 1985, the USDA contended that Mexican contract workers were involved in deliberately dispersing screwworm (*Cochliomyia hominivorax*) among livestock; In 2000, Palestinian media reported that Israeli settlers released sewer water into Palestinian agricultural fields. In 2011, a court sentenced a person to prison for endangering US and UK livestock with the deliberate spread of foot-and-mouth disease virus.

During the World War I, Germany attempted to attack draft horses utilising biological agents like *Bacillus anthracis* (anthrax) and *Burkholderia mallei* (glanders), and between the World Wars, both Germany and France researched agricultural pathogens such as rinderpest virus, *Phytophthora infestans* (causing late blight), *Puccinia spp.* (causing wheat rust), and numerous beetlepests. Various agroterrorism agents and diseases have been researched or weaponised in Russia (1935–1992), including African swine fever virus, avian influenza virus, *B. anthracis*, *Brucella spp.* (causing brucellosis), *Burkholderia mallei*, *Chlamydophila psittaci* (causing psittacosis), FMD virus, and the plant pathogenic viruses brown grass mosaic virus, potato virus Y, tobacco mosaic virus, *Puccinia sorghi* (causing maize rust), and *Puccinia graminis* (causing wheat stem rust). In the US too different biological agroterrorism agents were investigated or weaponised from 1943 to 1969 such as avian influenza virus (causing fowl plague), *B. anthracis*, *Brucella spp.*, *B. mallei*, *Chlamydophila psittaci* and *Phytophthora infestans* and the causative agents of wheat blast, wheat stem rust, rice blast and rice brown spot disease. In Iraq, aflatoxins and the causative agents of cover smut/bunt of wheat were experimented or weaponised. After World War II, the research on plant pathogens and anti-crop weapons progressed in several countries.

It is estimated that 75 per cent of the diseases that have arisen in the last 25 years are zoonotic in their origin and around 80 per cent of the top biological threat agents are zoonotic diseases. Zoonotic disease is an infectious disease that is transmitted between species from animals to humans or from humans to animals. Eleven of the last 12 outbreaks of global concern are zoonotic in inception. Some of these diseases, even if they do not make people sick, can present a challenge to the health and well-being of our human population. For example, foot and mouth disease or FMD affects only cows, swine, sheep, goats, deer and similar species. But the disease could have a very dramatic effect on our domestic and global economy. Should the disease stabilise itself in our wild species, such as feral swine, it would be almost impossible to eradicate.

Vectors, such as insects or ticks, are among the most common conduits for disease transmission from animals to humans. Diseases transmitted by vectors are especially difficult to control, as shown by the rapid spread of the West Nile virus, which has so far infected over 1.2 million Americans. Other examples of vector-borne diseases include plague, tularemia, and hemorrhagic viruses, like Rift Valley fever. Current examples of this hazard are the epidemic of chikungunya virus in the Indian Ocean, the leap of Rift Valley fever from Africa to Saudi Arabia, and eruptions of dengue along the US–Mexican border. While it is difficult to anticipate when and where the next zoonotic event will occur, all the crucial factors are in place to guarantee that this new era of emerging zoonoses – naturally or deliberately caused –will prevail or even speed up in the times to come.

Brucellosis, a zoonotic bacterial disease that devastates livestock worldwide is classifiable as a potential bioweapon. It causes substantial illness and death in animals and humans. We have made significant progress in eliminating brucellosis from cattle and swine populations over the past 50 years and in helping to control it in some wildlife species.

The Rift Valley fever virus transmitted by mosquitoes is a biological threat agent of high priority. Introduction of this pathogen, intentionally or even accidentally, would be catastrophic to the agricultural economy. The disease has already moved out of East Africa into Egypt, Yemen and Saudi Arabia.

Bacillus anthracis is a spore-forming bacterium found in soil and can cause a disease known as anthrax – in livestock and other animals. We could use anthrax spores as an agroterrorism agent in several ways. Without treatment, the mortality rate for pulmonary anthrax is 70–80 per cent. Most times, pulmonary and gastrointestinal anthrax is fatal if not treated immediately.

In the preceding five years, 'food defence' has received increasing interest in the counterterrorism and bioterrorism communities. Laboratory and reaction capability are being boosted to deal with the reality of agroterrorism, and national response plans now integrate agroterror. The vigilance from our farmers will be crucial. We would expect farmers to perform as both first responders and first preventers. They would be the first to recognise the emergence of zoonotic disease, the first to report an agroterrorist attack and the first to respond to it.

Agroterrorism has never been extensively used because accomplishing a political shift through terrorism requires more than the destruction of food and livestock; it requires a shocking loss of lives to provoke a modification in government policy. While agriculture may not be a terrorist's first choice because it lacks the 'shock factor' of more traditional terrorist targets, many analysts consider it a reasonable secondary goal. Therefore, agroterror could, however, be a secondary modus operandi to destabilise a society much more after a conventional attack. As this type of attack is dirt cheap, this form of attack gives terrorists a high cost/benefit payoff to overcome high power asymmetry. Further, in cities, population density is high. Therefore, extremists find it ideal, but farming gets spread out, making it difficult for terrorists to infect crops in vast areas. Yet another drawback of Agroterrorism is its difficulty in gaining the attention of media due to its inadequate visibility

Thus, agroterrorism is much more preferable to animal activists and other radical groups who aspire to destroy property than to al-Qaeda or other international terrorists who aim to destroy lives.

Whether a terrorist or a terrorist group uses bio-agents or bombs, they do so because they do not have an awareness of existence present everywhere, a sense of compassion or caring for the whole of humanity. Agroterrorism or terrorism in the name of religion or ideology exists because terrorists have not understood the spiritual dimension of their lives. Once they gain this consciousness, their awareness could become uplifted, leading to extinguishment of extremist tendencies.

Chapter 44
THE PROBLEM OF ENVIRONMENTAL CRIME

A 2004 American science-fiction film *The Day After Tomorrow* directed and produced by Roland Emmerich highlights what the world would look like if the greenhouse effect and global warming continued under the onslaught of environmental crimes being perpetrated by humankind. The film's protagonist, a climatologist named Professor Jack Hall, discovers that due to global warming, the polar ice caps are melting, lowering ocean temperatures and triggering a massive climate shift causing many natural disasters and eventually a new ice age.

Our environment has been the victim of all sorts of attacks. As a result, people are experiencing both the subtle and stark effects of climate change. Most of the attacks are human-made such as wars, explosions and chemical spills .

If there could be one person who could qualify as the world's worst environmental criminal, it would probably be Saddam Hussein. During the 1991 Persian Gulf War, Hussein knew he would lose Kuwait, so he sent men to blow up Kuwaiti oil wells. Approximately 600 were set ablaze, and the fires – towering infernos – burned for seven months plunging the Gulf in poisonous smoke, soot and ash. On 26 April 1986, one of the reactors at the Chernobyl power plant in Ukraine exploded. This was yet another human-made environmental disaster resulting in a nuclear meltdown that sent massive amounts of radiation into the atmosphere, reportedly more than the fallout from Hiroshima and Nagasaki. Around midnight on 2 December 1984, another human-made accident at a Union Carbide pesticide plant in Bhopal, India, resulted in 45 tons of poisonous methyl isocyanate escaping from the facility. Thousands died within hours.

As a result, Interpol decided to fight environmental crime in 1992. Crimes committed in violation of environmental laws are called ecological

Stephane Bidouze/Shutterstock.com

crimes. Interpol, United Nations Environment Programme and the United Nations Interregional Crime and Justice Research Institute have declared that any contravention to the Convention on International Trade in Endangered Species of Fauna and Flora (CITES) by way of illegal trade in endangered species, dumping and illicit business in hazardous waste in contravention of the 1989 Basel Convention on the Control of Transboundary Movement of Hazardous Wastes and Other Wastes and their Disposal, and Smuggling of ozone-depleting substances (ODS) in contravention to the 1987 Montreal Protocol on Substances that Deplete the Ozone Layer would constitute environmental crimes. It also recognises illegal logging and the associated trade in stolen timber in violation of national laws, as well as unreported and unregulated fishing as environmental crimes. These crimes are liable for prosecution. Interpol renders possible international police cooperation and supports its member states in the effective enforcement of national and international environmental laws and treaties.

In India, offences against the environment are registered under five laws namely Water (Prevention & Control of Pollution) Act, 1974, Air

(Prevention & Control of Pollution) Act, 1981, Environmental (Protection) Act, 1986, Wildlife Protection Act, 1972 and Forest Act, 1927.

As far as India is concerned, Uttar Pradesh topped the list of environment-related offences at (2,130 cases) in 2016, followed by Rajasthan (1,381 cases). Environment-related crimes across India have been on the steady decline – 5,835 cases in 2014, 5,156 in 2015 and 4,732 in 2016. Last year, the WHO list of 30 most polluted cities in the world, included Gwalior, Allahabad and Delhi.

In December 2016, the UN Environment and Interpol published a joint Strategic Report on Environment, Peace and Security titled 'A Convergence of Threats'. In the report, abuse of the environment was highlighted as the fourth most substantial criminal activity in the world. Exploitation of the situation was valued at USD 258 billion, and it was projected to increase by five to seven per cent every year. The environmental crime was, therefore, a growing threat to peace, security and stability besides being a national priority for 80 per cent of countries surveyed in the report.

Environmental offences today are the largest source of funding for non-state militias and terrorist organisations, contributing 38 per cent of their revenue, according to a new study released by Interpol and research workers. For instance, in the Central African Republic, illegal logging of trees earns more money than narcotic trafficking, kidnappings, pillaging, extortion, human trafficking and so on. 'Transnational organised-criminal groups targeting primarily natural resources and environmental crimes, in or near conflicts, get by far the largest slice of their revenue in conflict zones, often associated with corruption, and powerful political and military elites.' The study mentioned above estimates that total cash flow from illegal timber, illegal fishing, wildlife trafficking and illegal mining to be between US$110 and US$281 billion annually. Of this, between US$22.8 and US$34 billion finds its way to extremists and organised criminal gangs such as al-Shabaab, the Democratic Republic of Congo (DRC) rebels and the Taliban. Elephant ivory is reported to make between US$4 million and US$12.2 million for sub-Saharan militias each year and illegal logging, which sees revenues of up to US$152 billion annually worldwide, earns US$48 million for armed groups in the DRC.

The illegal wildlife trade – a severe environmental crime – is a significant contributor to species endangerment, often the second biggest threat to biodiversity after habitat loss. Illegal wildlife trade is widespread and constitutes one of the significant unlawful economic activities, comparable to the traffic of drugs and weapons. Wildlife trade is a serious conservation problem, hurts the viability of many wildlife populations and is one of the major threats to the survival of vertebrate species. Interpol has estimated the extent of the illegal wildlife trade between $10 billion and $20 billion per year. CITES (the Convention on International Trade in Endangered Species of Wild Fauna and Flora, also known as the Washington Convention) is a multilateral treaty to protect endangered plants and animals. It was drafted as a result of a resolution adopted in 1963 at a meeting of members of the International Union for Conservation of Nature (IUCN). CITES accords varying degrees of protection to more than 35,000 species of animals and plants. Members of terrorist organisations and criminal organisations illegally traffic in hundreds of millions of plants and animals to fund the purchase of weapons, finance civil conflicts, and launder money from illicit sources. The appeal, in part, is the low risk of detection and punishment compared to drug trafficking and a promise of significant profits. For example, a single Ploughshare tortoise from Madagascar (there are only 400 estimated left in the wild) can fetch US$24,000. Elephant ivory is a commonly trafficked contraband which fetches high prices in destination countries. Ivory prices and demand have skyrocketed. The cost for raw ivory in China was $2,100 per kilogram. Between 2010 and 2012, up to 33,000 elephants were poached and killed on average each year.

Illegal logging to get wood for furniture or construction purposes is another serious environmental crime. It is estimated that illegal logging on public land alone causes losses in assets and revenue more than US$10 billion annually. Although exact figures are difficult to calculate, estimates show that more than half of the logging that takes place globally is illegal, especially in open and vulnerable areas such as the Amazon Basin, Central Africa, Southeast Asia and the Russian Federation. The destruction of Amazon - the largest rainforest in the world -speeded up in 2013 at a 29 per cent rise in deforestation, according to the Brazilian government. Illegal logging not only contributes to deforestation but also to global warming and loss of biodiversity, besides undermining the rule of law. Furthermore, the illicit trade of forest resources threatens international security and is frequently associated with corruption, money laundering, organised crime, human rights abuses and, in some cases, violent conflict.

Illegal fishing, a major environmental crime, contributes to over-extraction of fish stocks, disruption of marine food chains and threats to marine biodiversity. Illegal fishing together with shark finning has brought about cataclysmic harm to the marine ecosystem. Shark finning is the practice of extracting the fins from sharks and casting away the remaining shark. The sharks are often still alive when discarded, but without their fins. Unable to swim effectively, they descend to the bottom of the ocean and die of suffocation. Shark fin is the most profitable part of the shark; fishing vessels find that finning helps them increase their lucrativeness by enabling them to transport more fins as the shark meat is bulky to carry. Roughly 73 million sharks die each year by finning, though some reckon that finning kills 100 million sharks each year. Many shark species have become endangered due to shark finning, including the threatened scalloped hammerhead shark. Shark fins are among the most expensive seafood products, commonly retailing at US$400 per kg. In China and its territories, there is a huge demand for shark fin soup and traditional cures.

Ozone depletion and the ozone hole have generated worldwide concern over increased cancer risks and other adverse effects. The leading cause of ozone depletion is manufactured chemicals, especially halocarbon refrigerants, solvents, propellants and chlorofluorocarbons (CFCs), HCFCs, and so on referred to as ozone-depleting substances (ODS). These compounds are transported into the stratosphere by the winds where they release halogen atoms through photodissociation, which catalyse the breakdown of ozone into oxygen. The ozone hole causes most harmful

UVB wavelengths of ultraviolet light to pass through which could cause skin cancer, sunburn and cataracts to human populations on earth. The adoption of the Montreal Protocol in 1987, which bans the production of CFCs, halons and other ozone-depleting chemicals is the most successful international environmental agreement to date as ozone hole is expected to reach pre-1980 levels by around 2075.

Dumping in rivers and aquifers is another severe environmental crime most often caused by irresponsible industries. Toxic wastes discharged from factories is being uncontrollably released into the environment, polluting rivers, lakes aquifers, and so on, which is a grave crime as the chemicals percolate into the soil, and cause groundwater pollution. Arsenic and fluoride have been recognised by the World Health Organization (WHO) as the most dangerous inorganic contaminants in drinking water. In the Gangetic Plains of northern India and Bangladesh severe contamination of groundwater by arsenic is seen in 25 per cent of water wells. Nitrates, fluorides, organic compounds and pathogens are often found contaminating the underground in India.

E-waste or electronic waste is created when an electronic product is discarded after the end of its useful life. In the developed countries up to 50 million tonnes of electronic waste is generated every year (computers, TV sets, mobile phones, appliances, etc.). And up to 75 per cent of it is estimated to be illegally exported to Africa, China or India. The rapid expansion of technology means that an enormous amount of e-waste is created every minute. The USA is reported to discard 30 million computers each year, and about 100 million phones are disposed of in Europe each year. Electronic scrap components, such as central processing units (CPUs), contain potentially harmful materials such as lead, cadmium, beryllium or brominated flame retardants.

Governments sometimes are known to be complicit with environmental criminals. The German government either had no role or was complicit in the Volkswagen emissions scandal famously called the 'dieselgate'. The United States Environmental Protection Agency (EPA), in September 2015, stumbled upon the scandal and issued a notice of violation of the Clean Air Act to the German automaker. Their investigation disclosed that Volkswagen had intentionally programmed turbocharged direct injection (TDI) diesel engines to activate their emissions controls only during laboratory emissions testing which caused the vehicles' NOx output to meet US standards during the normative trial, but discharge up to 40 times more NOx in real-world driving. Volkswagen deployed this programming software in about 11 million cars worldwide, including 500,000 in the USA., in model years 2009 through 2015.

Regulators in multiple countries started to investigate Volkswagen, and its stock price tumbled by a third in the days after the news broke out. Volkswagen Group CEO Martin Winterkorn resigned, and the head of brand development Heinz-Jakob Neusser, Audi R&D head Ulrich Hackenberg, and Porsche R&D head Wolfgang Hatz were suspended. Volkswagen announced plans in April 2016 to spend €16.2 billion on rectifying the emissions issues and planned to refit the affected vehicles as part of a recall campaign. In January 2017, Volkswagen pleaded guilty to criminal charges, and in April 2017, a US federal judge ordered Volkswagen 'to pay a $2.8 billion criminal fine for rigging diesel-powered vehicles to cheat on government emissions tests'. The scandal raised awareness over the higher levels of pollution emitted by all diesel-powered vehicles from a wide range of carmakers, which under real-world driving conditions exceeded legal emission limits. A study conducted by ICCT and ADAC showed the most significant deviations from Volvo, Renault, Jeep, Hyundai, Citroën and Fiat.

In the 1970s, Love Canal, located near Niagara Falls in upstate New York, was a charming little blue-collar enclave with several hundred houses and a school. It just happened to sit atop 21,000 tons of toxic industrial waste disposed of by Hooker Chemical and Plastics Company in the 1940s and 50s. After several years of unusually heavy rains, in 1976 the groundwater level started to rise, leaving house foundations overwhelmed with chemical waste. Gardens withered, pets died, and children suffered severe chemical burns on their hands and feet. High rates of congenital disabilities, miscarriage, cancer and blood disorders, together with other afflictions, were detected. When only 2 of 17 pregnant women in Love Canal gave birth to healthy babies, authorities evacuated the area in grave and imminent peril. Surveys indicated pollution several hundred times above safe levels. The local school was closed, over 200 houses were demolished, and over and above 1,000 families were evacuated. Cleanup and liability costs from the disaster exceeded $200 million.

The new millennium and the modern environmental crisis have created a need for ecologically based religion and spirituality called 'Eco-Spirituality' which draws together religion and ecological activism. Another nature-based religion called Paganism has been in existence since long. Many pagans put trust in interconnectedness among all living creatures, which allows them to foster moments of soul-searching before acting. These pagan ideas are coterminous with eco-spirituality because pagans understand the environment to be a part of the holy realm and part of their inner self. Therefore, in their view, harming the environment directly affects their well-being.

Chapter 45
SERVICE AND SACRIFICE IN THE LINE OF DUTY

Memories of the scene which I witnessed at Palar during my days as Assistant Superintendent of Salem (Training), where five police personnel and 17 others laid down their lives on 9 April 1993, in one of forest-brigand Veerappan's single-most massive killings is still raw in my mind. It consternates me to this day.

On the previous day, Veerappan after having slayed a police informer in Govindapadi, Mettur, had dared Rambo Gopalakrishnan, SP, STF to track and arrest his gang. Picking up the gauntlet, Rambo Gopalakrishnan along with a team of 41 members which included police from two states, forest officials, forest watchers and informers left in two vehicles, of which one was a bus carrying most of the team members, and the other a jeep in which Gopalakrishnan himself was travelling.

As the vehicles neared Palar near Malai Mahadeshwara hills, Simon Madaiah, a gang member of Veerappan gang detonated the IED land mines planted underneath the vehicles resulting in an explosion that hurled the bus hundreds of feet away massacring 22 people including 17 forest officials/informers and five police personnel. Rambo Gopalakrishnan, who was standing on the footboard of the jeep at the time of the explosion, sustained severe injuries to his head and legs because of the impact of the blast. Despite the explosion, the police personnel retaliated and returned the fire and staved off the gang from snatching arms and ammunition.

The history of the Indian Police is replete with several such acts of valour and supreme sacrifice. In 1939, the British constituted the Crown Representative's Police to quell the political unrest and help native states preserve Law and Order as a part of the imperial policy. Post-Independence, Sardar Vallabhbhai Patel, rechristened it as Central Reserve Police Force (CRPF) by an Act passed by the Constituent Assembly in 1949.

In 1959, China completed the construction of a highway passing from Sinkiang to Tibet via Aksai Chin. They not only proclaimed the completion of the highway but also published a map showing Aksai Chin as Chinese territory and deployed PLA there. India responded to this development by ordering the deployment of CRPF on the line where the Chinese presence had got registered.

MHA accordingly decided to establish the first outpost at Hot Springs. Despite the hardships encountered by the team at a time when there was no comfort of road, vehicle, warm clothing or fresh food as the last motorable road from Leh towards the border in Eastern Ladakh ended at Thiksey about 20 km from Leh, the Indian policemen plodded along a distance of 255 km from Leh to Hot Springs traversing a precarious terrain slicing across two snow-covered high mountain passes via 17,590-ft high Chang la and 18,953 ft-high Marsimik and established its outpost at Hot Springs.

After the post got established, the CRPF, on 20 October 1959, sent three reconnaissance teams from Hot Springs in north-eastern Ladakh to prepare for further movement of an Indian expedition proceeding to Lanak La, a pass located east of Hot Springs. While members of two parties returned to Hot Springs by the afternoon of that day, the third one comprising two police constables and a porter failed to return.

Undeterred Shri SP Tyagi, Dy. SP, CRPF and Shri. Karam Singh, DCIO, Indo-Tibetan Border Police (ITBF) leading a team of 20 cavalrymen left early in the morning searching for their lost party. However, the two groups lost contact when the first team following hoof impressions along the bank of Chang Chenmo went across a hill.

Unawares, the party headed by Karam Singh came into confrontation by the Chinese troops who gestured to them to surrender, but Karam Singh's party retaliated and the Chinese PLA being at an elevated position started firing at them from different directions scrunching the Indians into an ambush. Fighting gallantly nine men laid down their lives while ten others were left wounded. Later on, one of the injured also succumbed to his injuries. They took seven men as prisoners of war.

The supreme sacrifice by CRPF personnel during an unmatched battle turned the Hot Springs into a sacred place of pilgrimage for police officers from all over the country. Every year October 21 is in a befitting manner observed as 'Police Commemoration Day' and members of police forces from different parts of the country trek to Hot Springs which is now being manned by ITBP to pay homage to the brave hearts who made the supreme sacrifice on 21 October 1959. Similarly, the police forces all over the country to commemorate the event organise ceremonial parades in district and state headquarters on October 21, in remembrance of the police martyrs in the country.

Correspondingly, during the last 60 years, the blood of over 35,000 police heroes has drenched the soil of every nook and corner of our nation, not just in the metros but in distant rural areas, in dense jungles, wastelands and aquatic terrains. From September 2017 to August 2018, a total of 424 police personnel laid down their lives while performing their duties in India. Out of these, 67 belonged to the Uttar Pradesh Police, 46 from the Jammu and Kashmir Police, 42 belonged to the BSF, 34 belonged to ITBP and 27 were from the CRPF. Police personnel belonging to all religions and cultures be it Christian, Sikh, Hindu, Buddhist or Muslim have made the supreme sacrifice while dealing with violent mobs, or dangerous criminals, or combating terrorists, or dreaded mafias or while protecting VIPs which is way beyond the call of duty demanded in other professions.

Likewise in Tamil Nadu, several valiant police personnel have laid their lives while safeguarding the nation from the banned anti-national organisations like Liberation Tigers of Tamil Eelam (LTTE), Tamil Nadu Liberation Army (TNLA), Naxalites and Muslim Fundamentalist organisations like Al-Umma.

The assassination of former Prime Minister Rajiv Gandhi by LTTE claimed the lives of K.S. Mohammad Iqbal, SP, Kancheepuram and several other police personnel. When the Al-Umma carried out the Coimbatore bombings on 14 February 1998, 58 civilians and seven policemen got killed and over 200 injured in 12 bomb attacks.

Many police personnel have also lost their lives while maintaining law and order during various agitations, caste and communal riots, and agrarian disturbances. Going beyond the call of their duty, many police personnel have laid down their lives while trying to save people from drowning and rescuing people during catastrophes. It is therefore imperative that police officers and criminals know that the administration will leave no stone unturned to deliver justice in case anyone exterminates a policeman.

It is generally seen that all police personnel who served or are serving would have possibly lost a colleague in the line of duty. I have lost four from my batches in the line of duty. Two of them because of the Naxalites. Four Naxalites assassinated Umesh Chandra on 4 September 1999 in Hyderabad when his car stopped at a traffic light. Unidentified persons in Maoist-infested Rayagada district of south Orissa shot my batchmate Jaswinder Singh in October 2006. All the four batchmates of mine who made the supreme sacrifice were splendid officers. They are missed badly by the entire batch. Their sacrifices warrant respectful remembrance and homage from society and the nation as a whole.

Similarly, it is sometimes sad that when an officer gets slain in the line of duty, their families are sometimes forgotten once the funeral is over. For instance, Javed Iqbal son of Mohammad Iqbal, SP Kanchipuram who lost his father during Rajiv Gandhi's assassination was 17 years old at the time of his father's death, but he was forgotten soon after the Governor of Tamil Nadu offered him a seat in Anna University. Nobody ever bothered to learn about him and his family's welfare after the demise of his father. G.K. Moopanar alone called upon his family and got him a licence for an LPG distribution agency on which his livelihood is dependent to this day.

There is a necessity to have a healing dialogue between the family and the government and continued support to family members of martyrs long after the sacrifice. The death of policemen rarely incites public rage or empathy. Even the Police Commemoration Day is usually an all-police affair except in some districts/states.

Further, it is essential that police personnel who have placed duty above their most precious lives get recognition and are honoured for their supreme sacrifice. The 'National Police Memorial' that got built and consecrated to the Nation on the Police Commemoration Day (21st October 2018) by the Honourable Prime Minister of India is a befitting monument of their ultimate sacrifice. The National Police Memorial site is at the ridge of the Shantipath in the diplomatic neighbourhood of Chanakyapuri, New Delhi. This shrine in its architectural vision is a poem to the courageous guardians worthy of our eternal gratitude.

The Police Museum housed in its premises pays tribute to all policemen and policewomen exemplifying their martyrdom. It also allows the public to know about their police, with its rich history and a fantastic range of diversity.

Since 2012, Police Commemoration Day Parade at the national level is being organised at the National Police Memorial site in Chanakyapuri, New Delhi with participation of all the Central Armed Police Forces, Delhi Police and symbolic representation from state forces, though the Central Sculpture got eventually completed and consecrated to the nation last year. The names of all police martyrs get engraved and updated every year in stone on the Wall of Valour at the National Police Memorial.

Interestingly, our Honourable Union Home Minister, with the support of the MHA, has launched a website 'Bharat Ké Veer', where the community can show solidarity with the Government in looking after the families of our martyrs from the viewpoint of financial help. What is of significance is not the quantum of the financial support extended, but the essence and the vision behind it.

Finally, an inscription in a memorial stone at Hot Springs says it well – 'When you go home tell them of us and tell them we gave our today for their tomorrow.' There is and will never be any dearth of courageous men and women in uniform. The best tribute we can pay to our martyrs is to match their sacrifice with a greater sense of duty.

Abraham Lincoln understood that 'A country that does not honour its heroes will not long endure'. Therefore, the least we can do is to remember our heroes and cherish the values for which they stood, fought and eventually sacrificed their lives.

Chapter 46
SPIRITUAL WELL-BEING FOR LAW ENFORCEMENT

Taking care of the soul is crucial, but I kept procrastinating and deferring because it seemed the most irrelevant thing to nurture in this fast-paced, busy world. Hitting the gym occurred to me as the most pragmatic and prudent thing to do than sitting cross-legged on the ground with my eyes closed. So the decay and neglect of my soul went on until I ran into an old childhood friend of mine while boarding a flight a few years ago at the local airport, which made me realise that all the striving in the outer world had not fetched me any joy or lasting happiness. On the contrary, I figured out that all the grind was not only depleting me physically and mentally but also leaving me drained and spiritually parched.

Harking back to my childhood days, I can vividly reminisce several fond memories of time spent with this boyhood chum, either trapping guppies at the local pond with plastic bags or going catapult hunting in the fields or playing truant at school to binge on Clint Eastwood's movies at the local cinema. I lost touch with him when they left the neighbourhood after his father got transferred. After over four decades, on that random evening at the airport, we were suddenly staring at each other, thrilled beyond words at the reunion. There was something magnetic about his presence that instantly stupefied and hushed me. His saintlike demeanour radiated deep peace and expansive compassionate energy. Despite the hustle and bustle of milling crowds around us, I could sense his presence, exuding an energy of indescribable joy and peace unknown. A quick conversation with him revealed he had veered to a life of service and contemplation after jettisoning a glamorous profession. This brief interaction was so profound that I desperately wanted to gain all his hallowed qualities by subjecting my being to spiritual disciplines.

Over the years, especially after the tryst with my childhood buddy, I have since uncovered that tending to one's spirit is far more valuable

DeeaF/Shutterstock.com

than caring for one's body and mind. Because our spirit can be strong and glorious as ever even after age has atrophied our muscles, the skin has got shrunken and shrivelled; the brain has got permeated with plaques, and the blood vessels have got clogged despite our relentless quest for fitness and longevity.

Most police officers like me, at some stage of life, realise that there must be more to life than day-to-day existence, and some entertain thoughts of having a rich inner life. Contemporary policing has become more complex and challenging. It has become more demanding and stressful than before. Cultivating spiritual disciplines could help police officers grow and strengthen their souls, eventually bolstering the ability of a police officer to feel inner peace, demonstrate moral courage, get insights, conquer bad parts of oneself, endure hardships and act unselfishly. Inculcating spirituality in the lives of police officers does not mean making them religious. It implies helping them develop a deeper, more transcendent meaning of life which is untrammelled to roam and explore their life bereft of all calcified dogmas, tenets and traditions.

So, spiritual disciplines are specific habits that develop, grow, strengthen our spirit, build our character muscles and train our soul. Just as we grow our body in the gym by lifting weights or grow new neurons in the brain by challenging the brain with new tasks, we can consistently train our spiritual muscles with spiritual activities like meditation, service, prayer, gratitude, fasting, silence and journaling, to prevent us from becoming spiritually unfit, spiritually barren and spiritually stagnant.

Hence, to strengthen the soul, we would have to train consciously, like overcoming resistance by pushing weights in a gym. We need discipline in all walks of life. We need the field to learn a new art or craft, go to the gym, lose weight or achieve something in life. The same steadfast laws that underlie discipline in the physical world also apply in the spiritual realm. We must intentionally choose to train the soul consistently. Persistence is essential. Just as we earmark a specific time for physical exercise, we must make time for spiritual activities. Wellness and vitality that accrue from such practices could enhance the quality of service as law enforcement professionals.

My niece, trying to discover spirituality, recently asked me how religion differs from spirituality. The answer I gave her never convinced her. I reckon that religion believes in a power outside oneself called God, while spirituality is everyone's intrinsic spiritual nature and power. We all have the divine within ourselves that embodies our uniqueness our authenticity. Spirituality is an inward voyage rather than some form of external activity. Spirituality, therefore, is much more about inner awareness than outer worship. Religion and spirituality are not synonymous: Police personnel can stick to spiritual tenets following no particular belief.

Spirituality is also that part of oneself that helps one find meaning, connectedness and purpose in one's life. It can include the practice of philosophy, religion, or way of living. During tough times, people frequently look for meaning and connectedness in the greater scheme of things to help them comprehend and deal with their experiences.

We see this more in the life of police personnel who, in their day-to-day lives, get so caught up in catching criminals and protecting lives that they overlook they are spiritual beings. When the police personnel see the worst of society, such as irrational beatings, child abuse, murder or rape, they tend to forget their spiritual selves and their world gets crammed with anguish and hopelessness. The physical world cannot end their despair and hopelessness. Only the spiritual world can. The oneness, the connection with the essence alone, can heal by lending them purpose and reason for being. Then why the spiritual connection furnishes alone can give the wisdom to cope and flourish in this world going mad. When police officers unearth who they are inside, they can discover immense peace and solace.

Besides the physical demands and perils, the police job is spiritually demanding. A career in law enforcement can also take a hefty toll on police personnel's spiritual well-being. The law enforcement community is yet to address the magnitude of police stress in any meaningful way. Police job inflicts traumas and scars that are spiritual and not physical. Many police officers suffer deep psychological pain because of what they have observed during their duties. Police personnel experience the demise of their spirituality because of the negative aspects of the occupation. As a result, they need counsel and tools to tune themselves up regularly.

Much research is on emotional and psychological stressors is now being undertaken, and organisations have taken several steps to counteract them, like the 'Police Well-Being' programme in Tamilnadu. Still, we seem to be taking no actions to preempt spiritual stress. We are just starting to recognise the effects of spiritual well-being. The challenge now is to introduce spirituality with no religious underpinnings.

In India, several police officers die on duty every year. Also, police officers take their own lives as they suffer from depression, addictions, divorce, spiritual and psychological ailments at a rate higher than the general community.

The lack of spiritual resources available to battle the spiritual maladies that afflict the officers is even more alarming. We don't seem to be spending adequate resources developing strategies to ensure their spiritual well-being. Police personnel need guidance and counsel to reflect upon their spiritual condition and know-how to keep it healthy to respond to trials and tribulations in their lives at a higher and nobler moral level. If we commit resources to bolster the spiritual vision and expand them spiritually, they will develop spiritual resilience, maintaining a sense of reality and balance. We all need to make police personnel aware of their spiritual aspiration and help them reconnect to them to fortify them spiritually and buffer them against all vicissitudes of the police subculture.

That's because the police personnel who pursue a vocation in policing do so with rhetorical intentions. There can be no higher spiritual motivation than to protect and serve. The police profession conveys a profound aspiration of a noble human spirit to fulfil a transcendent purpose to attend to the welfare of human beings. What drives people to act and accomplish is the human spirit. What inspires police personnel to join the police force encompasses a yearning to make a positive difference in the world by safeguarding the weak and innocent, by endorsing noble ideals like the sanctity of human life and fighting evil. Many police personnel join the force compelled by such spiritual yearnings, but they are not conscious. Once they realise it, spirituality will automatically grow throughout their career. As soon as the recruits enter the police profession, they become distracted by the glamorousness of the uniform and the job. No one ever seems to make them aware of the spiritual rationales of the role that initially brought the recruits into the profession.

A policeman joins the profession with innocent idealism, but the hardships, predicaments and vicious acts can wreck that challenge. Everyday stressors on the job drain officers' faith and spiritual deposits. The spiritual reservoir of a police officer gets depleted with every brush with evil and suffering a person encounters on the job. Psychologist Carl Jung noticed a weird phenomenon of spiritual people; he found that those who failed to feed their spiritual side by withholding spiritual nourishment that their soul's desire often experience existential discomfort. Suppose such police personnel can identify their origin of pain. In that case, they can untangle it, but if they cannot recognise it, they indulge in hindering behaviours expecting that the pain will disappear. A person with an unfulfilled spiritual aspiration can wreak havoc when dealing with the pain because the effort to improve it can prove as disastrous as the effort to ease it often enhances it. During deadening their pain, many take to self-destructive addictive behaviours. Recruits enter law enforcement callings yearning to give expression, nurture, cultivate and rehearse their spiritual side, which needs regular, sustained replenishment for health. If they receive that sustenance, officers often become more profound human beings and attain a level of mature idealism. But if they do not accept that nourishment and don't realise they are spiritual beings, and if they don't know that they need help on that plane, they probably will end up disheartened, disturbed, depressed or sad.

Therefore, police personnel need spiritual coaching. Spiritual coaching can enable police personnel to unleash the divine within and make each one become conscious architects of their own lives. Unleashing the divine within them results in better health, happier relationships and more compassion. Helping the police reconnect can cause moving experiences resulting in awakening to the presence of the inner spirit, which can uncover the soul within each of them, holding forth the promise of eternal life and quickening the realisation that we are all one.

Hence, infusing spirituality in police personnel has many benefits. Spirituality will make the police personnel gracious. Spirituality will encourage the police to be positive, expressed as gratitude, optimism and generosity.

Spirituality will make police personnel compassionate. Showing compassion towards others is one correlate with living a spiritual life. Spirituality allows one to feel good about the little things in life and look at the world through empathetic eyes. Spiritual people have positive relationships, high self-esteem, optimism, and have meaning and purpose in life. When police personnel turn spiritual, they begin to self-actualise and consider personal growth and fulfilment as the primary goal. It compels them to focus on internal values and become better individuals. Spirituality will help police personnel cease dwelling on dark experiences, start taking time to savour life experiences and build lasting memories of positive experiences correlated with little pleasures in life.

Spirituality also connects with neuroscience; when our conditioned brains release the old limiting beliefs that have wired our brain to mediocrity, we can nullify the wiring as our minds are plastic and return to our original divinity.

We are aware that a policeman's life is more stressful than an ordinary man; a policeman is more liable to punishment rolls, suspension, job loss and anxieties of daily life which can prove debilitating. Practising spirituality can be a productive way to curtail stress levels and direct one's energy to something positive.

Studies have shown that meditation and mindfulness yield positive outcomes for the overwrought policeman. Suppose the personnel can find a calm spot to reflect for a few moments and forfeit control of whatever tormenting may be enough to quiet them down. Depression is widespread among many law enforcement personnel studies indicate that spiritual practices such as mindfulness and meditation can alleviate spiritual stress. Research shows that spirituality is also associated with better health outcomes. Spirituality appears to help people cope with disease, suffering and death. All people, with or without a connection to organised religion or any spiritual practices, seem to benefit from discovering their sense of meaning, purpose and connectedness.

Eventually, therefore, spiritual well-being is almost as crucial as physical and emotional health in police organisations. Suppose police organisations can effectively address employees' spiritual, physical and emotional needs. In that case, they will lend them the tools to find harmony in their personal and professional lives. Research has demonstrated that spiritually healthy persons experience less stress, avoid negative behaviours, and commit more to their duties and responsibilities.

Chapter 47
IN THE LINE OF KHAKI PSYCHACHE: PROBLEM OF POLICE SUICIDES AND SIMPLE SOLUTIONS FOR ITS PREVENTION

In Chennai, Constable Arun Raj of Armed Reserve, and Sub Inspector Satish Kumar of Ayanavaram Police station, who blew their brains with their guns recently, should have felt something akin to a 9/11 situation of being trapped and engulfed in a towering inferno of the gradually collapsing World Twin Towers, with the fire menacingly catching up with them and the blaze beginning to caress their backs. They are faced with two options – to jump out of the window and die instantaneously or be burnt excruciatingly to the bitter end, as in the proverbial hell? Death by jumping obviously seems a less painful way out. So, they haul themselves out of the window. That's precisely what suicide is. A person committing suicide finds exiting this world by killing oneself, herein by jumping out of the window, less painful and easy, when compared to the agony and heartache, of being charred and razed to the ground, fighting the demonic fires raging and ravaging one's personal or professional life.

India has earned the sobriquet of the 'Suicide capital' of the world from the World Health Organization [WHO]. India accounts for nearly a third of the global total, with the number of suicides here being twice as much as China, which is second on the list. It also has the highest rate of suicides among young people, in the age range of 15 to 29 years. Among the states, Tamil Nadu and Kerala had the highest suicide rates per 100,000 people in 2012. The male to female suicide ratio was around 2:1.

As far as the police is concerned, Tamilnadu has the highest number of suicides by police personnel among the Indian states. According to a report published in 2016, 166 police personnel in Tamilnadu, ended their lives between 2010 and 2014 followed by 161 in Maharashtra and 61 in Kerala. In a recent report published by National Crime Records Bureau (NCRB), suicides in the age group of 15 and 29 years accounted for 34.4 per cent and the age group between 30 and 44 years accounted for 33.8 per cent. The most worrisome fact being that about 70 per cent of suicides in the uniformed services too are committed by persons below the age of 44 years, imposing a huge social, economic and emotional burden on society.

The most probable precipitating factor connected with police suicide appears to be stress. Stress and policing affect officers and their families. A severe form of stress, known as traumatic stress, appears to be predominant in police work, and possibly plays a part in suicide. While ailments like PTSD (Post Traumatic Stress Disorder) are increasingly acknowledged within the armed forces, its prevalence in civilian police goes totally unnoticed.

Law enforcement is one of the most toxic, acerbic career fields under the sun. Police personnel put their lives on the line daily, they are always being called to situations that individuals would never want to deal with, such as murder, violence, accidents and disasters. Rotational shifts, long hours and exposure to life's catastrophes, exact a heavy toll on police personnel and their families. Poor working conditions, heavy workload, poor infrastructure including substandard equipment, poor police image, confrontation with the populace and the media on a daily basis, rigid police hierarchy, lack of job satisfaction and meager pay, not only complicate but compound the stress in one's work life, impacting family life as well. As a result, high divorce rates, suicides, domestic violence, heart attacks, cancer, depression and alcoholism are invariably the unfavorable outcomes amidst police personnel and their families.

The public and the media foster a macho image of the police personnel, often portraying their mythical ability to withstand trauma and violence without any suffering and ill effects, but the truth is however to the contrary. When police personnel are subjected to stresses over an extended period, their ability to cope becomes difficult. Police men and women as a group, tend not to cope well with psychological angst, they are often found to have maladaptive coping strategies. It's this coping disability which causes the police personnel to break easily, and contemplate suicide, much more easily, when things get unbearable.

Psychologists reckon that majority of the police personnel working in the field are either suffering from underlying depression or anxiety. Depression is a silent killer in the police force, exacting a psychosomatic toll on the mind and body of even the most resilient police officer. Most police men and women who are depressed are in denial regarding their condition, as the police subculture unfortunately, promotes silence. Besides, police officers do not want to be seen as weak. Speaking out plainly about one's problems in the police department is generally never encouraged and mostly stifled. So, if they are suffering from depression, or any other mental illness, they are extremely unlikely to get help. Most are also wary of seeking any type of professional assistance. This can prove harmful to police personnel in many ways, and turns into a Catch 22 situation for her/him. The reaction of colleagues, when a policeman is discovered to be psychologically unfit for duty, is generally not one of compassion and solidarity; in stark contrast, the stigma of being branded by subordinates, superiors or police management as possibly unstable or having a psychological issue may cause other staff to shun or not be willing to work with such person. The other consequences of being put on leave, reassigned to desk duty, having his gun taken away from him, the fear of being passed up for promotions makes the future seem even more scary and bleak. So, the great majority of depressed police brethren do nothing and remain at a high risk for suicide.

In the final analysis, a stressful job with untreated depression and a service gun at hand, is an extremely deadly mix. As police personnel are armed with a gun, a fatal suicide method is always readily available. Hence, more police officers die by their own hand than are killed in the line of duty.

Police leaders and supervisors must become conversant with depression, because it affects such high percentage of police personnel, especially when depression is linked with a significant risk of suicide. The symptoms of clinical depression include a decline in energy levels or increased fatigue and a loss of the ability to participate in enjoyable activities. A good police supervisor would easily be able to recognise these symptoms as portentous clues, and draw an inference that the person needs help. A feeling of sadness, worry and desperation tends to dominate a depressed police man's thoughts. Asking for emotional help in a time of crisis is not weakness. It should not be held against any person who desires to discuss issues that are bothering him. Emotional issues should never be repressed. The greatest prevention of depression apparently is a ridicule-free work ecosystem, where policemen can admit freely and share easily, in case they have had a rainy day, when life hurts, or whenever they are psychologically bruised from the confrontation with the public or by the abuses hurled at them by their superiors. Law enforcement officials must be allowed to feel free or to seek talk therapy, hospitalization or medical management, without any fear of reprisal or being looked upon as emotionally weak. Policemen need to be told that depression is common, it is treatable and there is no shame in being depressed. Police officers and men during training should be made aware of the emotional toll of depression on police work and must be taught coping techniques. Police men/officers should also be compulsorily required to undergo a thorough check-up periodically with a therapist who is adept at dealing with stress and trauma in just about the same way they get an annual medical examination. Training should be imparted to policemen in suicide awareness, not only to understand their feelings, but also identify and understand the feelings of persons vulnerable to suicide, and to cope with emotional adversities. Practice of theoretical psychological assessment, tracking high-risk police men, training the supervisors to recognise signs of suicide proneness and preparation of suicide prevention strategies for police organisations must be made obligatory.

A daily regimen of exercise and relaxation techniques is necessary to take on stress proactively in the life of policemen and women. Exercise is a great stress buster and it helps prevent chronic diseases such as blood pressure and depression. If other cities and states in our country are also able to switch over to a compact eight hour schedule, for the lower echelons as was done by the Mumbai Police in January this year, it would free up precious time for police personnel to take up more stress relieving activities or help police leadership incorporate more physical movement into their lives by reviving the practice of parade and physical training, which is facing neglect or has become almost defunct in the police stations due to exponential increase in law and order duties. This would not only improve discipline but also go a long way in combating depression and stress. Exercise has the added benefit of releasing endorphins, a great mood elevator. Every policeman/woman might have played some sport or game or practised yoga sometime in his/her life. Reviving his/her interest or encouraging him/her to pursue a new sport can also help matters a great deal by merging it in their work schedules.

The next big deal is laughter. 'Laughter being the best medicine' is not to be treated as a cliché. Children laugh about 300 times a day while adults laugh only 15 to 100 times per day. Laughing helps ease stress. And laughing hundred times equals 10 minutes of training oneself on a rowing machine or 15 minutes of cycling. To make policemen laugh is very difficult, as looking stern and tough is what their job demands. Punjab Armed Police recently has embarked upon Laughter Yoga programme for its constables at its training centre to make them stress free. The cops laugh their heart out, which fills them with a sense of calm and relaxation. They are also told to begin their day by looking into the mirror and start laughing at themselves in order to feel good and energised throughout the day. A similar laughter therapy session, before or after the roll call, could help police personnel kick-start their day in a cheery and positive frame of mind.

Practising meditation and breathing makes one more resilient to stress. But an average policeman finds it difficult to sit and meditate, or practise breathing or mindfulness as it feels majorly cumbersome to him/her. Any police personnel caught up in the frantic pace of the modern world can reap the benefits of meditation by chanting mantras to achieve relaxation and reduction of stress. Chanting is an easy, effective way to still the chatter of the mind and experience bliss. This prescription is found in all the scriptures of the world. Here is a sample from our Purana.

> Whatever is achieved in Satya-yuga by meditation, in Treta by offering ritual sacrifices and in the Dvapara by temple worship is achieved in Kali-yuga by chanting the names of Lord Kesava.
> (Padma Purana, Uttara Khanda 42nd Chapter)

When a policeman's outer world is cacophonous and disharmonious, that discordant vibration will configure his inner cosmos. Conversely, inner turbulence manifests as a psychotic outer world. Chanting mantra shifts this process and creates a more symphonic inner world which then harmonises his outer world. Police personnel of different faiths can have their own mantras. A Hindu might chant Om, while a Christian might find solace in the mantra 'Jesus have mercy on me' and a Muslim may chant 'Allah ho Akbar'. There can be no better prescription for stress and depression than the prescription of chanting. A policeman can do it any time – while patrolling, while on guard duty, while on bundobust duty or on any other duty – and experience bliss and harmony with his spiritual self, even while being engaged with the physical world.

Quite often it is noticed that loss of purpose and meaning in one's life may also force a policeman/woman to resort to the extreme step of taking his/her life. Many police personnel find it overwhelming to recreate purpose in life. Suicidal ideation in such individuals is preventable by providing proper guidance, good counsel and mentorship services. The missing purpose and meaning in policeman's life can be rekindled by helping them associate with their favourite cause, by renewed interest in their children and family, participation in volunteer services or by adoption of a pet.

To wrap it up, here's a small story highlighting the power of purpose to save a soul which had totally lost all hope in this world.

'A policeman was preparing to die. He loaded his revolver, and slowly, started to raise it to his head. Just before, he could pull the trigger, the door opened slowly. And his dog walked in. He abruptly stopped. Gradually, lowering the loaded revolver down, he pondered, "What will happen to my poor little dog after I die?" Seconds away from a suicide, the policeman opted not to die'.

Chapter 48
THE IMPORTANCE OF EMOTIONAL INTELLIGENCE FOR POLICING

The field of law enforcement is replete with good deeds and acts of compassion on one side of the spectrum, while brutality, excessive use of force and lack of empathy are rife on the other extreme of the expanse. On the positive side, for instance, in February last year, a woman Sub-Inspector K. Sirisha of Srikakulam district of Andhra Pradesh revealed her human side when she carried the corpse of an unknown person for two kilometres and also performed the last rites when the local people refused to accept the body and conduct the final ceremonies. Likewise, in Chennai city, in November last year, amidst torrential rains and waterlogging, TP Chatram Police Station Inspector Rajeshwari hauled an unconscious man on her shoulder to an autorickshaw and expeditiously shifted him to a hospital. While, on the negative side, a Special Sub-Inspector of police in the Salem district of Tamilnadu, despite the yells and pleas of the bystanders, beat a 47-year-old farmer to death near Pappinaickanpatti check-post. In the first two episodes, the women police officers epitomised grace and compassion due to an embodiment of high levels of Emotional Intelligence (EI). The latter, who failed to control his emotions in the Salem district, exhibited a total lack of EI.

EI is the ability to comprehend, detect, manage and handle emotions. Individuals with high emotional intelligence can discern their feelings and those of others. And deploy that knowledge to think and behave appropriately by distinguishing and labelling emotions. Even though EI first surfaced in 1964, it gained popularity in the 1995 best-selling book *Emotional Intelligence*, authored by Daniel Goleman. Goleman defined EI as the array of skills and characteristics that drive leadership performance.

EI is vital for law enforcement personnel as they need to acquire the ability to express and control their emotions and have the skill to understand, infer and respond to the feelings of others. Police officers who understand and rely on EI have pleasing manners and steer away from controversies, misconduct and other legal transgressions. Police officers with EI have better mental health, strong leadership skills and outstanding job performance. EI is also essential to maximise individual and professional success. EI and mindset training can enable law enforcement to focus on the task at hand and make better decisions under pressure. Besides, EI can help police officers manage stress, balance their lives and influence others to swivel around to their point of view through understanding and seamless modification of emotions.

Further, EI is a significant factor in day-to-day police work because a policeman's job involves dealing with hostile and aggressive criminal elements while maintaining good rapport and relationships with law-abiding citizens. A policeman's job also entails examining witnesses and comforting the victims; all of which requires good interpersonal skills, a high latitude of empathy and excellent communication skills. If a police officer can regulate his emotions and also comprehend the emotions of others, such an officer would be able to remain calm, collected and relaxed even in the face of the gravest provocation. Because when a policeman recognises the place from where the wrath is arising and makes the person hysterical, it would be easy to empathise with the plight of the individual even if it seems ridiculous. When a police officer empathises and accepts even a smattering of the outburst of the other, the outcome of the interaction most likely is a peaceful resolution to the encounter.

Furthermore, EI skills are crucial for efficient and effective maintenance of law and order. More so during crowd control, civil protests, riots, demonstrations and arrests. During my tenure as ADGP L&O last year, I saw some situations evolve and eventually go out of control because the police officers on the scene become emotionally entangled in an argument with the public, which then blew out of proportions into a physical confrontation, warranting the use of excessive force, tear gas or lethal weapons. Police officers with EI skills, on the other hand, recognise triggers of confrontation and violence immediately, and apply their

EI skills to manage crises or conflict situations. Being proactive, they nip things in the bud. EI skills can go a long way in preventing excessive use of force and misuse of firearms by some trigger-happy police personnel.

Police personnel with high intrinsic attributes of EI often manifest as Good Samaritans. During the COVID lockdown in April of 2020, Syed Abuthahir, a 23-year-old constable of the Trichy district, transported a stranded 24-year-old pregnant woman needing urgent medical attention. He also donated blood and saved her life when she developed complications during the C-section. Similarly, in March 2021, Inspector Rajeshwari of Chennai city helped an abandoned pregnant woman deliver a son and enabled her to start a new life. Likewise, Benny, a Sub Inspector of Chengamanad station in Kerala, noticing the predicament of an impoverished 85-year-old woman, decided to give her monthly monetary assistance of ₹2,000 from his salary. During the recent COVID lockdown, numerous Good Samaritan acts of police were witnessed in our country from police personnel manifesting a high degree of EI.

In contrast, police personnel with low EI skills are highly vulnerable to misconduct, high handedness and brutality. Police officers with high EI can regulate their emotions better and are less impulsive and irrational. In comparison, police personnel with low EI are highly susceptible to reckless and risky behaviour due to their inability to understand the behaviour due to a lack of empathy that predisposes them to police misconduct and high handedness. Hence, it is urgent to train every officer in EI as it is an essential component for law enforcement. Unlike IQ, we can improve the EI of police officers through training. Benefits of improved EI includes lesser use of excessive force, more satisfied citizens, better public opinion and image for the police.

CONCLUSION

In the preceding chapters of this volume, we have succinctly reconnoitred a few exponential technologies that have exploded in recent years and some technologies that are waiting to burst forth on the law enforcement scene. Of late, technologies are accelerating so rapidly that we are now accomplishing what took centuries in ancient history in one year. The degree of innovation occurring is genuinely staggering. The explosion of technologies in the next 50 years is unimaginable. The smartphones that are in our pockets today are almost a thousand times quicker than the mid-80s Cray-2 Supercomputer and several multiples faster than the computer installed onboard NASA's Perseverance Rover propelled to explore Mars. And most significantly, they have surpassed the speed of laptops most of us are carrying around today. In the past thirty years, the eruption of technologies has been more unprecedented than in the previous thousand years.

The sudden surge in exponential technologies facilitates and leads to integrating technologies. AI, Blockchain, Machine learning, robots, and so on are simultaneously converging, complementing and co-evolving into new groundbreaking technologies. So much so that it is becoming an intimidating task for the decision makers and the police administrators to consider all the technology options available today and all that is coming soon.

The exponential growth of technology so far seems to have followed the path of Moore's law advanced by Intel co-founder Gordon Moore in 1965, according to which transistors on processors would double every two years. Although Moore's law has lingered for nearly 50 years, its pertinence of late has diminished because of new ways of measuring processing power. So, Moore's Law, by the stringent explanation of doubling chip densities every two years, may not be happening anymore, despite that technology relentlessly continues to explode at a mind-blowing pace.

Heeding Moore's law, the explosion of technology that has occurred in recent years is something akin to the story of the Persian king and an inventor of the chess game. The story goes that the inventor of the chess game met the Persian king and presented him with a chessboard. The king was so delighted with the gift that he offered the inventor the freedom to demand any inheritance from him. The inventor placed a grain of rice on the first square and requested the King to add twice as much the number of rice grains for each following square. By the time the King arrived at the last yard, he owed the inventor 64 to the power of 2 grains, which translates to 18,446,744,073,709,551,616 grains. As the value of the wealth of the entire kingdom would still fall short to bear the cost of the rice, the king relinquished his whole wealth to the inventor. The story of the Persian king is an urgent call to action for humanity to take back control over our gadgets and channelise technology's tremendous power for the betterment of humankind before singularity dawns and allows machine intelligence to have control over us.

Surprisingly, our sense of technology appears to be linear when it is exponential. Although technology evolves exponentially, police organisations and societies have been adapting slower than a tortoise compared to the technology, sprinting like a hare. Hence, decision makers need to do some future casting to fill technological advancement and technology adoption gaps. Decision makers also need to question whether they are taking all steps necessary to harness the new technologies, check if they are budgeting adequately for innovation and whether the organisations would gain the know-how to benefit from and ride the tide of technology.

We have glimpsed that the exponential technologies that have exploded on the policing scene thus far are significantly augmenting the efforts of the police worldwide in the investigation, detection and prosecution of crimes. Technologies like FRT, DNA and ANPR have considerably accelerated the pace of police inquiry and detection of crimes. By making the police work accurate and efficient, the new technologies have helped make police work seem less dreary. Computer forensic technology is enormously helping law enforcement search and analyse crime data during investigations promptly and efficiently. Exponential technologies may have several positives, but they have several drawbacks or negatives.

For instance, most of the emerging new technologies collect and generate data. Police organisations worldwide face the problem of managing the data that the latest technologies are developing. Unlike the police equipment of the past, modern technology comes with the ability to amass, build, store and interpret data. Taking on these additional risks and responsibilities is costly. Departments should factor in such costs when considering the adoption of any new data-collection technology. Procuring data-collection technologies is unlike procuring analogue equipment because the expenses and downstream effects get linked to the physical hardware, and the resulting data compels management. Therefore, the new tools that police organisations adopt require controlling and managing resultant data.

Further, in several countries, including India, consent for implementing any new technology is seldom sought by the decision makers from the citizens. Police stand to gain legitimacy if they inform and gain feedback or support from the citizens before introducing any new technology. Citizens have concerns or misconceptions about the latest technology proposed for implementation, which the police must address and, if possible, gain their confidence. For example, the public may be concerned about AI-based Predictive Policing or FRT because of privacy concerns. Under such circumstances, police should clear the misconceptions and devise an operating policy to assure citizens that the technology will not be misused. The police may convince the public by guaranteeing that the SOP (Standard Operating Procedure) they are devising will adequately safeguard and address the suspicions and concerns of the citizens.

Some new technologies which police departments embrace with gusto and enthusiasm soon get discarded because the costs of using or maintaining the data could spiral out of control. For instance, many police agencies in the USA which took to body cams have discarded their use as the data maintenance costs became prohibitively expensive. The high storage costs of body cams due to the new data retention law in Nebraska State forced the police agency to abandon body cams altogether. Besides, when a police department collects and retains data, it is responsible for safeguarding it and ensuring that it is used appropriately, in compliance with applicable laws and regulations. Failure to do so means the department risks becoming legally, financially and publicly accountable when the data gets misused or a data breach occurs.

Another shortcoming that law enforcement authorities encounter is that the vendors of several modern technologies often tempt the police to acquire new technologies free of cost or at throwaway prices but later charge exorbitantly for AMC or service charges. Most new technologies also come with hidden fees and high recurring costs for decision makers to consider in advance. New technologies are sometimes randomly approved for implementation by the decision makers based on research papers or without pilot studies or flawed study reports. For instance, the performance of a new technology may not replicate the same results if deployed in a different culture or nation or setting. A technology that has proved successful in rural settings may not yield the same benefits in an urban environment. Modern policing technologies generate substantial financial costs beyond an initial hardware or software purchase that decision makers fail to anticipate. By anticipating these future expenses, police departments can make more informed choices about which technologies are worth adopting.

Yet another most significant technological challenge law enforcement and individuals face today is hacker intrusions into their devices. Hacker intrusions into devices often do not have telltale signs. The greatest puzzle is that we can't fight an invisible enemy. The intrusions maybe like the Coronaviruses. The hackers proliferate into anything and everything cyber like our PCs, tablets, laptops, mobiles, cars, bank accounts and watches. Law enforcement should proactively devise ways to chase such intruders away and hunt them down as a worthy goal.

In the future, law enforcement agencies embracing exponential technologies may encounter frequent cyberattacks like the corporates face today. The more data a police agency possesses, the more data it will have to protect. Most corporate companies don't appear to take stock of their data; they have no idea about the critical data that needs protection or where they have stored it. Smashing down the wall of silence over cyber-attacks is a crucial step towards augmenting our technological security. Companies don't admit or disclose cyberattacks because of the ramifications of being labelled as a cyber victim. The companies do all that is possible to stay silent to protect their reputation despite losses of millions of dollars. It's like a girl who has suffered rape not willing to report to the police for the simple fear of being ostracised by family and society. If the police do not identify and punish, the perpetrators will be encouraged to commit more rapes. This silence in the corporate companies is at the heart of cyber security problems. Retaining silence about such attacks does not prevent or deter future attacks. It only worsens as it empowers cybercriminals to operate with impunity and allow them to target the cyber-ware of law enforcement agencies.

All over the world, the governments collects taxes to provide internal security and security from external attacks and invasions in the physical space. Similarly, in an increasingly connected digital world, the government must provision cyber defence to its citizens and protect its citizenry from everything cyber coming at them. We may use CCTV, burglar alarms, weapons to defend ourselves in our house and install anti-virus software to safeguard our computers. Similarly, governments worldwide must ensure that security and privacy are inbuilt upfront at the design phase. And it must be guaranteed throughout the lifetime of the devices inhabiting our lives.

Further, one unintended fallout from our love for technology could be the challenges to the rule of law from several quarters. These litigations could hamper or postpone the implementation of technology. The other significant challenges which could arise are the displacement or substitution of personnel by automation, economic inequality, data privacy issues and ever more creative forms of electronic fraud and cyber espionage. Cybercriminals are already stealing and selling our personal information. While there is an upsurge of enthusiasm for technologies such as blockchain and facial recognition systems, several police stations and offices are yet to digitise paper records.

We may conclude that technology may be evil going by the criminals, terrorists, hackers and rogue governments subverting technology to harm others. Still, technology is neutral, like a fire or a knife. Technology like fire could keep us warm, cook our food, or bad actors could use it in evil ways to burn down the village next door or burn public properties. Another example is a knife in the hands of a surgeon and a murderer. In the hands of those with positive intentions, our rapidly evolving technologies can be a blessing and create abundance in society. But the same knife in the hands of a terrorist can kill innocent people and turn this world into hell. We should not surrender to the mistaken notion that there is nothing we can do to stop the negatives of technology. We should not befriend apathy; instead, take steps to overcome the upcoming technological catastrophe.

Exponentially hyper-accelerated technological change can figure out numerous problems very quickly, but this won't happen soon unless the decision makers or leaders respond to the challenges of the technology with urgency. Linear thinking will not work for exponential technologies because extraordinary challenges require unique solutions and exceptional will for implementation. The future we want will not happen on its own. To create it, we all need tremendous intention, determination and effort. If we put all that in with sincerity and dedication, we will endure technological advancement and thrive beyond our imagination.

LIST OF SOURCES

1	A Reality Check on Criminality in Virtual Reality	*DT Next*, Chennai, 31 January 2021
2	The Emerging Face of Facial Recognition Technology	*DT Next*, Chennai, 14 February 2021
3	Robotics in Law Enforcement	*Deccan Chronicle*, 9 March 2020
4	Unchaining Blockchain for Policing	*Deccan Chronicle*, 1 July 2019
5	The Growing Threat of A.I. Assisted Crimes	*DT Next*, Chennai, 16 May 2021
6	DNA Database in India to Boost Crime Detection	*Deccan Chronicle*, 25 August 2018
7	CRISPR: A Game-Changing Crisp Genetic Tool	*DT Next*, Chennai, 8 August 2021
8	3D Imaging Is a Picture Perfect Technology for Policing	*DT Next*, Chennai, 6 December 2020
9	Infrared – A Red-Hot Technology for Policing	*DT Next*, Chennai, 20 December 2020
10	Benefits and Risks of Nanotechnology	*Deccan Chronicle*, 1 April 2019
11	The Emerging Robot-Dog Eat Police-Dog World	*DT Next*, Chennai, 25 April 2021
12	DNA Fingerprinting Tech	*Deccan Chronicle*, 8 July 2019
13	The Burgeoning Impact of AI on Policing	*Deccan Chronicle*, 14 January 2019
14	Are We All Cyborgs Already?	*Deccan Chronicle*, 7 October 2019
15	Is Human Microbiome a Macroscopic Repository of Precious Legal Evidence?	*DT Next*, Chennai, 14 March 2021
16	Dark Cloud or a Cloud with a Silver Lining?	*Deccan Chronicle*, 4 November 2019
17	Astroturfing Can Have Astronomical Fallouts	*DT Next*, Chennai, 29 August 2021
18	Geographic Information System for Crime Prevention	*Deccan Chronicle*, 16 December 2019
19	Can Advanced Exoskeletons turn Cops into Robocops	*Deccan Chronicle*,13 January 2020

20	COVID Era Is All Ears to Voice Biometrics	*DT Next*, Chennai, 8 November 2020
21	3D Printing in Policing - Boon or Bane?	*Deccan Chronicle*, 22 October 2018
22	Is it Alright to Trust Algorithms Altogether?	*DT Next*, Chennai, 11 April 2021
23	Cognitive Computing – a Force Multiplier	*Deccan Chronicle*, 29 July 2019
24	Who Will Police the Metaverse?	*DT Next*, Chennai, 9 January 2022
25	Growing Threat of Sextortion from Cyber-Predators	*Deccan Chronicle*, 20 January 2020
26	Cyber-Stalking: Get Safe Online	*Deccan Chronicle*, 17 February 2020
27	The Emerging Threat of Cyber-Terrorism	*Deccan Chronicle*, 10 February 2020
28	Does Cloud Computing Have A Silver Lining?	*DT Next*, Chennai, 12 September 2021
29	Darknet Weapons Market	*Deccan Chronicle*, 6 May 2019
30	Human-Trafficking on the Dark-Web	*Deccan Chronicle*, 2 September 2019
31	The Dataveillance Bubble	*DT Next*, Chennai, 15 August 2021
32	Are Biometrics More Secure than Passwords?	*Deccan Chronicle*, 7 January 2019
33	Passwords to Biometrics to Behaviometrics	*Deccan Chronicle*, 25 November 2019
34	Data Is the New Oil	*Deccan Chronicle*, 14 October 2019
35	Crowdsourcing Policing	*Deccan Chronicle*, 15 April 2019
36	Proactive Policing Strategies for Crime Prevention	*Deccan Chronicle*, 2 March 2020
37	Evidence for Evidence Based Policing	*Deccan Chronicle*, 6 January 2020
38	Do Murderers Have Murder Genes?	*Deccan Chronicle*, 2 December 2019
39	Law Enforcement during a Pandemic	*Deccan Chronicle*, 23 March 2020
40	Policing the Pandemic with Technological Innovations	*DT Next*, Chennai, 18 October 2020
41	Is Coronavirus a Natural Mutant or a Manmade Bioweapon?	*Deccan Chronicle*, 4 February 2020
42	Bioterrorism in India	*Deccan Chronicle*, 18 March 2019
43	The Threat of Agroterrorism	*Deccan Chronicle*, 10 November 2019
44	The Problem of Environmental Crime	*Deccan Chronicle*, 11 February 209
45	Service and Sacrifice in the Line of Duty	*Deccan Chronicle*, 21 October 2019
46	Spiritual Well-Being for Law Enforcement	*Deccan Chronicle*, 23 December 2019
47	In the Line of Khaki Psychache: Problem of Police Suicides and Simple Solution for Its Prevention	*Deccan Chronicle*, 19 May 2018 and 21 May 2018
48	The Importance of Emotional Intelligence for Policing	*DT Next*, Chennai, 16 January 2022

NOTES

1. Just one Dark Web site: Patrick Howell O'Neill, 'Feds Dismantle Massive Deep Web Child Porn Ring', *Daily Dot*, 19 March 2014.
2. Moreover, the National Center: Thorn Blog, http://www.wearethorn.org/child-trafficking-statistics/.
3. Law enforcement sources report: Testimony of Ernie Allen, President of the National Center of Missing and Exploited Children, to the Institute of Medicine Committee on Commercial Sexual Exploitation and Sex Trafficking of Minors in the United States of the National Academies, http://storage.cloversites.com/thedaughterproject/documents/www.nao.edu/catalog.php?record-id=18358.
4. All or most of the information: Mat Honan, 'How Apple and Amazon Security Flaws Led to My Epic Hacking', *Wired*, 6 July 2012.
5. Mat Honan, 'Kill the Password: Why a String of Characters Can't Protect Us Anymore', *Wired*, 15 November 2012.
6. Over the past hundred years: Peter Diamandis, 'Abundance Is Our Future', *TEDTalk*, February 2012.
7. For centuries, the Westphalian system: Marc Goodman 'The Power of Moore's Law in a World of Geotechnology', *National Interest*, January/February 2013.
8. Marc Goodman, *Future Crimes-Inside the Digital Underground* (Transworld Publishers, 2015).
9. While the potential humanitarian benefits: Tim Adams, 'The "Chemputer" That Could Print Out Any Drug', *Guardian*, 21 July 2012.

10. Wilson created the Wiki Weapon Project: Carole Cadwalladr, 'Meet Cody Wilson, Creator of the 3D-Gun, Anarchist, Libertarian', *Guardian*, 8 February 2014.
11. The lower receiver: Andy Greenberg, 'Here's What It Looks Like to Fire a (Partly) 3D-Printed Gun', *Forbes*, 3 December 2012.
12. In May 2013: Andy Greenberg, 'Meet the "Liberator": Test-Firing the World's First Fully 3D-Printed Gun', *Forbes*, 5 May 2013.
13. Wilson's efforts have left: Andy Greenberg, 'How 3-D Printed Guns Evolved into Serious Weapons in Just One Year', *Wired*, 15 May 2014.
14. These plastic firearms: Cheryl K. Chumley, 'Israeli TV Crew Sneaks Printed 3-D Gun into Knesset-Twice', *Washington Times*, 4 July 2013.
15. Other repositories: Greenberg, 'How 3-D Printed Guns Evolved into Serious Weapons in Just One Year'.
16. Later it was discovered: Joel O. Wertheim, 'The Re-emergence of HINI Influenza Virus in 1977: A Cautionary Tale for Estimating Divergence Times Using Biologically Unrealistic Sampling Dates', *PLoS ONE* 5, no. 6 (2010): ell184, doi:10.1371/journal pone.0011184.
17. You could take: Marc Goodman, 'A Vision for Crimes in the Future', *TED Talk*, July 2012.
18. Facebook's automatic: Adam Clark Estes, 'Facebook's Doing Face Recognition again and This Time America Doesn't Seem to Mind', *Motherboard*, 5 February 2013.
19. In mid-2011: Amir Efrati, 'Google Acquires Facial Recognition Technology Company', Digits (blog), *Wall Street Journal*, 22 July 2011.
20. Kit Eaton, 'How Google's New Face Recognition Tech Could Change the Web's Future', *Fast Company*, 25 July 2011.
21. Such facial-recognition apps: Michelle Starr, 'Facial Recognition App Matches Strangers to Online Profiles', *CNET*, 7 January 2014.

22. The FBI's billion-dollar: Jeremy Hsu, 'FBI'S Facial Recognition Database Will Include Non-criminals', *IEEE Spectrum*, 16 April 2014.
23. Perhaps nanotech's greatest contributions: 'HowStuffWorks' Nanotechnology Cancer Treatments', *HowStuffWorks*, accessed 14 September 2014, http://health.howstuffworks.com.
24. Dean Ho, 'Fighting Cancer with Nanomedicine', *Scientist*, 1 April 2014.
25. Nanotechnology will also be immensely impactful: John Gehl, 'Nanotechnology: Designs for the Future', *Ubiquity*, July 2000, http://ubiquity.acm.org.
26. There is another way: Jenny Awford, 'Student Accused of Murder Asked Sun Where to Hide Body, Say Police', *Mail Online*, 13 August 2014.
27. Just three years: 'IBM Watson', *IBM Website*, http://www03.ibm.com/pres/usen/presskit/27297.wss.
28. The M. D. Anderson Cancer Center: '1BM Watson Hard at Work', Memorial Sloan Kettering Cancer Center, 8 February 2013; Larry Greenemeier, 'Will IBMs Watson Usher in a New Era of Cognitive Computing', *Scientific American*, 13 November 2013.
29. Ray Kurzweil has popularised: Ray Kurzweil, *The Singularity Is Near When Humans Transcend Biology* (New York: Penguin Books, 2006), 7.
30. The lack of algorithmic transparency: Gabriel Hallevy, 'The Criminal Liability of Artificial Intelligence Entities', Social Science Research Network scholarly paper, 15 February 2010, http://papers.ssrn.com/.

ABOUT THE AUTHOR

Dr K. Jayanth Murali, IPS (Retd.), is a dynamic and charismatic leader who has left an indelible mark in the realm of law enforcement and beyond. Hailing from the vibrant city of Golconda Fort, India, Dr Murali's career has been nothing short of extraordinary, brimming with excitement, accomplishments, and unwavering dedication to public service.

A trailblazer from the very beginning, Dr Murali's insatiable thirst for knowledge led him to pursue a PhD in microbiology from the prestigious Indian Agricultural Research Institute, New Delhi where he emerged as a brilliant scientific scholar. However, destiny had other plans for him, and he was handpicked for the prestigious Indian Police Service in 1991, setting the stage for an illustrious career that spanned over three decades of unparalleled achievements.

With his larger-than-life personality and exceptional leadership skills, Dr Murali served in a diverse array of policing assignments that left a lasting impact. From tackling complex law and order situations to spearheading high-stakes crime investigations and providing VIP security, Dr Murali's unwavering commitment to duty earned him widespread recognition and admiration. As Chief of Crime Branch CID, Director of Vigilance and Anti-Corruption, and Additional Director General of Police, Law and Order, and Director General of Police for the Government of Tamil Nadu, he carved a niche for himself as an exemplary law enforcement professional.

But Dr Murali's contributions go far beyond his official duties. He is a prolific writer, whose thought-provoking articles have graced the pages of leading newspapers and e-magazines, capturing the imagination of readers with his diverse interests and deep insights. As a gifted writer, Jayanth's words resonate with depth and insight. His critically acclaimed book, "42 Monday's: On Emerging Technologies in Policing," is a testament to his profound understanding of the evolving landscape of law enforcement. In addition, he has authored three other captivating books, namely "Soliloquies on Future Policing," "Enkindling the Endorphins of Endurance," and "Marathon" (Tamil). His writings on policing, security, technology, sports, science fiction, health, and fitness are nothing short of captivating, igniting a spark of inspiration in the hearts of his readers.

In addition to his literary pursuits, Dr Murali is a man of many talents. An avid farmer, he nurtures his passion for the land and has a green thumb that is the envy of many. He is also a renowned coach for running, nutrition, and health, helping countless individuals achieve their fitness goals and lead healthier lives. As a painter and cook, he unleashes his creative genius, delighting others with his artistic flair and culinary expertise.

Dr Murali's indomitable spirit and unwavering determination are further exemplified by his exceptional achievements in the field of marathon running. He has completed over 50 half and full marathons, and holds prestigious records in the India Book of Records and Asia Book of Records, showcasing his unparalleled prowess as an athlete. His dedication to the cause of organ donation, through marathons and other initiatives, is a testament to his compassionate heart and desire to make a positive impact on society.

Beyond his professional accomplishments and athletic pursuits, Dr Murali's humanitarian endeavors are truly awe-inspiring. As ADGP, Armed Police, he launched the www.letsfightcorona.com initiative during the ongoing pandemic, leading a remarkable effort to distribute relief worth more than Rs 50 lakhs in just 40 days, providing much-needed aid to those in need. His selfless acts of kindness and unwavering commitment to serving humanity have earned him the respect and admiration of people from all walks of life.

In his personal life, Jayanth is a loving husband to his college mate Dr. Jayanthi, IFS, and a proud father to two accomplished daughters, Anisha, an architect in Mumbai, and Anussha, a postgraduate student at Jawaharlal

National University, New Delhi. Jayanth's extraordinary journey is a shining example of resilience, determination, and compassion, making him a true inspiration to all. To learn more about this remarkable individual and his incredible achievements, visit www.jayanthmurali.com and prepare to be inspired.

In conclusion, Dr K. Jayanth Murali, IPS, is a trailblazer and an inspiration to many. His unwavering commitment to public service, exceptional leadership skills, diverse talents, and humanitarian endeavors make him a true force to be reckoned with. His journey is a testament to the power of determination, resilience, and unwavering passion to make a positive impact on society

Website - https://www.jayanthmurali.com/

www.ingramcontent.com/pod-product-compliance
Lightning Source LLC
LaVergne TN
LVHW041146150826
845673LV00001B/87

* 9 7 9 8 8 9 2 3 3 5 7 2 0 *